# Lecture Notes in Computer Science 15428

Founding Editors

Gerhard Goos
Juris Hartmanis

The series Lecture Notes in Computer Science (LNCS), including its subseries Lecture Notes in Artificial Intelligence (LNAI) and Lecture Notes in Bioinformatics (LNBI), has established itself as a medium for the publication of new developments in computer science and information technology research, teaching, and education.

LNCS enjoys close cooperation with the computer science R & D community, the series counts many renowned academics among its volume editors and paper authors, and collaborates with prestigious societies. Its mission is to serve this international community by providing an invaluable service, mainly focused on the publication of conference and workshop proceedings and postproceedings. LNCS commenced publication in 1973.

Yuchao Zhang · Liang-Jie Zhang
Editors

# Web Services – ICWS 2024

31st International Conference
Held as Part of the Services Conference Federation, SCF 2024
Bangkok, Thailand, November 16–19, 2024
Proceedings

 Springer

*Editors*
Yuchao Zhang (iD)
Beijing University of Posts
and Telecommunications
Beijing, China

Liang-Jie Zhang (iD)
Shenzhen University
Shenzhen, China

ISSN 0302-9743        ISSN 1611-3349 (electronic)
Lecture Notes in Computer Science
ISBN 978-3-031-77071-5        ISBN 978-3-031-77072-2 (eBook)
https://doi.org/10.1007/978-3-031-77072-2

# Preface

The International Conference on Web Services (ICWS) is a prime international forum for both researchers and industry practitioners to exchange the latest fundamental advances in the state of the art and practice of Web-based services, identify emerging research topics, and define the future of Web-based services. All topics regarding Internet/Web services lifecycle study and management are aligned with the theme of ICWS.

ICWS 2024 was a member of the Services Conference Federation (SCF). SCF 2024 had the following 10 collocated service-oriented sister conferences: 2024 International Conference on Web Services (ICWS 2024), 2024 International Conference on Cloud Computing (CLOUD 2024), 2024 International Conference on Services Computing (SCC 2024), 2024 International Conference on Big Data (BigData 2024), 2024 International Conference on AI & Multimodal Services (AIMS 2024), 2024 International Conference on Metaverse (METAVERSE 2024), 2024 International Conference on Internet of Things (ICIOT 2024), 2024 International Conference on Cognitive Computing (ICCC 2024), 2024 International Conference on Edge Computing (EDGE 2024), and 2024 International Conference on Blockchain (ICBC 2024).

This volume presents the accepted papers of the 2024 International Conference on Web Services (ICWS 2024), held in Bangkok, Thailand during November 16 – 19, 2024. For this conference, each paper was single-blind reviewed by three independent members of the International Program Committee. After carefully evaluating their originality and quality, we accepted 9 papers from the original 16 submissions.

We are pleased to thank the authors whose submissions and participation made this conference possible. We also want to express our thanks to the Organizing Committee and Program Committee members for their dedication in helping to organize the conference and reviewing the submissions. We owe special thanks to the keynote speakers for their impressive speeches.

Finally, we would like to thank operations team members Jing Zeng, Sheng He, Yishuang Ning, and Zhuolin Mei for their excellent work in organizing this conference. We look forward to your future great contributions as a volunteer, author, and conference participant in the fast-growing worldwide services innovations community.

September 2024

Yuchao Zhang
Liang-Jie Zhang

# Organization

## Program Chair

Yuchao Zhang       Beijing University of Posts and
Telecommunications, China

## Services Conference Federation (SCF 2024)

### General Chairs

Ali Arsanjani       Google, USA
Wu Chou       Essenlix Corporation, USA

### Coordinating Program Chair

Liang-Jie Zhang       Shenzhen University, China

### CFO and International Affairs Chair

Min Luo       Georgia Tech, USA

### Operation Committee

Jing Zeng       China Gridcom Co., Ltd., China
Yishuang Ning       Tsinghua University, China
Sheng He       Kingdee International Software Group Co., Ltd., China
Zhuolin Mei       Jiujiang University, China

### Steering Committee

Calton Pu (Co-chair)       Georgia Tech, USA
Liang-Jie Zhang (Co-chair)       Shenzhen University, China

**ICWS 2024 Program Committee**

| | |
|---|---|
| Keke Gai | Beijing Institute of Technology, China |
| Hakim Hacid | Technology Innovation Institute, United Arab Emirates |
| Dhaval Patel | IBM T. J. Watson Research Center, USA |
| Lei Yang | South China University of Technology, China |
| Haibo Zhang | University of Otago, New Zealand |
| Ikbal Taleb | Zayed University, United Arab Emirates |
| Marios-Eleftherios Fokaefs | Polytechnique Montréal, Canada |
| Hyuk-Yoon Kwon | Seoul National University of Science & Technology, South Korea |
| Young-Kyoon Suh | Kyungpook National University, South Korea |

# Conference Sponsor – Services Society

The Services Society (S2) is a non-profit professional organization that has been created to promote worldwide research and technical collaboration in services innovations among academia and industrial professionals. Its members are volunteers from industry and academia with common interests. S2 is registered in the USA as a "501(c) organization", which means that it is an American tax-exempt nonprofit organization. S2 collaborates with other professional organizations to sponsor or co-sponsor conferences and to promote an effective services curriculum in colleges and universities. S2 initiates and promotes a "Services University" program worldwide to bridge the gap between industrial needs and university instruction.

The Services Sector accounted for 79.5% of the GDP of the USA in 2016. The Services Society has formed 5 Special Interest Groups (SIGs) to support technology- and domain-specific professional activities.

- Special Interest Group on Services Computing (SIG-SC)
- Special Interest Group on Big Data (SIG-BD)
- Special Interest Group on Cloud Computing (SIG-CLOUD)
- Special Interest Group on Artificial Intelligence (SIG-AI)
- Special Interest Group on Metaverse (SIG-Metaverse)

# About the Services Conference Federation (SCF)

As the founding member of the Services Conference Federation (SCF), the first **International Conference on Web Services (ICWS)** was held in June 2003 in Las Vegas, USA. Meanwhile, the First International Conference on Web Services - Europe 2003 (ICWS-Europe 2003) was held in Germany in October 2003. ICWS-Europe 2003 was an extended event of the 2003 International Conference on Web Services (ICWS 2003) in Europe. In 2004, ICWS-Europe was changed to the European Conference on Web Services (ECOWS), which was held at Erfurt, Germany. Sponsored by the Services Society and Springer, SCF 2018 and SCF 2019 were held successfully in Seattle and San Diego, USA. SCF 2020 and SCF 2021 were held successfully online and in Shenzhen, China. SCF 2022 and 2023 were held successfully in Hawaii, USA. To celebrate its 21st birthday, SCF 2024 was held on November 16–19, 2024, in Bangkok, Thailand.

In the past 21 years, the ICWS community has expanded from Web engineering innovations to scientific research for the whole services industry. Service delivery platforms have been expanded to mobile platforms, Internet of Things, cloud computing, and edge computing. The services ecosystem has gradually been enabled, value added, and intelligence embedded through enabling technologies such as big data, artificial intelligence, and cognitive computing. In the coming years, all transactions with multiple parties involved will be transformed to blockchain.

Based on technology trends and best practices in the field, the Services Conference Federation (SCF) will continue serving as the conference umbrella's code name for all services-related conferences. SCF 2024 defined the future of New ABCDE (AI, Blockchain, Cloud, BigData & IOT) and entered the 5G for Services Era. The theme of ICWS 2024 was Web-based Services for Metaverse Era. We are very proud to announce that SCF 2024's 10 co-located theme topic conferences all centered around "services", with each focusing on exploring different themes (web-based services, cloud-based services, Big Data-based services, services innovation lifecycle, AI-driven ubiquitous services, blockchain-driven trust service ecosystems, industry-specific services and applications, and emerging service-oriented technologies).

– Bigger Platform: The 10 collocated conferences (SCF 2024) were sponsored by the Services Society, which is the world-leading not-for-profit organization (501(c)(3)) dedicated to the service of more than 30,000 worldwide Services Computing researchers and practitioners. A bigger platform means bigger opportunities for all volunteers, authors, and participants. Meanwhile, Springer provided sponsorship of the best paper awards and other professional activities. All the 10 conference proceedings of SCF 2024 were published by Springer and indexed in the ISI Conference Proceedings Citation Index (included in Web of Science), Engineering Index EI (Compendex and Inspec databases), DBLP, Google Scholar, IO-Port, MathSciNet, Scopus, and ZBlMath.

– Brighter Future: While celebrating the 2024 version of ICWS, SCF 2024 highlighted the International Conference on Blockchain (ICBC 2024) and the International Conference on Metaverse (Metaverse 2024) to build the fundamental infrastructure for enabling secure and trusted services ecosystems and cover immersive services for all vertical industries and area solutions. It put its focus on the industry-specific services for digital transformation. This will lead our community members to create their own brighter future.
– Better Model: SCF 2024 continued to leverage the invented Conference Blockchain Model (CBM) to innovate the organizing practices for all the 10 theme conferences. Senior researchers in the field are welcome to submit proposals to serve as CBM Ambassador for an individual conference to start better interactions during your leadership role in organizing future SCF conferences.

# Contents

# An Evolutionary Game Theoretic-Based Approach to Task Offloading in Hybrid Vehicular Cloud-Edge Environment

Jinpeng Li[1], Yunni Xia[1(✉)], Hui Liu[2], Jiafeng Feng[3], Ke Zhang[3], Zhaoguang Ding[3], Yumin Dong[4], Yang Yu[5], Yu Wang[1], Qinglan Peng[6], and Xifeng Xu[1]

[1] School of Computer, Chongqing University, Chongqing 400030, China
xiayunni@hotmail.com
[2] School of Computer Science and Technology, Beijing Institute of Technology, Beijing 100083, China
[3] China Huadian Corporation Guangdong Branch, Guangdong, China
[4] Chongqing Normal University, Chongqing, China
[5] Nanjing Nanzi Huadun Digital Technology Co.,Ltd., Nanjing, China
[6] Henan University, Henan, China

**Abstract.** Vehicle Edge Computing (VEC) is a novel computing paradigm that addresses the computational demands of intelligent vehicles by offloading tasks to edge servers. In a VEC environment, edge servers limited storage and processing capacity require a sensible task offloading strategy, where only a part of computing requirement can be offloaded directly to the VEC server and the remaining to the remote cloud. A primary challenge in this context is the creation of an effective and responsive task offloading algorithm that improves the utility. This study proposes an evolutionary game theoretic-based approach, utilizing a Dynamical-Resource Evolutionary Game (DREG) algorithm for decentralized task offloading. DREG leverages the Evolutionary Stable Strategy(ESS) and Adaptive Resource Allocation(ARA) method to optimize response delay and energy cost while increasing success rate. Experimental results indicate that DREG outperforms traditional methods across various performance metrics.

**Keywords:** Vehicle edge computing · Evolutionary game theoretic · Task offloading · Fault tolerant · Resource allocation

## 1 Introduction

With the rapid advancement of artificial intelligence and 5G networks, the market share of smart vehicles has expanded significantly, catalyzing exten-

This work was supported in part by the grants from Science and Technology Program of Sichuan Province under Grant No.2024NSFTD0008, and in part by the Young Scientists Fund of the Natural Science Foundation of Henan Province under Grant No.242300421700.

sive research and development in vehicle computing [1]. In traditional central-ized computing environments, tasks rely on a remote cloud that uses a central-ized model to distribute computing resources. The cloud offers notable benefits including scalability, virtualization, high reliability, and cost-effectiveness. How-ever, in the context of the Internet of Things (IoT), tasks generated by vehicles are typically computation-intensive and delay-sensitive, making the traditional cloud paradigm insufficient to meet the computing demands [2]. The VEC relo-cates computing and storage functions from cloud to the edge, providing a solu-tion for the challenge of vehicle computing. In a VEC environment, tasks can be offloaded from moving vehicles to roadside VEC servers, obtaining low-latency services and reducing the workload of cloud.

Despite the many benefits of VEC, it faces some challenges, such as limited storage space in edge devices and the computational reliability of VEC servers [3]. A key challenge is to reduce task response time and energy consumption while ensuring accuracy.

In this study, we propose the DREG algorithm to yield dynamic task offload-ing schemes in the VEC environment, the main contributions are as follows:

1) To minimize task response delay under long-term energy constraints, we model the task offloading problem in VEC as a composite optimization prob-lem. The model captures long-term energy consumption and provides an avail-able prototype for evolutionary game formulation.
2) We develop a decentralized task offloading algorithm, termed DREG, which utilizes the ESS [4] and ARA algorithm for generating task offloading sched-ules dynamically.
3) To evaluate the performance of DREG, we conduct extensive simulations using a real-world data set and show that our proposed method outperforms its peers in terms of multiple performance indicators.

## 2    Related Work

Research on VEC primarily aims to optimize response delays and energy costs. Karimi *et al.* [5] developed a strategy using multi-access edge computing to enhance service response times in vehicular networks via deep reinforcement learning. Gilly *et al.* [6] investigated latency reduction in vehicular services through edge computing coordinators with a focus on layered dynamic resource management. Xue *et al.* [7] tackled the integrated optimization of service caching and computation offloading through a long-term mixed-integer nonlinear pro-gramming (MINLP) model, employing an algorithm rooted in deep reinforce-ment learning to curtail task processing delays, thereby markedly enhancing performance and response efficiency in VEC networks. Zhou *et al.* [8] exam-ined energy-efficient workload offloading in vehicular networks employing the Alternating Direction Method of Multipliers (ADMM), which simplifies complex problems into separable consensus issues, facilitating low-energy, high-efficiency distributed solutions. Zhu *et al.* [9] proposed a multi-agent deep reinforcement learning framework to optimize task offloading decisions in a mobile edge computing environment for vehicles, aimed at minimizing long-term task processing delays and boosting overall system efficiency.

Recently, studies have focused on balancing multiple objectives in the VEC environment. Du *et al.* [10] utilized TV White Space (TVWS) bands to jointly optimize vehicular terminal offloading decisions and wireless resource allocation, thereby minimizing costs for vehicles and mobile edge computing servers. Liu *et al.* [11] developed a multi-user vehicular computation offloading game to optimize vehicles' computation offloading decisions and resource allocation, aimed at minimizing computation costs and delays. Tang *et al.* [12] introduced an optimized scheme for task caching and computation offloading that reduces service time and energy consumption by genetic algorithms. Dai *et al.* [13] enhanced offloading decisions and resource allocation in a data-driven manner. Huang *et al.* [14] built a vehicle speed-aware task offloading and resource allocation strategy to decrease energy consumption costs and augment task processing revenue. Liu *et al.* [15] devised a location-view based intelligent decision process using the Asynchronous Advantage Actor-Critic (A3C) algorithm from the asynchronous gradient deep reinforcement learning framework.

## 3    System Models and Problem Formulation

### 3.1    System Model

As shown in Fig. 1, we propose a fault-tolerant VEC environment that integrates mobile vehicles, roadside base stations, VEC servers, an edge center, and a cloud server, utilizing the Vehicle-to-Infrastructure (V2I) network [16]. Mobile vehicles communicate with base stations via Dedicated Short Range Communications (DSRC) and with the edge center through Long Term Evolution (LTE). Importantly, we introduce a cloud-based fault detection center capable of dynamically adjusting the resource allocations of VEC servers during failures. We consider that VEC servers may occasionally provide unstable services due to potential failures in edge nodes or communications, influencing the execution of tasks under fault conditions.

The set of vehicles is $V = v_1, v_2, ..., v_m$, and we define $v_i$ as a triplet $(l_i, A_i, d_i)$, where $l_i$ represents the vehicle's location information (composed of longitude and latitude), $A_i$ the set of tasks, and $d_i$ the date volume of tasks in $A_i$. The set of servers is represented as $S = s_1, s_2, s_3, ..., s_n$, where $s_j$ denotes the $j$-th server, and $|S| = n$ the number of servers. Similarly, $s_j$ is defined as a triplet $(C_j, e_j, b_j)$, where $C_j$ represents the coverage area of $s_j$, $e_j$ the task processing capability, which is related to task processing delay, and $b_j$ the transmission capability, which is related to transmission delay. All key symbols used in this section are summarized in Table 1.

### 3.2    Task Response Delay Model

Task response delay comprises transmission delay, processing delay, and migration delay. We adopt bandwidth resource usage as a standard, consider a dynam-

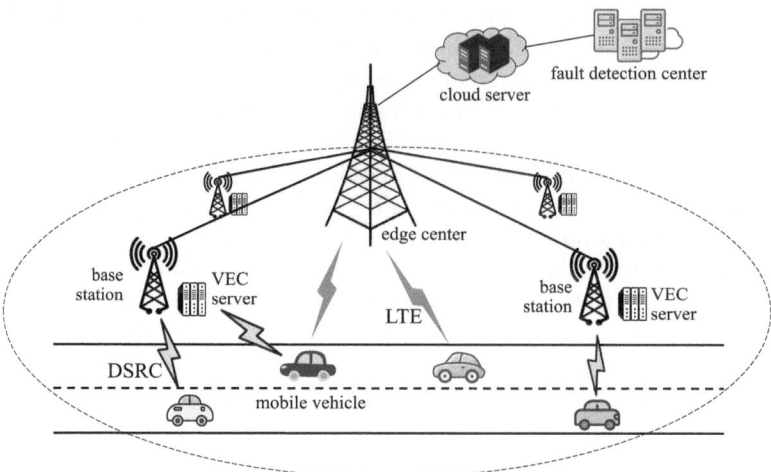

**Fig. 1.** Hybrid vehicular cloud-edge environment.

**Table 1.** Notion table

| Variable | Description |
| --- | --- |
| $m$ | The number of mobile vehicles |
| $V$ | A set of mobile vehicles |
| $v_i$ | The $i$-th mobile vehicle |
| $l_i$ | The geographical position of $v_i$ |
| $A_i$ | A set of tasks of $v_i$ |
| $d_i$ | The amount of resources required by $v_i$ |
| $n$ | The number of VEC servers |
| $S$ | A set of VEC servers |
| $s_j$ | The $j$-th VEC server |
| $C_j$ | A set of coverage locations of $s_j$ |
| $e_j$ | The computing capacity of $s_j$ |
| $b_j$ | The transmission capacity of $s_j$ |
| $x_{i,j}(t)$ | The transmission delay from $v_i$ to $s_j$ at time $t$ |
| $y_{i,j}(t)$ | The computing delay from $v_i$ to $s_j$ at time $t$ |
| $z_{j,j'}(t)$ | The migration delay from $s_j$ to $s_{j'}$ at time $t$ |
| $h(t)$ | The total task response delay at time $t$ |
| $et_{i,j}(t)$ | The transmission energy cost from $v_i$ to $s_j$ at time $t$ |
| $ec_{i,j}(t)$ | The computing energy cost from $v_i$ to $s_j$ at time $t$ |
| $eo(t)$ | The total energy cost at time $t$ |
| $sc_i(t)$ | The average task success rate of $v_i$ at time $t$ |
| $ul(t)$ | The average system utility at time $t$ |

ically changing communication model, and design a latency calculation formula based on the Shannon formula.

*Transmission Delay:* The bandwidth allocated for executing tasks is variable and subject to environmental influences. The computation of transmission delay depends on the total bandwidth resources allocated by the VEC server. According to the Shannon formula, the transmission rate when vehicle $v_i$ offloads tasks to server $s_j$ at time $t$ can be expressed as:

$$r_{i,j}(t) = b_j(t) \log \left( 1 + \frac{p_i(t)g_{i,j}(t)}{o^2 + q_{i,j}(t)} \right) \tag{1}$$

where $r_{i,j}(t)$ represents the transmission rate when vehicle $v_i$ offloads tasks to server $s_j$ at time $t$, $p_i(t)$ the transmission power of vehicle $v_i$, $g_{i,j}(t)$ the channel gain between $v_i$ and $s_j$, $o^2$ the background noise power, and $q_{i,j}(t) = \sum_{v_i \in \{v_i | l_i \in C_j\}} p_i(t)g_{i,j}(t)$ the infinite interference generated by communication. The transmission delay for the VEC server at time $t$ is defined as:

$$x_{i,j}(t) = \frac{d_i(t)}{r_{i,j}(t)} \tag{2}$$

*Processing Delay:* The task processing delay is determined by the requirements of vehicles and the computing capacity of the server and can be expressed as:

$$y_{i,j}(t) = \frac{d_i(t)}{e_j(t)} \tag{3}$$

*Migration Delay:* Migration delay exhibits a selective characteristic, indicating that the migration of computational tasks from server $s_j$ to $s_{j'}$ results in a delay. We denote the migration delay of a task from $s_j$ to $s_{j'}$ as $z_{j,j'}$:

$$z_{j,j'}(t) = \frac{\min(c_j, c_{j'})}{f} \tag{4}$$

where $\min(c_j, c_{j'})$ denotes the minimum distance between servers, which is due to the deployment method between edge servers, $f$ represents the signal propagation speed, equivalent to the speed of light in fiber optic cables.

Overall, the task response delay in the environment can be represented as:

$$h(t) = \sum_{i=1}^{m} \sum_{j=1}^{n} \sum_{j'=1}^{n} (\alpha_{i,j}(t)(x_{i,j}(t) + y_{i,j}(t)) + \beta_{j,j'}(t)z_{j,j'}(t)) \tag{5}$$

where $\alpha_{i,j}(t)$ is an indicator that equals one when the vehicle $v_i$ offloads tasks to server $s_j$ and 0 otherwise, and $\beta_{j,j'}(t)$ equals one when a task migration occurs between $s_j$ and $s_{j'}$.

### 3.3   Energy Cost Model

The energy cost model comprises transmission and computing energy costs. Transmission energy cost results from bandwidth costs incurred during task transmission, and computing energy cost comes from the occupation of computing resources.

*Transmission Energy Cost:* The energy cost of bandwidth during transmission is influenced by the unit cost, the data volume, and the transmission speed, and is represented as follows:

$$et_{i,j}(t) = ue_{i,j}(t)x_{i,j}(t) + ut_{j,j'}(t)z_{j,j'}(t) \tag{6}$$

where $ue_{i,j}(t)$ denotes the unit transmission energy cost between $v_i$ and $s_j$ at time $t$, and $ut_{j,j'}(t)$ the unit transmission energy cost between servers at time $t$.

*Computational Energy Cost:* The cost of computing is determined by the required amount of resources, the computational delay, and the unit computing energy cost, and is expressed as:

$$ec_{i,j}(t) = y_{i,j}(t)d_i(t)uc_j(t) \tag{7}$$

where $uc_j(t)$ represents the unit computing energy cost of $s_j$ at time $t$. Overall, the energy consumption in the environment can be represented as:

$$eo(t) = \sum_{i=1}^{m}\sum_{j=1}^{n}\alpha_{i,j}(t)\left(et_{i,j}(t) + ec_{i,j}(t)\right) \tag{8}$$

### 3.4   Fault-Tolerant Model

In the fault-tolerant VEC environment, the system may experience partial or complete failures of VEC servers, potentially impacting the processing of vehicle requests. These failures fall into three main categories: 1) Failures due to hardware or software issues within the computing nodes themselves; 2) Network connectivity failures, often occurring when mobile vehicle equipment exits the coverage area of a particular edge node; 3) Task execution failures, which occur when computing tasks assigned to edge nodes are not successfully completed for various reasons. Notably, the frequency of task execution failures varies across different observation time windows, fitting well with a Poisson probability mass function distribution. The probability of a failure occurring at edge node $s_j$ at time $t$ is denoted by $fa_j(t)$, and the average task offloading success rate for vehicle $v_i$ is expressed as:

$$sc_i = \frac{1}{T}\sum_{t=1}^{T}\sum_{j=1}^{n}\prod_{k=t}^{t+ac_{i,j}(t)}(1 - fa_j(k)) \tag{9}$$

where $ac_{i,j}(t) = x_{i,j}(t) + y_{i,j}(t) + z_{i,j}(t)$ denotes the total response delay, and $T$ the upper limit of time $t$.

## 3.5   Problem Formulation

We propose a multi-objective optimization method that encompasses various performance indicators. Specifically, this method utilizes average response delay, energy cost, and task success rate to construct a multi-objective optimization framework. The objective function is defined as:

$$ul(t) = a_1 \ln(a_2 - u_1 h(t) - u_2 eo(t) + u_3 \frac{1}{m} \sum_{i=1}^{m} sc_i) \tag{10}$$

where $a_1$ represents a satisfaction coefficient affecting utility perception, and $a_2$ is a normalization constant. $u_1$ $u_2$ $u_3$ are determined based on the importance and relative priority of each objective and following the constraint:

$$u_1 + u_2 + u_3 = 1 \tag{11}$$

In the fault-tolerant VEC environment, we aim to optimize task offloading strategies to achieve the following objectives: minimize task response delay and energy cost while maximizing the offloading success rate. The problem formulation is described as follows:

$$\text{Max} : \sum_{t=1}^{T} ul(t) \tag{12}$$

$$s.t. \quad \textbf{C1.} \quad sc_i > sc_{min} \qquad \forall i$$
$$\textbf{C2.} \quad l_i(t) \in C_j \qquad \forall i, \forall j, \forall t$$

$\textbf{C1}$ indicates that the success rate must exceed the predetermined threshold $sc_{\min}$, since a success rate below $sc_{\min}$ could severely jeopardize vehicle safety. $\textbf{C2}$ represents that vehicles must be within the service range of VEC servers.

## 4   The Proposed Method

In this section, we introduce the evolutionary game formulation of the task offloading problem in VEC, which incorporates players, strategies, population, and payoff function. Analyzing the payoff of players under various strategies, we guide them to gradually refine their offloading strategies. Building on the above concepts, we propose a fault-tolerant task offloading algorithm for hybrid edge-cloud environments.

### 4.1   Game Formulation

Evolutionary game models typically comprise four components: players, strategies, a population, and a payoff function. We now introduce the standard form of the evolutionary game:

**Player:** All vehicles distributed around the VEC servers are players in our environment.

**Strategy:** Offloading tasks to VEC servers or the cloud represents a competitive and selective process. Therefore, the server selection strategy includes all combinations where participants choose between cloud and edge servers, represented as $\mathcal{K} = \{(v, s, p)|v \in V, s \in S, p \in \{0, 1\}\}$.

**Population:** Players are divided into $k$ different populations based on geographical location. We represent the overall set as $\mathcal{N} = \{N_1, N_2, ..., N_k\}$, with players in each population located in the same geographical area.

**Payoff:** Selecting different strategies leads to varying costs, thereby influencing the magnitude of the payoff. We employ the composite overall satisfaction metric, $ul(t)$, to quantify the participants' payoff.

### 4.2 DREG Algorithm

Task offloading decisions and resource management are crucial for enhancing computational performance and service experience. Traditional methods generally rely on static strategies that fail to account for dynamic fluctuations in resource status and the immediate demands of tasks in the VEC environment. To enhance the systems adaptability and robustness, we propose the DREG algorithm, integrating dynamic resource scheduling with evolutionary game theory, to optimize the real-time effectiveness of task offloading decisions and resource allocation.

As shown in Algorithm 1, we initialize the offloading strategy $\mathcal{K}$ based on the ESS, and then offload tasks according to $\mathcal{K}$ and the state of the VEC servers (Lines 5–6). If a failure occurs which indicates that the current resource allocation strategy and task offloading are unreasonable, we need to reallocate resources and adjust $\mathcal{K}$ (Lines 7–10). The specific resource allocation algorithm will be introduced in Sect. 4.3. Following the completion of task computing in the current episode, the utility of all VEC servers is evaluated, prompting immediate adjustments to resource allocation (Lines 13–18).

### 4.3 Adaptive Resource Allocation Algorithm

Algorithm 2 is designed to optimize the success rate of task execution in the VEC environment. The ARA algorithm initiates by setting an initial resource quota (Line 2), which allocates starting resources for each task on the edge server. This initial allocation ensures that each task has adequate resources to commence execution and establishes a baseline for subsequent adaptive resource adjustments. Then, ARA proceeds to execute each task, adjusting the resource quota based on performance outcomes. If a task is executed successfully, ARA reduces the resource quota to determine the optimal conditions (Lines 7–10). Conversely, if a task fails, ARA increases the resource quota in the hope that additional resources will enhance the success rate of subsequent tasks (Lines 11–16). When it is not possible to increase the success rate by increasing the resource quota, the algorithm will record the error and return the initial resource quota (Lines 19–22).

---

**Algorithm 1:** DREG Algorithm

---

   **Input**: task request queue $B$, mobile vehicles $V$, VEC servers $S$, application
        services $S$
   **Output**: task offloading strategy $\mathcal{K}$

1  **Initialize** resource quota $R$
2  **foreach** *episode* **do**
3     |  **while** $B \neq \varnothing$ **do**
4     |    |  **foreach** $N_i \in \mathcal{N}$ **do**
5     |    |    |  generate the offloading strategy $\mathcal{K}_i$ according to the ESS
6     |    |    |  offload user tasks to VEC servers based on $\mathcal{K}_i$ and the resource
                 status of VEC servers
7     |    |    |  **if** *failure occured* **then**
8     |    |    |    |  $R_i =$Adaptive_resource_allocation()
9     |    |    |    |  update the offloading strategy $\mathcal{K}_i$ based on the latest $R_i$
10    |    |    |  **end**
11    |    |    |  update the resource status of VEC servers
12    |    |  **end**
13    |    |  **foreach** $s_j \in S$ **do**
14    |    |    |  evaluate the resource status of $s_j$
15    |    |    |  **if** *low utilization occured* **then**
16    |    |    |    |  Adaptive_resource_allocation()
17    |    |    |  **end**
18    |    |  **end**
19    |  **end**
20 **end**

---

## 5   Performance Evaluation

### 5.1   Experiment Setting

We build a real-world simulation environment based on the Shanghai Telecom's dataset and the Shanghai Taxi dataset. Shanghai Telecom's dataset contains 7.2 million internet access logs from 3,233 edge stations for 9,481 mobile users over 6 months [17]. Figure 2 shows the distribution of VEC servers in the dataset. The Shanghai Taxi dataset records the driving trajectories of taxis in the central urban area of Shanghai. Figure 3 visually represents the driving trajectories of different vehicles within a specific timeframe of the dataset. The parameters related to the simulation are shown in Table 2.

All the experiments are conducted on the same computer with an Intel Core i9-13700H 4.20 GHz processor, 32.0 GB of RAM, NVIDIA GeForce RTX 4090 and using Python 3.11.

### 5.2   Comparison Algorithms

To evaluate the performance of the DREG algorithm, we selected the following four benchmarks:

---

**Algorithm 2:** ARA Algorithm

---

**Input**: initial resource quota $R_{it}$, resource increase factor $\gamma_{in}$, resource reduction factor $\gamma_{de}$, maximum number of retries $m_r$, task request queue $B$

**Output**: updated resource quota $R$

1   **Initialize** retry count $rc \leftarrow 0$
2   $R \leftarrow R_{it}$
3   **foreach** $b \in B$ **do**
4      **while** $rc < m_r$ **do**
5          **foreach** $v_i \in V$ **do**
6              execute $b$ in the condition of resource quota $R$
7              **if** *successfully executed* **then**
8                  $R \leftarrow \max(R_{it}, R * \gamma_{de})$
9                  return $R$
10              **end**
11              **else**
12                  $rc \leftarrow rc + 1$
13                  **if** $rc < m_r$ **then**
14                      $R \leftarrow R * \gamma_{in}$
15                  **end**
16              **end**
17          **end**
18      **end**
19      **if** $rc == m_r$ **then**
20          mark failure occured
21          return $R_{it}$
22      **end**
23 **end**

---

1) Mobility Aware Task Offloading Algorithm(MATOA) [18]: This algorithm proposes a mobility-aware adaptive offloading framework to achieve adaptive task offloading with mobility and fault tolerance awareness in heterogeneous mobile cloud-edge environments.

2) Energy-Efficient Fault-Tolerant Offloading Algorithm(EFTA) [19]: This algorithm introduces an offloading strategy processed by DNA combination and genetic algorithms to achieve energy-saving fault-tolerant task offloading in mobile cloud-edge computing environments.

3) Fault-Tolerant Edge Computing Task Offloading Algorithm(FT-TOA) [20]: This approach designs an efficient and robust computational offloading solution for edge nodes, with a special emphasis on maintaining system operation in the event of partial failures.

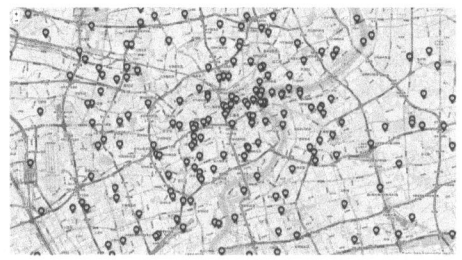

**Fig. 2.** VEC server distribution.

**Fig. 3.** Taxi data set vehicle driving trajectory.

**Table 2.** Parameter table

| Parameters | Value |
|---|---|
| population number | 8 |
| vehicle transmission power: $p_i(t)$ (mW) | 100–150 |
| channel gain between vehicle and VEC server: $g_{i,j}(t)$ | $10^{-4}$-$20^{-4}$ |
| background noise power: $o^2$ (mW) | $10^{-9}$ |
| computing capacity: $e_j$ (GHz) | 0.5–2 |
| transmission capacity: $b_j$ (GHz) | 2–4 |
| amount of resources: $d_i$ | 0.5–3 |
| server coverage locations: $C_j$ (km) | 2–3 |
| speed of light: $f$ (km/s) | 299792 |
| Total rounds of simulation | 2000 |

4) Checkpoint-based Fault-Tolerant Offloading Framework(CFTOF) [21]: This algorithm constructs a fault-tolerant offloading framework to address various failure scenarios potentially encountered in mobile computing offloading systems, thus effectively extending the availability and stability of mobile devices.

## 5.3  Performance Evaluation

To minimize the impact of experimental errors on the results, we calculated the average data from at least 20 trials to evaluate the algorithm's performance.

**Convergence:** Figure 4 shows the convergence behavior in a specific regional population when the number of vehicles m = 200. It is observed that: 1) With increasing iterations, the total computational cost of the system decreases progressively and eventually stabilizes; 2) At 630 iterations, the computational resource consumption of the system minimizes and tends towards convergence.

Figure 5 depicts the relationship between system utility and the number of iterations for a population region with 200 vehicles. The findings indicate that:

1) The average completion time of vehicle task offloading, energy cost, and task success rate achieve equilibrium, and the overall utility of the system progressively improves and stabilizes; 2) System utility reaches convergence at 1050 iterations.

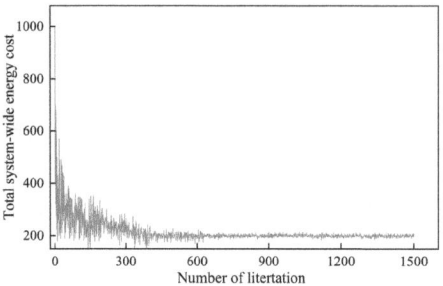

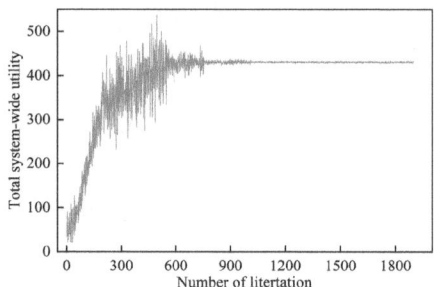

**Fig. 4.** System-wide cost and iteration.     **Fig. 5.** System-wide utility and iteration.

**Number of Vehicles:** We use a normalization method to compare the key performance indicators of different algorithms. Figure 6 shows the performance comparison of the DREG algorithm with other competing algorithms under different vehicle numbers.

*Response Delay Perspective:* The DREG algorithm's fault-tolerant strategies, grounded in historical data, significantly enhance the delay control in all test scenarios. Specifically, DREG outperforms the next best algorithm, MATOA, by 32.55%, 35.13%, 31.27%, and 28.69% for vehicle counts of 150, 200, 250, and 300, respectively. Unlike traditional methods, FT-TOA and CFTOF, which rely on post-fault recovery tactics like backup and checkpoint, DREG preemptively mitigates faults, thereby improving time efficiency and enhancing system stability in error-prone offloading environments.

*Energy Cost Perspective:* The DREG algorithm significantly reduces energy costs, outperforming MATOA, FT-TOA, and CFTOF by 18.48%, 42.91%, and 55.51%, respectively. However, at 250 vehicles, the margin narrows to only 3.19% over the EFTA algorithm, and at 300 vehicles, it underperforms EFTA by 1.524%. This variation likely stems from EFTA's effective utilization of sleep mechanisms and genetic algorithms, which are particularly adept at managing resources in large-scale vehicle scenarios, thereby optimizing energy efficiency.

*Success Rate Perspective:* On average, the DREG algorithm achieves the highest success rates in multiple scenarios, showing improvements of 17.65%, 21.60%, and 22.58% compared to CFTOF, EFTA, and MATOA, respectively. The FT-TOA algorithm also shows commendable performance, achieving a success rate of 0.928 at 250 vehicles, marginally better than DREG's 0.919, indicating the robust fault tolerance of FT-TOA's unique consistency strategy.

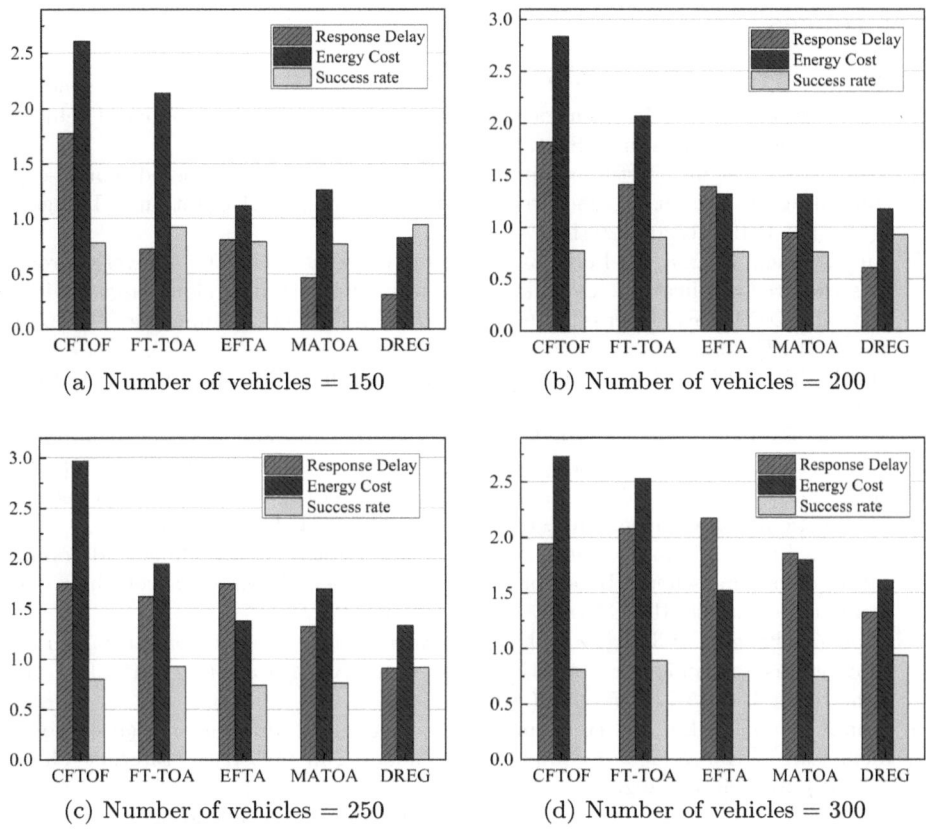

**Fig. 6.** Normalization indicators and number of vehicles

## 6   Conclusion

In this work, we propose a fault-tolerant method for delay-cost aware task offloading in the VEC environment. This method synthesizes the ESS and ARA algorithm for developing the DREG algorithm, which models the task offloading problem as a composite optimization problem. Numerical results demonstrate that our proposed method surpasses traditional algorithms on multiple metrics and adapts effectively to increases in vehicle numbers while maintaining a high level of availability. For further research, we intend to: 1) Develop complex task offloading models from the perspectives of task migration methods and service caching. 2) Utilize more sophisticated evolutionary game method to improve performance. 3) Explore the potential of the fault-tolerant mechanism in the VEC environment.

# References

1. Zhang, D., Wang, W., Zhang, J., Zhang, T., Du, J., Yang, C.: Novel edge caching approach based on multi-agent deep reinforcement learning for internet of vehicles. IEEE Trans. Intell. Transp. Syst. (2023)
2. Truong, T.P., et al.: Partial computation offloading in Noma-assisted mobile-edge computing systems using deep reinforcement learning. IEEE Internet Things J. **8**(17), pp. 13196–13208 (2021)
3. Xu, X., Chen, P., Xia, Y., Long, M., Peng, Q., Long, T.: MRoCO: a novel approach to structured application scheduling with a hybrid vehicular cloud-edge environment. In: 2022 IEEE International Conference on Services Computing (SCC), pp. 84–92. IEEE (2022)
4. Smith, J.M., Price, G.R.: The logic of animal conflict. Nature **246**(5427), 15–18 (1973)
5. Karimi, E., Chen, Y., Akbari, B.: Task offloading in vehicular edge computing networks via deep reinforcement learning. Comput. Commun. **189**, 193–204 (2022)
6. Gilly, K., Mishev, A., Filiposka, S., Alcaraz, S.: Offloading edge vehicular services in realistic urban environments. IEEE Access **8**, 11491–11502 (2020)
7. Xue, Z., Liu, C., Liao, C., Han, G., Sheng, Z.: Joint service caching and computation offloading scheme based on deep reinforcement learning in vehicular edge computing systems. IEEE Trans. Vehic. Technol. (2023)
8. Zhou, Z., Feng, J., Chang, Z., Shen, X.: Energy-efficient edge computing service provisioning for vehicular networks: a consensus ADMM approach. IEEE Trans. Veh. Technol. **68**(5), 5087–5099 (2019)
9. Zhu, X., Luo, Y., Liu, A., Bhuiyan, M.Z.A., Zhang, S.: Multiagent deep reinforcement learning for vehicular computation offloading in IoT. IEEE Internet Things J. **8**(12), 9763–9773 (2020)
10. Du, J., Yu, F.R., Chu, X., Feng, J., Lu, G.: Computation offloading and resource allocation in vehicular networks based on dual-side cost minimization. IEEE Trans. Veh. Technol. **68**(2), 1079–1092 (2018)
11. Liu, Y., Wang, S., Huang, J., Yang, F.: A computation offloading algorithm based on game theory for vehicular edge networks. In: 2018 IEEE International Conference on Communications (ICC), pp. 1–6. IEEE (2018)
12. Tang, C., Wu, H.: Joint optimization of task caching and computation offloading in vehicular edge computing. Peer-to-Peer Netw. Appl. **15**(2), 854–869 (2021). https://doi.org/10.1007/s12083-021-01252-w
13. Dai, P., Hu, K., Wu, X., Xing, H., Yu, Z.: Asynchronous deep reinforcement learning for data-driven task offloading in MEC-empowered vehicular networks. In: IEEE INFOCOM 2021-IEEE Conference on Computer Communications, pp. 1–10. IEEE (2021)
14. Huang, X., He, L., Chen, X., Wang, L., Li, F.: Revenue and energy efficiency-driven delay-constrained computing task offloading and resource allocation in a vehicular edge computing network: a deep reinforcement learning approach. IEEE Internet Things J. **9**(11), 8852–8868 (2021)
15. Liu, S., Yang, Q., Zhang, S., Wang, T., Xiong, N.N.: MIDP: an MDP-based intelligent big data processing scheme for vehicular edge computing. J. Parallel Distrib. Comput. **167**, 1–17 (2022)
16. Xu, X., Xia, Y., Zeng, F., Li, F., Xie, H., Fu, X., Wang, M.: A novel vehicular task deployment method in hybrid MEC. J. Cloud Comput. **11**(1), 88 (2022)

17. Li, J., et al.: A multi-armed bandits learning-based approach to service caching in edge computing environment. In: Zhang, Y., Zhang, L.J. (eds.) ICWS 2023. LNCS, vol. 14209, pp. 3–17. Springer, Cham (2023). https://doi.org/10.1007/978-3-031-44836-2_1
18. Lakhan, A., Li, X.: Mobility and fault aware adaptive task offloading in heterogeneous mobile cloud environments. In: EAI Endorsed Transactions on Mobile Communications and Applications, vol. 5, no. 16 (2019)
19. Abd, S.K., Al-Haddad, S.A.R., Hashim, F., Abdullah, A.B., Yussof, S.: Energy-aware fault tolerant task offloading of mobile cloud computing. In: 2017 5th IEEE International Conference on Mobile Cloud Computing, Services, and Engineering (MobileCloud), pp. 161–164. IEEE (2017)
20. Droob, A.: Fault tolerant horizontal computation offloading. In: 2023 IEEE International Conference on Edge Computing and Communications (EDGE), pp. 177–182. IEEE (2023)
21. Chowdhury, C., Roy, S., Ray, A., Deb, S.K.: A fault-tolerant approach to alleviate failures in offloading systems. Wirel. Pers. Commun. **110**(2), 1033–1055 (2020)

# Securing Child Health Records with RSA-Encrypted NFTs and Smart Contract on the Blockchain

H. V. Khanh[1], M. N. Triet[1], H. G. Khiem[1(✉)], L. K. Bang[1], N. N. Hung[1], T. B. Nam[1], D. P. Trinh[1], and K. T. N. Ngan[2]

[1] FPT University, Can Tho city, Vietnam
khanhvh@fe.edu.vn, khiemhgce160922@fpt.edu.vn
[2] FPT Polytechnic, Can Tho city, Vietnam

**Abstract.** The landscape of pediatric healthcare management is undergoing significant transformation with the adoption of digital technologies. Traditional health record systems, characterized by their reliance on paper-based documentation and manual processes, are increasingly being viewed as inadequate for the demands of modern healthcare. This paper introduces a novel framework that utilizes blockchain technology, RSA-encrypted Non-Fungible Tokens (NFTs), and smart contracts to address the critical need for enhanced security and accessibility in child health records management. Drawing on the decentralization, transparency, and immutability of blockchain, along with the robust data protection offered by RSA encryption, our framework proposes a secure, efficient, and tamper-proof method for managing and accessing pediatric health information. Evaluation scenarios underscore the framework's effectiveness in RSA key generation, encryption/decryption processes, and integration with decentralized storage solutions like the InterPlanetary File System (IPFS). Our findings highlight the framework's potential to improve the management of child health records significantly, ensuring data integrity, confidentiality, and easy access for authorized parties.

**Keywords:** Pediatric Healthcare · Blockchain · Data Management · Electronic Health Records (EHRs) · Non-Fungible Tokens (NFTs) · InterPlanetary File System (IPFS) · Decentralized Storage · Smart Contracts

## 1 Introduction

The evolution of pediatric healthcare management is witnessing a paradigm shift towards the integration of advanced digital solutions [18]. This transition is underscored by the growing recognition of the limitations inherent in traditional health record systems, which rely heavily on paper-based documentation and manual processes. In response, our research proposes a novel framework that leverages blockchain technology, RSA-encrypted Non-Fungible Tokens (NFTs), and smart contracts to revolutionize the security and accessibility of child health records. This introduction sets the stage for a comprehensive discussion on how

Y. Zhang and L.-J. Zhang (Eds.): ICWS 2024, LNCS 15428, pp. 16–30, 2025.
https://doi.org/10.1007/978-3-031-77072-2_2

these technologies collectively offer a robust solution to the challenges faced by the existing healthcare record management systems.

The blockchain's inherent characteristics of decentralization, transparency, and immutability make it an ideal platform for securing sensitive health data. Previous studies, such as those by Quynh et al. [22] or Duong et al. [12,13], demonstrate blockchain's applicability in enhancing data security and patient privacy in healthcare. These studies provide a solid foundation for our investigation into the use of blockchain technology for managing child health records. Our work aims to build upon these initial explorations by integrating RSA encryption with NFTs, thereby ensuring the highest standards of data security and privacy. RSA encryption offers a robust mechanism for securing digital data, making it an ideal choice for protecting health information. By encrypting health records before they are stored on the blockchain, we can ensure that only authorized individuals have access to sensitive information. Furthermore, the use of NFTs allows for the unique representation of each child's health record on the blockchain, providing a secure and tamper-proof method for managing medical data.

Our evaluation scenarios, as outlined in Sect. 4, demonstrate the practicality and efficiency of the RSA-Encrypted NFT framework in managing child health data. Through systematic analysis and empirical testing, we have assessed the framework's performance in key areas such as RSA key generation, encryption and decryption times, and the overall process flow from data entry to retrieval. Our findings confirm the framework's potential to significantly enhance the security and efficiency of child health record management.

Moreover, the integration of decentralized storage systems like the Inter-Planetary File System (IPFS) with our RSA-Encrypted NFT framework further strengthens the security and reliability of the system. By storing encrypted health records on a distributed and redundant storage platform, we mitigate the risks of data loss, tampering, and unauthorized access. This approach not only ensures the integrity and confidentiality of child health information but also facilitates easy and secure access to medical data by authorized parties.

The testing of our framework on Ethereum Virtual Machine (EVM)-supported platforms, including Binance Smart Chain, Polygon, Fantom, and Celo, has provided valuable insights into the operational efficiency and cost-effectiveness of deploying smart contracts for managing child health records. Our analysis of transaction fees across these platforms reveals the economic viability of our approach, highlighting the potential for widespread adoption in the healthcare sector.

The rest of our paper is structured as follows: Sect. 2, *Related Work*, delves into the existing literature, examining various contributions and advancements relevant to our study. Section 3, *Approach*, details the methodologies and techniques employed in our research, providing a comprehensive understanding of the proposed solutions. In Sect. 4, *Evaluation*, we critically analyze the effectiveness of our approach through various metrics and benchmarks, demonstrating the practical implications and outcomes. Finally, Sect. 6, *Conclusion*, summarizes the key findings, discusses the implications of our work, and suggests potential avenues for future research.

## 2    Related Work

### 2.1    Blockchain Technology in Child Health Records

The application of blockchain technology in securing child health records is explored by Jain et al. [16], who present a blockchain-based system for safeguarding dyslexia health records. Their approach utilizes machine learning to detect dyslexia in early childhood, aiming for timely interventions. This system supports the secure sharing of data, which is critical for ongoing research and analysis in a language-independent framework.

In the dental healthcare domain for children, Al et al. [1] and Mohammed [19] implement smart contracts on the blockchain to manage patient privacy and treatment plans. Their systems, built on Ethereum and using Solidity, demonstrate how blockchain can preserve patient confidentiality while streamlining healthcare services. These contributions reflect the growing trend of integrating blockchain to enhance the reliability and security of child health records.

In more general, Bang et al. [3] present a Blockchain-Enhanced Internet of Healthcare Things (IoHT) platform. Their approach emphasizes a patient-centric model where smart contracts are used for efficient data management. In the same spirit, Nam et al. [20] and Lam et al. [27] present a system designed to secure patient medical records in the cloud - collecting medical data via IoT devices. These approaches utilizes a microservice and brokerless architecture, leveraging blockchain technology to ensure the privacy and security of patient data in cloud-based environments.

### 2.2    Advancements and Challenges of EHRs in Pediatric Care

The contribution of Electronic Medical Records (EMR) to the field of healthcare, particularly in enhancing quality and efficiency, is substantial. For instance, Son et al. [25] and Le et al. [17] both focus on employing blockchain technology for emergency situations in patient-centered healthcare systems. Moreover, Haskew et al. [15] showcase the pivotal role of cloud-based EMR in improving maternal and child health data completeness in rural Kenya, emphasizing the potential for EMRs to overcome geographical and resource barriers. Brady et al. [5] demonstrate how EMR alerts can significantly enhance the recognition of high blood pressure in children, a critical step towards proactive healthcare interventions. This is complemented by Smith et al. [24], who validate the accuracy of body weight and height data within EMRs, underscoring the reliability of EMRs in pediatric health monitoring.

The use of EMR data extends beyond routine healthcare delivery, as illustrated by Denburg et al. [11], who developed an EMR algorithm to rapidly identify children with glomerular disease for clinical research, thereby facilitating targeted studies in a niche patient population. Carsley et al. [9] explore

EMRs for epidemiological surveillance, revealing temporal trends in severe obesity among children and youth, which can inform public health strategies. Su et al. [26] leverage machine learning on EMR data to predict suicide risk in children and adolescents, showcasing the advanced analytical capabilities EMRs can provide in identifying at-risk populations.

The global health crisis underscored by Bourgeois et al. [4] through an international analysis of EMRs of children hospitalized with COVID-19 reflects the crucial role of EMRs in managing and understanding pandemics. Meanwhile, Do et al. [8] discuss the ergonomic considerations in EMR design to support collaborative mental care for children and youth, indicating the importance of user-centric approaches in EMR development. Bruns et al. [7] evaluate the impact of a web-based EMR on behavioral health service delivery, providing insights into the potential and limitations of EMRs in specialized care settings.

Brooks et al. [6] highlight the challenges and opportunities in using administrative health data within EMRs for identifying children and youth with autism spectrum disorder, stressing the need for accurate data coding and algorithm development. Choudhary et al. [10] illustrate the benefits of EMR templates in improving diabetes care for children, showcasing how structured EMR content can support clinical guideline adherence. Nguyen et al. [21] offer a perspective on the implementation challenges and strategies for EMRs in developing countries, focusing on child health in Vietnam, which is critical for understanding the broader implications of EMR adoption globally.

Furthermore, Hagstrom et al. [14] provide a comprehensive review of the varying experiences and views on web-based EMR access for children, adolescents, and parents, emphasizing the importance of stakeholder engagement in EMR policy and design. The application of EMR in specialized settings like the intensive care unit is discussed by Al et al. [2], who assess system use and effectiveness, contributing to the discourse on EMR customization for acute care environments. Lastly, Shaikh et al. [23] investigate the impact of EMR-presented BMI on weight assessment and counseling practices, highlighting the potential of EMRs to facilitate critical health conversations.

# 3   Approach

## 3.1   Traditional Model for Pediatric Healthcare

The flowchart illustrates the conventional method of managing child health records, a process characterized by its reliance on human intervention and paper-based documentation. This traditional model delineates a series of steps beginning with healthcare providers, such as nurses, who are responsible for the initial creation of medical records. These records serve as foundational documents, capturing critical health data for children who are, by nature of their age and development, dependent on adult guardians for their healthcare management.

Once these records are established, they are transferred to the guardians, typically the parents, who hold the primary responsibility for their child's well-being. This handoff signifies a shift in the custody of information, placing the

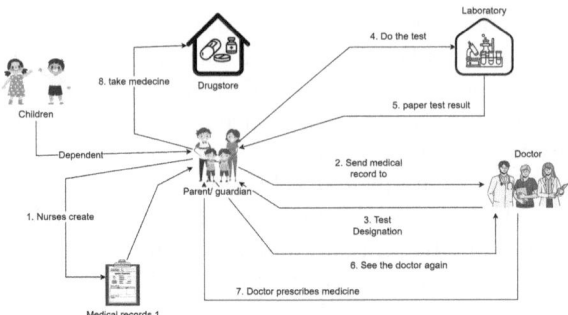

**Fig. 1.** Classic model for pediatric healthcare

onus on the parent or guardian to maintain and transport these records to subsequent healthcare appointments. The records are then presented to doctors, who assess the child's health and determine if further medical tests are necessary (Fig. 1).

Should testing be required, a designation for the specific tests is made, directing the next phase of the process to a laboratory setting. Here, the ordered tests are conducted, resulting in a tangible, paper-based outcome. These test results, often critical to the child's ongoing medical assessment, are then returned to the doctor for review. The tangible nature of these records, while straightforward, presents numerous challenges, including the risk of loss, damage, or misplacement. Upon reviewing the test results, the child is typically brought back to see the doctor. This subsequent consultation allows for the assessment of the test outcomes and determination of the next steps in the child's medical care. If medication is prescribed, the process then extends to a drugstore, where the prescription is filled, and medicine is dispensed for administration to the child.

This model is marked by its linear and segmented progression, where each stakeholder operates within their defined role, and the medical records act as a physical token of information exchange. While this method has been the standard for decades, it inherently lacks the dynamism to quickly adapt to changes, and it is susceptible to inefficiencies stemming from its paper-based nature. The reliance on physical documents can also lead to increased risk of errors, a gap in real-time updates, and challenges in maintaining the confidentiality and integrity of the sensitive health information of the child.

### 3.2 Phase One: Establishing the Foundation for Secure Child Health Management with Blockchain and RSA-Encrypted NFTs

The diagram presents a structured approach to child health record-keeping by incorporating blockchain technology. At the core of this system is the allocation of a unique global identifier for each individual, which serves as a foundational element in the creation and maintenance of medical records by healthcare profes-

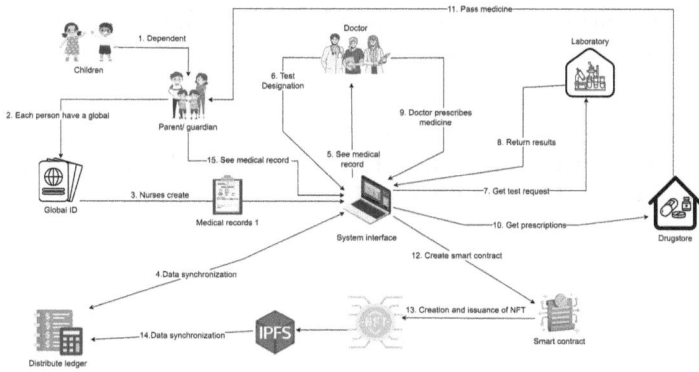

**Fig. 2.** Innovative Blockchain Model for Child Care

sionals, such as nurses. These identifiers are pivotal in ensuring that the health records are securely linked to the correct individual, thereby eliminating common errors associated with traditional record-keeping methods (Fig. 2).

The records created are then subject to a synchronization process with a distributed ledger, a hallmark of blockchain technology. This process is bidirectional and continuous, ensuring that all entries and modifications are consistently reflected across the system, thereby maintaining the integrity and up-to-dateness of the records. The distributed nature of the ledger allows for a decentralized form of data management, which intrinsically enhances the security and accessibility of the records.

Parents and guardians play a critical role in this ecosystem, acting as custodians of their children's health data. They interact with the system through an interface that enables them to review medical records, thus maintaining an informed position on their child's health status. In the event of a medical consultation, doctors access these records through the same system interface, ensuring that the most current health data informs their clinical decisions. When medical tests are prescribed, the system facilitates the seamless transmission of test requests to laboratories. Upon completion of the requested tests, results are returned through the system and synchronized with the distributed ledger, thus updating the child's health record in real-time. In scenarios where medication is prescribed, the system supports the electronic transmission of prescriptions to drugstores, streamlining the process of medication dispensation.

The advanced capabilities of this model are further extended through the creation of smart contracts. These contracts are programmed to execute specific actions within the blockchain when predefined conditions are met, such as the automatic renewal of prescriptions or the release of test results to authorized parties. Additionally, the system incorporates the IPFS for decentralized storage, enhancing data availability and persistence. Moreover, NFTs are used as a novel method of representing ownership and access rights to individual health records within the blockchain. The creation and issuance of these NFTs are governed by smart contracts, ensuring that each NFT is uniquely linked to a child's health record and that access is securely controlled and compliant with privacy regulations.

### 3.3  Phase Two: Integration of RSA-Encrypted NFTs and Smart Contracts for Secure Child Health Accessibility

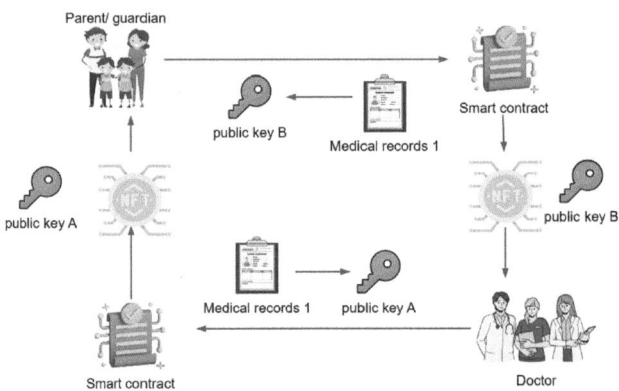

**Fig. 3.** Schematic representation of a child health record-keeping model using RSA-encrypted NFTs

The diagram provides an overview of a methodical approach to managing child health records employing RSA-encrypted Non-Fungible Tokens (NFTs) to ensure secure and private access. In this system, the guardians, such as parents or legal custodians, and healthcare providers like doctors, are the primary users who interact with the medical records through distinct public keys within the blockchain framework (Fig. 3).

At the outset, each guardian is assigned a unique public key (referred to as public key A in the diagram), which is essential for accessing the child's health records. The NFTs, which represent the child's health records, are encrypted using RSA encryption - a widely recognized method for securing sensitive data. The encrypted NFT is linked to the guardian's public key, ensuring that only they can access and manage their child's health data.

In parallel, healthcare providers are allocated a separate public key (public key B). When a doctor needs to access a childs health record, the NFT is decrypted using the corresponding private key that matches public key B. This decryption process allows for the secure and controlled viewing of medical records by healthcare professionals. The RSA encryption ensures that the data is transmitted and viewed without the risk of unauthorized access or exposure.

Smart contracts within the blockchain manage the permissions and actions associated with these NFTs. They execute predefined rules that govern who can access the health records, under what conditions, and what actions can be taken. For instance, a smart contract may be programmed to grant access to a new doctor when a child visits a new healthcare facility, or to update the medical records upon receiving new health information.

The architecture ensures that all interactions with the child's health records are logged and traceable. The use of blockchain technology provides an immutable ledger of transactions, which adds a layer of accountability and traceability to the record-keeping process. This method mitigates the risk of record tampering and provides a clear audit trail for all activities surrounding the child's health data.

This model represents a structured mechanism to safeguard the sensitive health data of children. By using RSA-encrypted NFTs, it addresses critical concerns around data security and privacy. The clear delineation of access rights via public and private keys, managed by smart contracts, provides a secure framework for managing child health records. This approach aims to enhance the integrity and confidentiality of health data, creating a more secure environment for managing the critical health information of minors.

## 4    Evaluation Scenarios

### 4.1    Evaluation of RSA-Encrypted NFT Framework for Efficiency in Managing Child Health Data

In evaluating the efficiency of the RSA-Encrypted NFT framework within the context of healthcare data management, particularly in the stewardship of child health records, a systematic analysis was undertaken. The framework's performance was scrutinized by simulating the encryption and decryption of two types of data: a digital image of size 120KB, representative of medical imaging, and a text string "Hello, RSA encryption!", exemplifying routine data entry.

The Table 1 presents the time metrics for RSA key generation, encryption, and decryption in the context of image data encryption, measured in microseconds. The key generation process shows variability, with times ranging from 44,450 µs to 105,556 µs, reflecting the complexity of RSA key generation. Encryption times for the image file are significantly faster, ranging from 4,660 µs to 15,391 µs, indicating a relatively quick encryption process. However, the decryption process is notably longer, with times spanning from 178,141 µs to 210,368 µs. This trend aligns with RSA's computational demands, where decryption is typically more time-intensive than encryption. These results highlight the efficiency trade-offs in the RSA encryption mechanism for handling image data.

Table 2 illustrates the time metrics for RSA key generation, encryption, and decryption in the context of text data encryption, measured in microseconds. The key generation times range from 41,933 µs to 215,695 µs, reflecting a significant variability similar to the image encryption context. Interestingly, the encryption process consistently shows 0 µs across all attempts, indicating either extremely rapid encryption or a possible measurement discrepancy. For decryption, most entries also show 0 µs, with only a few recorded times ranging from 516 µs to

**Table 1.** Assessment of Time Metrics for RSA Key Generation, Encryption, and Decryption in the Context of Image Data Encryption in Microseconds

| RSA image | 1 | 2 | 3 | 4 | 5 | 6 | 7 | 8 | 9 | 10 |
|---|---|---|---|---|---|---|---|---|---|---|
| Generating key | 66090 | 44450 | 91012 | 32803 | 50220 | 38981 | 51384 | 37016 | 105556 | 102577 |
| Encrypting image | 10402 | 10220 | 14418 | 12062 | 6190 | 7692 | 15391 | 13336 | 7613 | 4660 |
| Decrypting image | 196868 | 210368 | 184415 | 189742 | 178141 | 181396 | 188253 | 186014 | 188950 | 186903 |

1,327 µs. This suggests that the decryption process for text data is either very efficient or did not require substantial processing time.

**Table 2.** Assessment of Time Metrics for RSA Key Generation, Encryption, and Decryption in the Context of Text Data Encryption in Microseconds

| RSA (text) | 1 | 2 | 3 | 4 | 5 | 6 | 7 | 8 | 9 | 10 |
|---|---|---|---|---|---|---|---|---|---|---|
| Generating key | 215695 | 58710 | 93249 | 85934 | 41933 | 62422 | 52182 | 60206 | 62067 | 155582 |
| Encrypting text | 0 | 0 | 0 | 0 | 0 | 0 | 0 | 0 | 0 | 0 |
| Decrypting text | 0 | 0 | 0 | 516 | 0 | 1327 | 1112 | 1034 | 0 | 998 |

The implications of these results are two-fold. Firstly, the RSA encryption and decryption process exhibits a dependable performance for both text and image data, which are common data types within child health records. Although the times for key generation and decryption are considerable, they remain within the practical limits for applications that prioritize data security and integrity, such as those in the healthcare sector. Secondly, the relatively shorter duration of the encryption process is beneficial for operations that demand promptness, like updating health records in real-time following consultations or procedures.

The integration of the RSA-Encrypted NFT framework into the management of child health records necessitates a balance between robust security measures and operational efficiency. The empirical data gleaned from these experiments offer a substantive basis for the framework's application within the healthcare domain. It informs the understanding that while the RSA algorithm may introduce latency in key generation and decryption, its application in the safeguarding of sensitive health data is justified. The introduction of smart contracts alongside this encryption mechanism could provide automated oversight, ensuring that access to encrypted health records via NFTs is governed by predefined rules, thereby enhancing the system's overall efficacy and reliability.

## 4.2 Analysis of RSA-Encrypted NFTs in Conjunction with Decentralized Storage Systems

The first step in the process of securing child health records involves the careful structuring of data. This initial structure, as depicted in Fig. 4, outlines a

JSON object that holds key information pertinent to child health records. The object includes fields for test types, results, times, and places of testing, alongside identifiers for the medical professionals involved. This structured data is the foundation upon which security measures are applied.

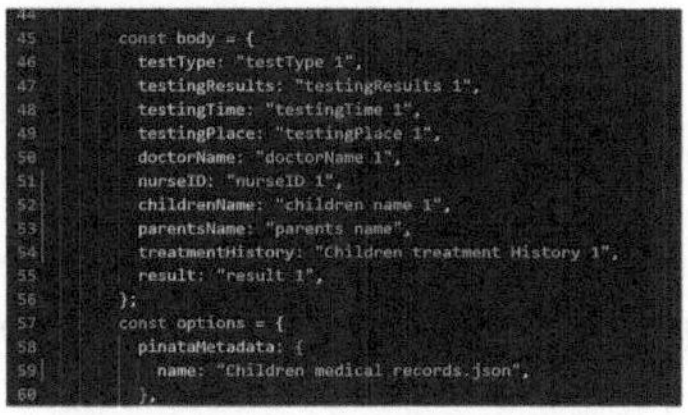

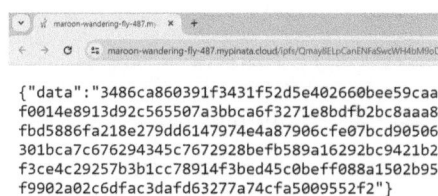

**Fig. 4.** Data structure for child health records to be RSA-encrypted and tokenized into NFTs

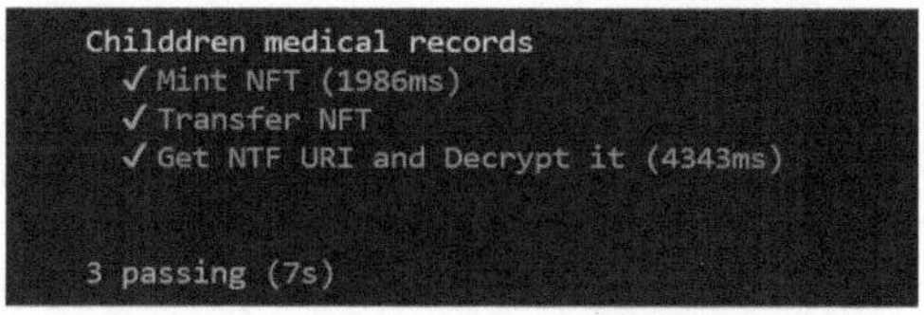

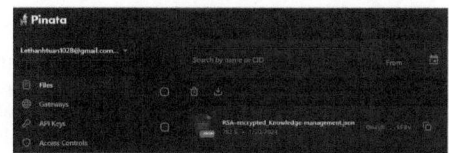

**Fig. 5.** Performance metrics of NFT minting and decryption processes in a child health record system.

Following data structuring, RSA encryption is used to secure the information. The application of RSA encryption transforms the data into a secure format, making it accessible only to those with the corresponding decryption keys. This step is crucial in preserving the confidentiality of sensitive child health information. Once encrypted, this data is tokenized into a Non-Fungible Token (NFT), creating a unique and secure representation of the child's health record on the blockchain (Fig. 5). This tokenization process includes minting the NFT—a procedure that embeds the encrypted data into a blockchain transaction—and measuring the time efficiency of the process, ensuring it meets the performance standards necessary for practical application.

The third step involves uploading the encrypted data to the InterPlanetary File System (IPFS), a decentralized and distributed file storage system. IPFS serves as a resilient and redundant platform to store and access the RSA-encrypted health records. This system is particularly suited to handle such sensitive data due to its robustness against data loss and tampering. Within the IPFS, the encrypted file is displayed with a clear reference to its content, indicating its purpose as a child health record (Fig. 7) (Fig. 6).

{"data":"3486ca860391f3431f52d5e402660bee59caa f0014e8913d92c565507a3bbca6f3271e8bdfb2bc8aaa8 fbd5886fa218e279dd6147974e4a87906cfe07bcd90506 301bca7c676294345c7672928befb589a16292bc9421b2 f3ce4c29257b3b1cc78914f3bed45c0beff088a1502b95 f9902a02c6dfac3dafd63277a74cfa5009552f2"}

**Fig. 6.** Representation of RSA-encrypted child health data retrieved from IPFS.

**Fig. 7.** Display of an RSA-encrypted child health record JSON file within the IPFS platform.

Lastly, the retrieval of this data is shown in Fig. 4, where the encrypted health record is fetched from the IPFS using its unique content identifier. The displayed data is in its encrypted form, signifying that the integrity of the data remains intact during storage and retrieval operations. This encrypted data represents the child's health record and is a testament to the security measures applied throughout the process.

## 4.3   Testing on EVM-Supported Platforms

The Ethereum Virtual Machine (EVM) serves as the foundational technology for the deployment of smart contracts, providing a consistent runtime environment across various blockchain platforms. In the pursuit of a secure child health record management system, our study has harnessed the capabilities of four EVM-compatible platforms: Binance Smart Chain, Polygon, Fantom, and Celo. These platforms have been meticulously selected to evaluate the critical functions integral to our system's operation.

The primary function under examination is the entry of new data, which constitutes the recording of child health records onto the blockchain. This process is fundamental, as it dictates the system's ability to efficiently incorporate new records. Our analysis focuses on the transaction initiation's speed, resource consumption, and the user-friendliness of the interface—parameters essential for a system that health professionals will interact with regularly.

The creation of Non-Fungible Tokens (NFTs) for each health record is the second pivotal function we assess. This step is essential for securing the uniqueness and confidentiality of each child's health data within the blockchain. Our assessment considers how effectively and securely these platforms can convert health records into NFTs, providing a robust mechanism for managing sensitive information.

Lastly, we appraise the transferability of NFTs across the network, a feature that mirrors the necessary exchange of medical records between entities. This transferability is a critical component in managing child health records, ensuring smooth transitions while maintaining high security and integrity. Our evaluation measures the ease, speed, and reliability of these NFT transfers, which are crucial for maintaining a seamless flow of accurate health data within the healthcare ecosystem.

**Table 3.** Transaction fee

| | Transaction Creation | Create NFT | Transfer NFT |
|---|---|---|---|
| BNB Smart Chain | 0.0273134 BNB ($8.27) | 0.00109162 BNB ($0.33) | 0.00057003 BNB ($0.17) |
| Fantom | 0.00957754 FTM ($0.00) | 0.000405167 FTM ($0.00) | 0.0002380105 FTM ($0.00) |
| Polygon | 0.006840710032835408 MATIC ($0.01) | 0.000289405001852192 MATIC ($0.00) | 0.000170007501088048 MATIC ($0.00) |
| Celo | 0.007097844 CELO ($0.005) | 0.0002840812 CELO ($0.000 ) | 0.0001554878 CELO ($0.000 ) |

The Table 3 provided offers a structured overview of the transaction fees incurred for specific operations pertinent to the management of child health records via blockchain technology. These operations, fundamental to the function of our system, include the creation of transactions-signifying the recording of new health data, the minting of Non-Fungible Tokens (NFTs)-representing the individual health records, and the transfer of NFTs-indicative of the shifting access rights between authorized parties. Furthermore, we provide an overview of the token prices for the platforms under review, as of January 27, 2024, at 7:00:00 AM UTC, aiming to offer a snapshot of the economic context surrounding these networks.

Starting with the BNB Smart Chain, the transaction creation fee is 0.0273134 BNB (equivalent to approximately $8.27), while creating an NFT incurs a fee of 0.00109162 BNB (approximately $0.33). The transfer of an NFT involves a slightly lower fee of 0.00057003 BNB (around $0.17). These fees, although relatively higher compared to other networks, need to be factored into the overall cost structure of implementing a system for securing child health records. However, it's worth noting that the BNB Smart Chain offers robust functionality and relatively high throughput, which could be advantageous for applications requiring quick and efficient transaction processing.

Moving to the Fantom network, the transaction fees are notably lower. Transaction creation costs 0.00957754 FTM (roughly $0.00), NFT creation is priced at 0.000405167 FTM (also negligible), and NFT transfer incurs a fee of 0.0002380105 FTM (virtually zero). These negligible fees could be attractive for applications with stringent cost constraints, such as managing sensitive health records, where minimizing operational expenses is paramount.

On the Polygon network, the transaction fees are similarly low. Transaction creation amounts to 0.006840710032835408 MATIC (approximately $0.01), NFT creation costs 0.000289405001852192 MATIC (almost negligible), and NFT transfer requires 0.000170007501088048 MATIC (also almost negligible). The low fees coupled with Polygon's scalability and interoperability features make it an appealing choice for implementing systems like securing child health records, ensuring cost-effectiveness without compromising on performance.

Lastly, the Celo network imposes modest transaction fees. Transaction creation comes at a cost of 0.007097844 CELO (roughly $0.005), while NFT creation and transfer incur fees of 0.0002840812 CELO and 0.0001554878 CELO, respectively (both negligible). Although slightly higher than Fantom and Polygon, Celo's fees remain relatively low and could be justified by its focus on accessibility and inclusivity, which align well with the goal of securing child health records in a decentralized and equitable manner.

In summary, when considering the implementation of a system to secure child health records with RSA-encrypted NFTs and smart contracts on the blockchain, evaluating transaction fees across different networks is essential. While some networks may offer lower fees, others might provide additional features or advantages that could outweigh the slightly higher costs. Therefore, a careful analysis of both the economic and technical aspects is crucial in selecting the most suitable blockchain network for such a critical application.

## 5	Discussion

### 5.1	Threats to Validity

While the evaluation presented in the preceding sections offers valuable insights into the performance and feasibility of the proposed RSA-Encrypted NFT framework for securing child health records, several threats to validity must be acknowledged. Firstly, the evaluation scenarios were conducted in a simulated environment, which may not fully capture the complexities and nuances of real-world usage. The simulated data used for encryption and decryption may not fully reflect the diversity and variability of actual child health records, potentially impacting the generalizability of the findings. Additionally, the evaluation focused primarily on the technical aspects of the framework, overlooking potential socio-economic factors that could influence its adoption and effectiveness in real-world healthcare settings.

### 5.2	Limitations

Several limitations inherent to the proposed framework warrant consideration. Firstly, the computational overhead associated with RSA key generation and decryption, as evidenced by the evaluation results, may pose scalability challenges, particularly in scenarios involving large volumes of health records. Moreover, while the integration of smart contracts enhances the security and automation of access control, it introduces additional complexity to the system, potentially impacting its usability and maintenance. Furthermore, the reliance on blockchain technology introduces dependencies on external factors such as network congestion and gas fees, which could affect the system's reliability and cost-effectiveness over time.

## 6	Conclusion

This study presents a comprehensive framework for the secure management of child health records, leveraging the synergies of blockchain technology, RSA encryption, and smart contracts. The integration of these technologies provides a secure and efficient solution to the challenges inherent in traditional health record systems. Through detailed evaluation, our research demonstrates the practicality and efficiency of using RSA-encrypted NFTs for health data management, supported by decentralized storage systems for enhanced data integrity and accessibility. The deployment of this framework on EVM-compatible platforms further validates its operational efficiency and economic viability. Our contribution to the field of healthcare technology marks a significant step towards redefining the management of pediatric health records, ensuring a higher standard of data security, privacy, and accessibility. The implications of this research promise to enhance the quality and safety of healthcare delivery for children and set a new benchmark for the application of blockchain technology in healthcare.

# References

1. Al-Rubaye, W.M.A., Kurnaz, S.: Blockchain and smart contracts to improve dental healthcare for children in primary school. In: 2021 International Conference on Advanced Computer Applications (ACA), pp. 62–67. IEEE (2021)
2. Al-Shammari, M.A.G., Yasir, A.A., Al-Doori, N.M.: Application of electronic medical record at intensive care unit in maternity and children hospital (2009)
3. Bang, N., et al.: Blockchain enhanced IoHT: a patient-centric internet of healthcare things platform with smart contract driven data management. In: Haghighi, P.D., Khalil, I., Kotsis, G., ER, N.A.S. (eds.) Advances in Mobile Computing and Multimedia Intelligence, MoMM 2023. Lecture Notes in Computer Science, vol. 14417, pp. 50–56. Springer, Cham (2023). https://doi.org/10.1007/978-3-031-48348-6_4
4. Bourgeois, F.T., et al.: International analysis of electronic health records of children and youth hospitalized with COVID-19 infection in 6 countries. JAMA Netw. Open 4(6), e2112596–e2112596 (2021)
5. Brady, T.M., Neu, A.M., Miller, E.R., III., Appel, L.J., Siberry, G.K., Solomon, B.S.: Real-time electronic medical record alerts increase high blood pressure recognition in children. Clin. Pediatr. 54(7), 667–675 (2015)
6. Brooks, J.D., et al.: Assessing the validity of administrative health data for the identification of children and youth with autism spectrum disorder in Ontario. Autism Res. 14(5), 1037–1045 (2021)
7. Bruns, E.J., et al.: Impact of a web-based electronic health record on behavioral health service delivery for children and adolescents: randomized controlled trial. J. Med. Internet Res. 20(6), e10197 (2018)
8. do Carmo Alonso, C.M., et al.: Contributions of activity ergonomics to the design of an electronic health record to support collaborative mental care of children and youth: preliminary results. Work 65(1), 187–194 (2020)
9. Carsley, S., Pope, E.I., Anderson, L.N., Tremblay, M.S., Tu, K., Birken, C.S.: Temporal trends in severe obesity prevalence in children and youth from primary care electronic medical records in Ontario: a repeated cross-sectional study. Canadian Med. Assoc. Open Access J. 7(2), E351–E359 (2019)
10. Choudhary, D., Brown, B., Khawar, N., Narula, P., Agdere, L.: Implementation of electronic medical record template improves screening for complications in children with type 1 diabetes mellitus. Pediatric Health Med. Therapeut. (2020)
11. Denburg, M.R., et al.: Using electronic health record data to rapidly identify children with glomerular disease for clinical research. J. Am. Soc. Nephrol. 30(12), 2427 (2019)
12. Duong-Trung, N., et al.: On components of a patient-centered healthcare system using smart contract. In: Proceedings of the 2020 4th International Conference on Cryptography, Security and Privacy, pp. 31–35 (2020)
13. Duong-Trung, N., et al.: Smart care: integrating blockchain technology into the design of patient-centered healthcare systems. In: Proceedings of the 2020 4th International Conference on Cryptography, Security and Privacy, pp. 105–109 (2020)

14. Hagström, J., Blease, C., Haage, B., Scandurra, I., Hansson, S., Hägglund, M.: Views, use, and experiences of web-based access to pediatric electronic health records for children, adolescents, and parents: scoping review. J. Med. Internet Res. **24**(11), e40328 (2022)

15. Haskew, J., et al.: Implementation of a cloud-based electronic medical record for maternal and child health in rural Kenya. Int. J. Med. Inform. **84**(5), 349–354 (2015)

16. Jain, M., Pandey, D., Sharma, K.K.: A blockchain approach on security of health records for children suffering from dyslexia during pandemic COVID-19. In: Artificial Intelligence, Machine Learning, and Mental Health in Pandemics, pp. 343–363. Elsevier (2022)

17. Le, H.T., et al.: Patient-chain: patient-centered healthcare system a blockchain-based technology in dealing with emergencies. In: Shen, H., et al. (eds.) PDCAT 2021. LNCS, vol. 13148, pp. 576–583. Springer, Cham (2022). https://doi.org/10.1007/978-3-030-96772-7_54

18. Le, H.T., et al.: Bloodchain: a blood donation network managed by blockchain technologies. Network **2**(1), 21–35 (2022)

19. Mohammed Araby Al Rubaye, W.: Blockchain in healthcare: Smart contracts to improve dental healthcare for children in mixed dentition period. Master's thesis, Altınbaş Üniversitesi, Lisansüstü Eğitim Enstitüsü (2021)

20. Nam, T., et al.: SPaMeR: securing patient medical records in the cloud-a microservice and brokerless architecture approach. In: Zhang, Y., Zhang, L.J. (eds.) ICWS 2023. LNCS, vol. 14209, pp. 32–46. Springer, Cham (2023). https://doi.org/10.1007/978-3-031-44836-2_3

21. Nguyen, T.N.: Institutional perspectives on implementing health information systems in developing countries: the case of electronic medical records (EMR) for children health in Vietnam (2010)

22. Quynh, N.T.T., et al.: Toward a design of blood donation management by blockchain technologies. In: Gervasi, O., et al. (eds.) ICCSA 2021. LNCS, vol. 12956, pp. 78–90. Springer, Cham (2021). https://doi.org/10.1007/978-3-030-87010-2_6

23. Shaikh, U., Nelson, R., Tancredi, D., Byrd, R.S.: Presentation of body mass index within an electronic health record to improve weight assessment and counselling in children and adolescents. Inform. Primary Care **18**(4) (2010)

24. Smith, N., et al.: Body weight and height data in electronic medical records of children. Int. J. Pediatr. Obes. **5**(3), 237–242 (2010)

25. Son, H.X., Le, T.H., Quynh, N.T.T., Huy, H.N.D., Duong-Trung, N., Luong, H.H.: Toward a Blockchain-Based Technology in Dealing with Emergencies in Patient-Centered Healthcare Systems. In: Bouzefrane, S., Laurent, M., Boumerdassi, S., Renault, E. (eds.) MSPN 2020. LNCS, vol. 12605, pp. 44–56. Springer, Cham (2021). https://doi.org/10.1007/978-3-030-67550-9_4

26. Su, C., Aseltine, R., Doshi, R., Chen, K., Rogers, S.C., Wang, F.: Machine learning for suicide risk prediction in children and adolescents with electronic health records. Transl. Psychiatry **10**(1), 413 (2020)

27. Thanh, L.N.T., et al.: IoHT-MBA: an internet of healthcare things (IoHT) platform based on microservice and brokerless architecture. Int. J. Adv. Comput. Sci. Appl. **12**(7) (2021)

# A Novel Redundant Service Caching and Task Offloading Method in Mobile Edge Computing

Zhaobin Ouyang[1], Yunni Xia[1(✉)], Jingpeng Li[1], Jiafeng Feng[2], Yang Yu[3], Ke Zhang[4], Xifeng Xu[1], Yong Ma[5(✉)], Peng Chen[6], and Xiaobo Li[7]

[1] School of Computer, Chongqing University, Chongqing 400030, China
xiayunni@hotmail.com
[2] China Huadian Corporation Guangdong Branch, Guangdong, China
[3] Nanjing Nanzi Huadun Digital Technology Co., Ltd., Nanjing, China
[4] School of Computer Science and Technology, Beijing Institute of Technology, Beijing 100083, China
[5] School of Computer and Information Engineering, Jiangxi Normal University, Nanchang 330000, China
may@jxnu.edu.cn
[6] School of Computer and Software Engineering, Xihua University, Chengdu, China
[7] Chongqing Animal Husbandry Techniques Extension Center, Chongqing, China

**Abstract.** Edge caching is a promising technologies, which enhances content delivery and reduces service latency by caching potentially interested content and services on edge nodes near users. Due to constraints such as limited edge server capacities and unstable communications in a highly dynamic MEC environment, caching and content delivery are prone to failures and inconsistencies. Consequently, redundant caching mechanisms are in high need as counter measures in this paper, we proposes a novel redundant service caching and task offloading Decision (FT-STD) method. Specifically, we utilize the primary backup (PB) approach for offloading fault tolerance and employ a learning-based algorithm for yielding redundant service caching schedules in MEC. Simulation results demonstrate thatclearly outperforms its peers across multiple performance metrics.

**Keywords:** Service caching · Task offloading · Redundancy · Primary Backup

## 1 Introduction

Recently, with the rapid growth of user-centric computing applications and the increasing popularity of novel services such as cloud computing and edge computing [1,2], a significant amount of attention has been paid to the emergence

This work was supported by the grants from Sichuan Provincial Natural Science Foundation under Grant No. 2024NSFTD0008.

of numerous latency-sensitive or computationally intensive dependent applications, which requires high system responsiveness and low communication latency. Edge caching is a promising solution to the above requirement. By caching service applications on edge servers close to users and offloading service requests to the edge servers where the corresponding service applications are cached, edge caching and offloading strategy can reduce communication overhead and alleviates the workload of central cloud servers [3–5].

Nevertheless, due to the highly dynamic and error prone natures of MEC, computation and caching activities performed at the edge are prone to inconsistency and faults caused by, e.g., instability of inter-edge-node communications. [6]. These failures can have a disruptive impact on task execution. When these dependent tasks are collaboratively processed on distributed edge servers, the vulnerabilities and impacts caused by such failures become more pronounced. Therefore, it is crucial to develop fault-tolerance strategies to mitigate these negative impacts. Fault-tolerance and redundant mechanisms fall into two categories, namely proactive redundancy and passive one [7,8]. Proactive redundancy involves taking measures to prevent failures before task execution, such as task redundancy and real-time monitoring. Passive redundancy involves recovery after a failure occurs, with the most popular passive redundancy method being the Primary-Backup (PB) approach [9,10]. Which creates a primary replica and a backup replica for each service application and places the replicas on different edge nodes, so that when the primary replica fails, the backup replica can take over the task execution. However, achieving high-quality redundancy is challenging, mainly due to (1) the caching capacity of edge servers is usually limited, (2) caching decisions should be made at runtime with near-0 delays but the corresponding optimization problems are usually NP-hard.

In this paper, we propose a novel redundant service caching and task offloading decision (FT-STD) method. Specifically, we employ the PB model and yielding high-quality service caching and task offloading schedules in an fault-prone MEC environment.

## 2   Related Work

In recent years, caching is receiving extensive attention from both academy and industry. For example, Cai *et al.* [11] studied the joint 3C control problem for efficiently delivering data-intensive services. Chu *et al.* [12] proposed a novel two-stage algorithm solution based on approximation and decomposition theory for jointly optimizing service caching, resource allocation, and task offloading decisions. Qin *et al.* [13] proposed an efficient joint optimization algorithm, JO-CDSD, based on Lyapunov optimization and Generalized Benders Decomposition (GBD), for jointly optimizing base station clustering and service caching decisions. Zhang *et al.* [14] proposed a caching scheme based on content importance, where caching decisions are made according to the evaluated importance of the content. Yao *et al.* [15] proposed a multi-agent reinforcement learning algorithm based on graph attention to learn the optimal service caching and task offloading strategies. Xu *et al.* [16] proposed an online algorithm to jointly optimize dynamic service caching and task offloading. Zhao *et al.* [17] proposed an efficient algorithm based on convex programming to address the offloading problem of dependent tasks.

The above research do not consider handling the failure of dependent tasks. Chen *et al.* [18] proposed a novel deep neural network model training method, incorporating a fault-tolerance mechanism for training on distributed hetero-geneous devices. Cai *et al.* [19] proposed a redundancy strategy to address the high availability of cloud applications in a cloud-edge collaborative environment. Long *et al.* [20] proposed a semi-online redundancy offloading method based on the PB model and formulated offloading decisions using the DQN algorithm. The application of the PB model in passive fault tolerance is a hot topic in various fault-tolerance research fields, but there is limited research on edge service caching and task offloading.

## 3   System Models

As shown in Fig. 1, we assume a MEC computing configuration comprising a central cloud server (CS) and multiple base stations (BSs) $B = \{b_1, b_2, \ldots, b_n\}$, where $b_i$ is the $i$-th base station. We define $U_i^t = \{u_1^t, u_2^t, \ldots, u_m^t\}$ to represent a set of user equipment (UEs) connected to base station $b_i$ at time $t$, where $u_j^t$ is the $j$-th user equipment connected to base station $b_i$.

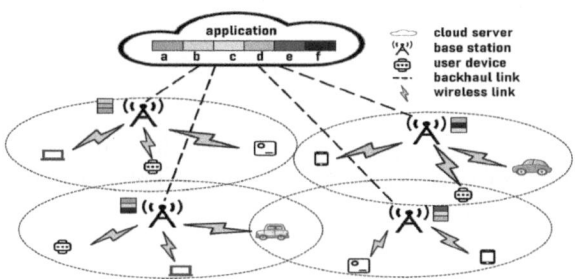

**Fig. 1.** System model.

Each BSs is equipped with an edge servers (ES) $E = \{es_1, es_2, \ldots, es_n\}$, the edge server $es_i$ is equipped with storage resources $RS_i$ and computing resources $RC_i$, and uses docker to store service applications $A = \{a_1, a_2, \ldots, a_l\}$ and run service applications, where $a_k$ is the $k$-th service. We use $rs_k$ to represent the storage resources required and $rc_k$ to represent the computing resources (CPU cycles) required by service application $a_k$. Due to the limited resources of the edge server, it can only deploy part of the service applications, while the CS can deploy all the service applications. We define $S = \{s_1, s_2, \ldots, s_l\}$ as the

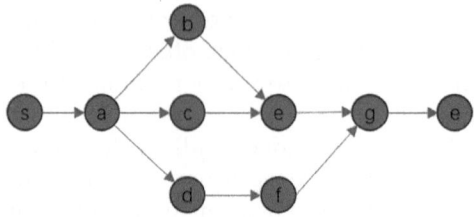

**Fig. 2.** An example of dependent subtask.

set of minimum tasks, each task $s_k$ can only be processed in specific service applications $a_k$.

As shown in Fig. 2, the service request task $s_k$ sent by each user equipment consists of multiple interdependent subtasks. In high-load environments, errors may occur in both the task processing and transmission processes. If the result of a predecessor subtask is not obtained or subsequent subtasks cannot be processed at a certain stage, the remaining tasks need to be handed over to the CS for processing.

## 3.1   Service Caching Model

Due to the limited storage and computing resources of edge servers, we define a binary variable $x^t_{i,k} \in \{0,1\}$ to indicate whether the service application $a_k$ is cached in edge server $es_i$ at time $t$. Then the storage resource constraint for edge server $es_i$ is:

$$\sum_{s_k \in S} x^t_{i,k} \cdot rc_k \leq RC_i \tag{1}$$

Define a binary variable $y^t_{i,k} \in \{0,1\}$ to indicate whether the service application $a_k$ is running in edge server $es_i$ at time $t$. Then the computing resource constraint for edge server $es_i$ is:

$$\sum_{a_k \in A, x^t_{i,k}=1} y^t_{i,k} \cdot rc_k \leq RC_i \tag{2}$$

## 3.2   Computation and Communication Model

In this paper, we define a binary variable $z^{t,c}_{x,i} \in \{0,1\}$ to indicate whether channel $c$ is allocated by $b_i$ in time $t$ to describe the channel allocation, each channel can only be assigned to one user equipment or other base station. Therefore, in time $t$, the transmission rate $r^{t,c}_{x,i}$ from $u_x$ or $b_x$ to base station $b_i$ on channel $c$ is

$$r^{t,c}_{x,i} = w\log_2\left(1 + \frac{p_x g^{t,c}_{x,i}}{\sigma^2 + I^{t,c}_i}\right), \tag{3}$$

where $g_{x,i}^{t,c}$ is the channel gain of user equipment $u_x$ or base station $b_x$ transmitting on channel $c$ to $b_i$, $w$ the channel bandwidth, $p_x$ the transmission power of device $x$, $\sigma^2$ the noise power, and $I_i^{t,c}$ the interference received on channel $c$ from other user equipment or base stations to $b_i$.

$$I_i^{t,c} = \sum_{\substack{y \in (B \cup U_i) \\ y \neq x}} z_{y,i}^{t,c} p_x g_{x,i}^{t,c} \tag{4}$$

where $B$ and $U_i$ respectively represent the base stations connected to base station $b_i$ and the user equipment.

We define $lt_{x,i}^t$ as the transmission latency of data $d_{x,i}^t$ between $u_x$ or $b_x$ and base station $b_i$, and $lc_{k,i}^t$ as the processing latency of service $s_k$ on the base station $b_i$:

$$lt_{x,i}^t = \begin{cases} 0, & \text{if } x = b_n \\ \dfrac{d_{x,i}^t}{r_{x,b_i}^{t,c}}, & \text{if } x \neq b_n \end{cases} \tag{5a}$$

$$lc_{k,i}^t = \frac{d_{x,i}^t \cdot \rho_k}{f_i} \tag{5b}$$

where $\rho_k$ is the computational intensity of subtask $s_k$ and $f_i$ is the computational capacity of the $e_i$.

### 3.3  Redundant Task Offloading Model

The service request task $T_s$ from the user needs to be processed by several subtasks, and the final processing results are returned to the user. For each type of subtask $s_k$, its corresponding service application $a_k$ needs to be started for processing. Here, we assume that the processing combination of subtasks is formally a Directed Acyclic Graph (DAG), which can satisfy the constraints of subtask combinations. The DAG is formally $W = \{T, D\}$, where $T_s = \{s_1, s_2, ..., s_k\}$ indicates a set of tasks, and $D = \{D_{u,v} \mid s_u, s_v \in T_s\}$ a set of dependencies, where $D_{u,v} = 1$ indicates that $s_v$ can only be executed after $s_u$ is completed, otherwise $D_{u,v} = 0$. For a partial subtask set $T_s = \{s_g, s_u, s_v\}$ satisfying $D_{g,u} = 1, D_{u,v} = 1$, the direct predecessor subtask set of $s_v$ is $DP_{s_v} = \{s_u\}$, and the predecessor subtask set of $s_v$ is $P_{s_v} = \{s_g, s_u\}$.

According to the PB model, each subtask $s_k$ owns a primary replica $pt_k$ and a backup replica $bt_k$, which are delivered to two different $docker_i$ and $docker_j$ for processing. For any set of dependent subtasks where $D_{u,v} = 1$, the subtask $s_v$ is first classified into strong primary replica or weak primary replica based on whether the start time of the primary replica $pt_v$ is after the completion time of the backup replica $bt_u$ of the preceding subtask. Figure 3a illustrates the case where $pt_v$ as a strong primary replica, meaning $s_v$ can receive the processing results from both the primary replica $pt_u$ and the backup replica $bt_u$ of the predecessor task $s_u$. Figure 3b illustrates the scenario where $s_v$ is a weak primary replica. For example, when the edge server fails to execute the primary replica,

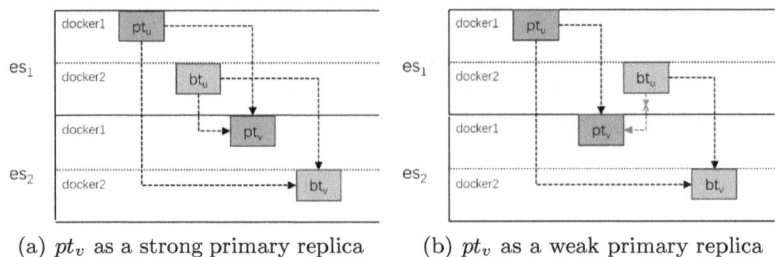

(a) $pt_v$ as a strong primary replica    (b) $pt_v$ as a weak primary replica

**Fig. 3.** The example of strong and weak primary replica.

the backup replica $bt_u$ is executed. Since $bt_u$ cannot reach $pt_v$, $pt_v$ cannot receive the processing result of the predecessor subtask $bt_u$, so $pt_v$ is a weak primary replica. We define $l_{u,v}$ to represent the relationship between $x_u$ and $y_v$, where $x_u$ can be $pt_u$ or $bt_u$, and $y_v$ can be $pt_v$ or $bt_v$.

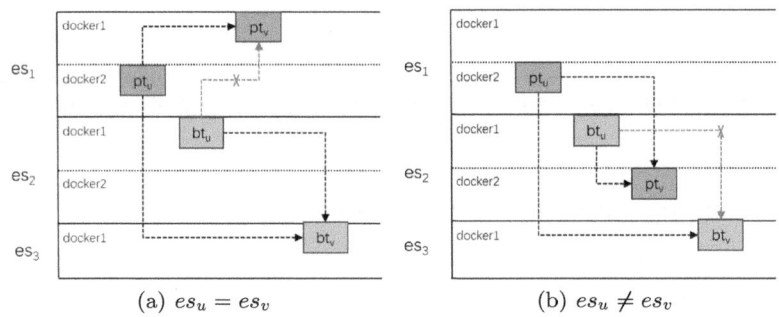

(a) $es_u = es_v$    (b) $es_u \neq es_v$

**Fig. 4.** $pt_u$ as a strong primary replica and $pt_v$ as a strong primary replica.

As shown in Fig. 4, when $pt_u$ indicates a strong primary replica and $pt_v$ a strong primary replica, when $es_u = es_v$, $l_{b_i p_j}$ represents redundant links, so the earliest start time of $bt_v$ is $st_{bt_v} = max(ft_{pt_u} + lt^t_{1,3}, ft_{bt_u} + lt^t_{2,3})$, where $ft_{pt_u}$ is the completion time of the primary replica $pt_u$, and $ft_{bt_u}$ is the completion time of the backup replica $bt_u$. When $es_u \neq es_v$, $l_{b_i b_j}$ represents redundant links, and the earliest starting time of $bt_v$ is $st_{bt_v} = ft_{pt_u} + lt^t_{1,3}$.

As shown in Fig. 5, when $pt_u$ indicates a strong primary replica and $pt_v$ is a weak primary replica, regardless of whether $es_u$ and $es_v$ are the same, the earliest start time of $bt_j$ is $st_{bt_v} = max(ft_{pt_u} + lt^t_{1,3}, ft_{bt_u} + lt^t_{2,3})$.

As shown by Fig. 6, $pt_u$ is the weak primary replica, and $pt_v$ is the strong primary replica. When $es_1 \neq es_2$ and $bt_v$ has not been assigned to the edge server in which the previous subtask was assigned, i.e., state (1), $l_{bt_u bt_v}$ is a redundant link.

As shown in Fig. 7a, when $pt_u$ indicates a weak primary replica and $pt_v$ a weak primary replica, when $es_u = es_v$, $l_{pt_u bt_v}$ represents redundant links. When

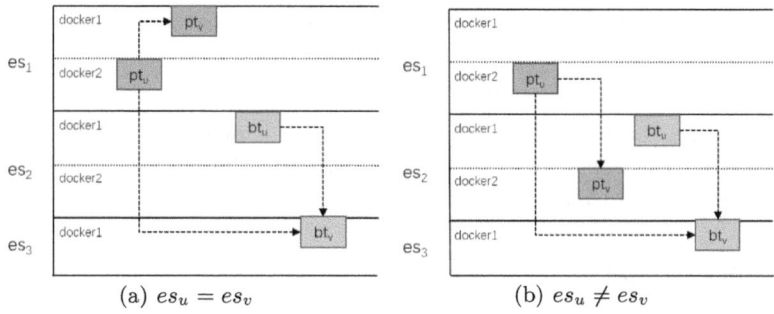

**Fig. 5.** $pt_u$ as a strong primary replica and $pt_v$ as a weak primary replica.

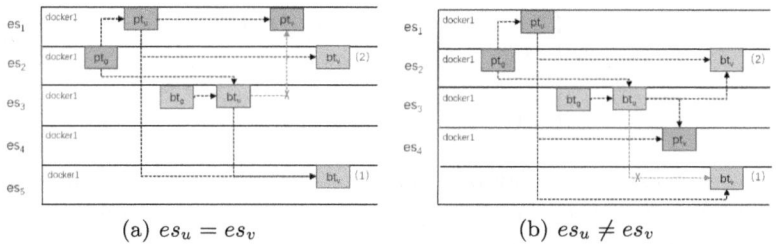

**Fig. 6.** $pt_u$ as a weak primary replica and $pt_v$ as a strong primary replica.

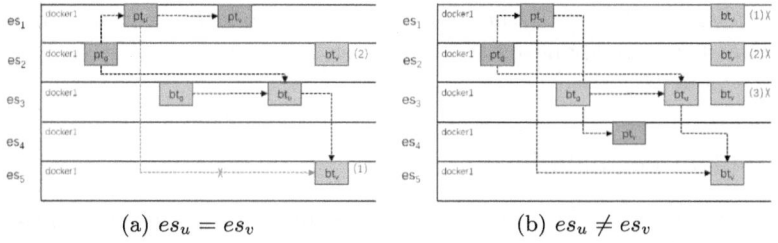

**Fig. 7.** $pt_u$ as a weak primary replica and $pt_v$ as a weak primary replica.

$es_u \neq es_v$, as shown in Fig. 7b, weak primary replica $bt_v$ is not allowed to select the edge service chosen by the predecessor subtask.

Based on the above observations, we estimate the available edge server set for $bt_v$ based on all its predecessor sub-tasks. $WT_{s_v}$ represents the subset of subtasks in $DP_{s_v}$ for which $pt_v$ is a weak primary replica, for example, $WT_{s_v} = \{s_u\}$. $HT_{s_v}$ represents the set of tasks in $DP_{s_v}$ and $P_{s_v}$ for which $pt_u$ is a weak primary replica.

$$HT_{s_v} = WT_{s_v} \cup \{\cup_{s_u \in WT_{s_v}} T_u\} \tag{6}$$

$SD_{s_v}$ and $ST_{s_u}$ respectively represent the edge servers allocated to the primary replica in $WT_{s_v}$ and $\cup_{s_u \in WT_{s_v}} T_u$. The set of edge servers allocated to tasks that make $s_v$ a weak primary replica and subtasks that could make $t_v$ a weak primary replica are:

$$\Gamma_v = \{SD_{s_v}\} \cup \{ST_{s_u}\} \cup \{s_v\} \tag{7}$$

This formula indicates that when $pt_v$ is a weak primary replica, $bt_v$ cannot be deployed on the edge servers in the set $\Gamma_v$, and the earliest starting time of $bt_v$ cannot be earlier than max.

### 3.4   Utility Model

To better assess the Quality of Service (Qos) of user, we have defined a utility function, as follows:

$$U_{j,k}^t = \begin{cases} 1, & 0 < l_{j,k}^t \le l_{j,k}^{t,min} \\ \frac{l_{j,k}^{t,max} - l_{j,k}^t}{l_{j,k}^{t,max} - l_{j,k}^{t,min}}, & l_{j,k}^{t,min} < l_{j,k}^t \le l_{j,k}^{t,max} \\ -1, & \text{otherwise} \end{cases} \tag{8}$$

As shown in Eq. (8), we adopt a non-increasing piecewise linear function to map the service processing Latency $l_{j,k}^t = lt_{j,i}^t + lc_{k,i}^t$ to the opinion scorecard of each user. Specifically, when $0 < l_{j,k}^t \le l_{j,k}^{t,min}$, we consider this service processing as high-quality, $U_{j,k}^t = 1$; when $l_{j,k}^{t,min} < l_{j,k}^t \le l_{j,k}^{t,max}$, the Qos of user decreases with the increase of service processing Latency, thus the Qos of user is between 0 and 1; when $l_{j,k}^t > l_{j,k}^{t,max}$, the QoE of UE exceeds the coverage range, which implies that the corresponding service processing fails, and U is represented as a negative value, $U_{j,k}^t = -1$.

### 3.5   Problem Formulation

Based on the above model, our goal is to maximize utility, and the optimization formulation is:

$$\mathbf{P}: \quad \max_{X,Z,Y} \frac{1}{|T| \cdot \sum_{b_i \in B} |U_i| \cdot |S|} \sum_{t \in T} \sum_{b_i \in B} \sum_{u_j \in U_i} \sum_{s_k \in S} U_{j,k}^t \tag{9}$$

$$\text{s.t.} \quad x_{i,k}^t \in \{0,1\}, \quad \forall i,k,t \tag{C1}$$

$$y_{i,k}^t \in \{0,1\}, \quad \forall i,k,t \tag{C2}$$

$$z_{y,i}^{t,c} \in \{0,1\}, \quad \forall i,k,t \tag{C3}$$

$$\sum_{s_k \in S} x_{i,k}^t \cdot rc_k \le RC_i, \forall i,k,t, \tag{C4}$$

$$\sum_{a_k \in A, x_{i,k}^t = 1} y_{i,k}^t \cdot rc_k \le RC_i, \forall i,k,t, \tag{C5}$$

$$\sum z_{y,i}^{t,c} \le 1, \quad \forall i,c,t. \tag{C6}$$

where $X = \{x_{i,k}^t\}_{b_i \in B, s_k \in S, t \in T}$ indicates a set of service application cache decisions, $Z = \{z_{y,i}^{t,c}\}_{b_i \in B, s_k \in S, t \in T}$ a set of the channel allocation decisions, $Y = \{y_{i,k}^t\}_{b_i \in B, s_k \in S, t \in T}$ a set of subtasks uninstall decisions. Constraint C4 indicates that the cached service application is bounded by storage resource capacity of BS, constraint C5 indicates that the activated subtask cannot exceed the computing resource capacity of BS, and constraint C6 indicates that each channel in one BS can be allocated to one UE or one BS at most.

The above optimization problem can be formulated as a decentralized observable Markov decision process (Dec-OMDP) known to be NP-hard.

---

**Algorithm 1:** Redundant Task Offloading

**Input**: $TL$ for the list of dependent subtasks, $PSL$ for the edge servers associated with the primary replica of the application server, and $BSL$ for the edge servers associated with the backup replica of the application server

**while** $TL$ *is not null* **do**

    select the first subtask from $TL$.

    select the edge server $es_{p_k}$ where $s_{p_k}$ is located, and the edge server $es_{b_k}$ where $s_{b_k}$ is located

    **if** *edge server* $es_{p_k}$ *in* $PSL$ *not failed* **then**

        $ft_{pt_k} = st_{sp_k} + lc_{k,i}^t$

        **if** $ft_{pt_k} < ft_{s_k}$ **then**

            $ft_{s_k} = ft_{pt_k}$

        **end**

    **end**

    **else if** *edge server* $es_{b_k}$ *in* $BSL$ *not failed* **then**

        $ft_{bt_k} = st_{bt_k} + lc_{k,i}^t$

        **if** $ft_{bt_k} < ft_{s_k}$ **then**

            $ft_{s_k} = ft_{bt_k}$

        **end**

    **end**

    **else**

        $ft_{s_k} = st_{s_k} + 2 \cdot lt_{cs,i}^t + lc_{k,cs}^t$

    **end**

**end**

---

## 4 The Proposed Methods

### 4.1 Redundant Task Offloading

As shown in Algorithm 1, the objective of this algorithm is to meet user service requests as early as possible with redundancy. Specifically, we define three queues: $TL$ for the list of dependent subtasks, $PSL$ for the edge servers associated with the primary replica of the application server, and $BSL$ for the edge servers associated with the backup replica of the application server. Each subtask needs to execute the primary subtask first and calculate the earliest completion time of the current primary subtask processing. If the primary replica fails, the backup replica is executed, and the earliest completion time of the backup replica is calculated. If the backup replica processing also fails, we consider that the subtask cannot be processed at the base station and needs to be offloaded to the cloud for processing. Since the transmission time at this point is much greater than the computation time for subtask processing, to simplify the model, we consider the earliest subtask completion time as the transmission time for subtask offloading.

### 4.2 DRL-Based Service Caching and Task Offloading Decision Algorithm

The problem can be described as a Dec-OMDP with N base stations, where each base station corresponds to an agent. We use a set $\{S, O, A, R\}$ to describe the interaction process of the Dec-OMDP, where $S$ describes all possible environment states of the agents, $A_n$ indicates a set of available actions for agent $a_n$, $O_n^t$ the local observation of agent $a_n$ at time $t$, and $R$ the reward function. At each time $t$, each agent obtains the local observation $O_n^t$ and takes action $a_n^t$, then after obtaining the joint actions $a^t$ of all agents, the environment grants a global reward $r^t = R(s^t, a^t)$ and transitions the state $s^t$ to the next state $s^{t+1}$.

**Environment State Space.** At each time $t$, the environment state space includes the current service request situation of users in the MEC environment, the wireless channel conditions of communication links, the service cache status of all current base stations, and the startup status of service applications at all current base stations. Therefore, the environment state $s^t$ is represented as $\{K^t, Z^t, X^{t-1}, Y^{t-1}\}$.

**Local Observation Space.** In the Mobile Edge Computing (MEC) environment, the local observation space of each base station $b_i$ can be represented as $O_i^t = \{K_i^t, Z_i^t, X^{t-1}, Y^{t-1}\}$. At the beginning of each time $t$, each base station can exchange service cache status and service application execution status with other base stations. Therefore, through the local observation space, each $b_i$ can offload task requests to idle edge servers.

**Action Space.** We define the action space as $a = \{a_1, a_2, ..., a_n\}$, where $a_n^t = \{X_n^t, Y_n^t, Z_n^t\}$. The calculation formula is

$$a^t = argmax(Q(s^t, a; \theta)) \tag{10}$$

**Reward Function.** when fed with the joint action $a^t$, the environment returns a reward $r^t$ for estimating the effectiveness of the joint action. With the goal of maximizing user QoS, we define the reward function as:

$$r^t = R\left(s^t, a^t\right) = \sum_{\substack{b_i \in B \\ u \in U_i}} \sum_{s \in S} U_{u,s}^t \tag{11}$$

---

**Algorithm 2:** DRL-Based Service Caching and Task Offloading Decision Algorithm

---

**foreach** *episode* **do**
    **foreach** $t \in T$ **do**
        **foreach** *agent n* **do**
            obtain the state $s_n^t$ according to environment
            obtain $A_n = \{a_n\}$ and select $a_n^t$ according to Eq. (10)
            obtain the next state $s^{t+1}$ and reward $r^t$ after execute $a_n^t$
            store the tuple $(s_n^t, a_n^t, r_n^t, s_n^{t+1})$ and randomly sample a minibatch
            calculate the loss function by Eq. (14)
            calculate the gradient by Eq. (15)
            update $\theta$ according to Eq. (16)
        **end**
    **end**
    obtain the service caching and task offloading decisions according to $\theta$
    **if** *the number of time is z* **then**
        $\theta = \theta'$
    **end**
**end**

---

In our study, each base station $b_n$ serves as an agent $a_n$ in the DQN framework. The program first takes action $a^t$ based on the current state $s^t$ to make decisions on caching, channel allocation, and task offloading. After this action, the base station receives a reward value $r^t$ and transitions to the next state $s^{t+1}$. The entire process forms a state transition, represented as $(s_i^t, a_i^t, r_i^t, s_i^{t+1})$. We store it in a replay buffer, then randomly select k tuples from the replay buffer to form a minibatch, where the i-th tuple is represented as $(s_i, a_i, r_i, s_{i+1})$. Therefore, the update of the action-value function is represented as:

$$Q\left(s_{i+1}, a_{i+1}; \theta\right) = Q\left(s_i, a_i; \theta\right) + \alpha\left[y_i - Q\left(s_i, a_i; \theta\right)\right] \tag{12}$$

where $\alpha$ represents the learning rate; the parameters $\theta'$ of the target network are periodically updated to match the predicted target network parameters $\theta$. $y_i$ represents the target Q-value of the target network, expressed as:

$$y_i = r_i + \gamma \max \hat{Q}\left(s_{i+1}, a_{i+1}; \theta'\right) \tag{13}$$

where $\gamma$ indicates the discount factor, the loss function for updating parameters is:

$$L(\theta_i^n) = \mathbb{E}\left[(y_i - Q(s_i, a_i; \theta))^2\right] \tag{14}$$

The gradient of the loss function for all sampled tuples is computed as:

$$\nabla_\theta L(\theta) = \mathbb{E}\left[(y_i - Q(s_i, a_i; \theta))\nabla_{\theta^i} Q(s_i, a_i; \theta)\right] \tag{15}$$

At the end of time $t$, the parameters of network $\theta$ are updated as:

$$\theta \leftarrow \theta - \eta_\theta \nabla_\theta L(\theta) \tag{16}$$

## 5  Case Studies

### 5.1  Simulation Configuration

We build a simulation environment based on the Shanghai Telecom Dataset [21–23], which includes 7 million records of Internet content requests from 9,481 mobile phones through 3,233 base stations over a period of six months. We assume that service task requests are divided based on the duration of each record. The method proposed in our study is implemented in Python.

### 5.2  Baselines

We consider the following baselines:

1) GatMARL: It leverages a multi-agent reinforcement learning framework and graph attention mechanisms for yielding service caching schedules [15].
2) OREO: This baseline method is based on an online algorithm that jointly optimizes dynamic service caching and task offloading [16].
3) CP: This baseline method proposes solving service caching and task offloading for dependent task pairs using an optimal successor algorithm [17].

### 5.3  Performance Analysis

We conducted experiments under three scenarios:

1) We compared the impact of different task processing failure rates on algorithm performance, with the base station resource capacity set to 100 and 1000 service types.
2) We compared the impact of base station resource capacity on algorithm performance, with a 30% task processing failure rate and 1000 service types.
3) We compared the impact of the number of service types on algorithm performance, with a 30% task processing failure rate and a base station resource capacity set to 100.

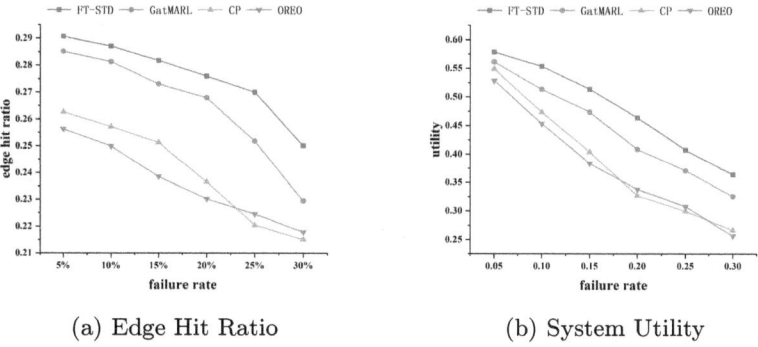

(a) Edge Hit Ratio                    (b) System Utility

**Fig. 8.** Algorithmic performance under different error rates.

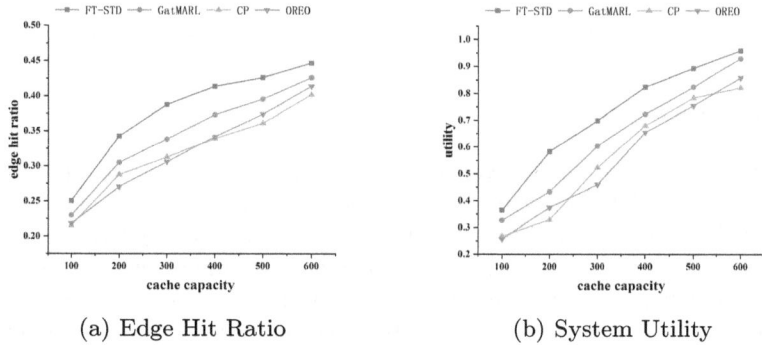

(a) Edge Hit Ratio                    (b) System Utility

**Fig. 9.** Algorithmic performance under different resource capacities.

As shown in Fig. 8, the FT-STD algorithm performs the best performance in the MEC environments with high error rates. By incorporating the PB model, the system can significantly reduce the impact of task processing failures, especially in scenarios with high error rates, where the performance of FT-STD is higher than that of traditional algorithms, about 10%–20%.

As shown in Fig. 9, it is evident that the performance of the FT-STD algorithm excels across various resource capacities. Furthermore, as the resource capacity increases, the performance of the FT-STD algorithm improves more significantly. This is attributed to the enhanced efficiency of the FT-STD algorithm in cache and offloading decisions as the resource capacity expands, enabling more effective utilization of available resources.

As shown in Fig. 10, it is evident that the performance of all algorithms with redundancy decreases with the increases in the number of service types. However, FT-STD the highest tolerance to such increases.

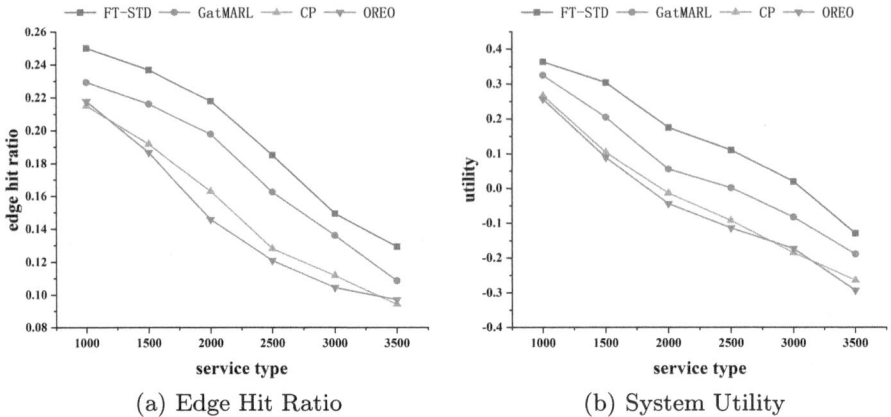

(a) Edge Hit Ratio  (b) System Utility

**Fig. 10.** Algorithmic performance under different numbers of service types.

## 6 Conclusion

In this paper, we propose a novel redundant service caching and task offloading (FT-STD) method for meeting content requests in an error-prone MEC environments. Specifically, the FT-STD method incorporates a PB mechanism in offloading and decides, optimizes the placement scheme of primary and backup task replicas when caching content upon MEC nodes. Empirical results clearly demonstrate that FT-STD exhibits better tolerance and scalability than its peers across multiple performance metrics. In future study, we plan to incorporate failure prediction mechanisms and develop failure occurrency prediction-based service caching algorithms, which are probably capable of achieving even higher success rate of service delivery in a failure-prone MEC environment.

## References

1. Al-Hammadi, I., Li, M., Islam, S.M.N., Almosharea, E.: Collaborative computation offloading for scheduling emergency tasks in SDN-based mobile edge computing networks. Comput. Netw. **238**, 110101 (2024)
2. Lin, H., Yang, L., Guo, H., Cao, J.: Decentralized task offloading in edge computing: an offline-to-online reinforcement learning approach. IEEE Trans. Comput. **73**(6), 1603–1615 (2024)
3. Tütüncüoglu, F., Dán, G.: Optimal service caching and pricing in edge computing: a Bayesian Gaussian process bandit approach. IEEE Trans. Mob. Comput. **23**(1), 705–718 (2024)
4. Ke, H., Wang, H., Yang, K., Sun, H.: Service caching decision-making policy for mobile edge computing using deep reinforcement learning. IET Commun. **17**(3), 362–376 (2023)
5. Fan, S., Hou, I., Mai, V.S.: Dynamic regret of randomized online service caching in edge computing. In: IEEE Conference on Computer Communications, IEEE INFOCOM 2023, New York City, NY, USA, 17–20 May 2023, pp. 1–10. IEEE (2023)

6. Pang, S., Hou, L., Gui, H., He, X., Wang, T., Zhao, Y.: Multi-mobile vehicles task offloading for vehicle-edge-cloud collaboration: a dependency-aware and deep reinforcement learning approach. Comput. Commun. **213**, 359–371 (2024)
7. Chen, J., et al.: Fault tolerance oriented SFC optimization in SDN/NFV-enabled cloud environment based on deep reinforcement learning. IEEE Trans. Cloud Comput. **12**(1), 200–218 (2024)
8. Kirti, M., Maurya, A.K., Yadav, R.S.: Fault-tolerance approaches for distributed and cloud computing environments: a systematic review, taxonomy and future directions. Concurr. Comput. Pract. Exp. **36**(13) (2024)
9. Al-Omari, R., Somani, A.K., Manimaran, G.: Efficient overloading techniques for primary-backup scheduling in real-time systems. J. Parallel Distrib. Comput. **64**(5), 629–648 (2004)
10. Balasangameshwara, J., Raju, N.: Performance-driven load balancing with a primary-backup approach for computational grids with low communication cost and replication cost. IEEE Trans. Comput. **62**(5), 990–1003 (2013)
11. Cai, Y., Llorca, J., Tulino, A.M., Molisch, A.F.: Joint compute-caching-communication control for online data-intensive service delivery. IEEE Trans. Mob. Comput. **23**(5), 4617–4633 (2024)
12. Chu, W., Jia, X., Yu, Z., Lui, J.C.S., Lin, Y.: Joint service caching, resource allocation and task offloading for MEC-based networks: a multi-layer optimization approach. IEEE Trans. Mob. Comput. **23**(4), 2958–2975 (2024)
13. Qin, L., Lu, H., Lu, Y., Zhang, C., Wu, F.: Joint optimization of base station clustering and service caching in user-centric MEC. IEEE Trans. Mob. Comput. **23**(5), 6455–6469 (2024)
14. Zhang, Z., St-Hilaire, M., Wei, X., Dong, H., El-Saddik, A.: How to cache important contents for multi-modal service in dynamic networks: a DRL-based caching scheme. IEEE Trans. Multimed. **26**, 7372–7385 (2024)
15. Yao, Z., Xia, S., Li, Y., Wu, G.: Cooperative task offloading and service caching for digital twin edge networks: a graph attention multi-agent reinforcement learning approach. IEEE J. Sel. Areas Commun. **41**(11), 3401–3413 (2023)
16. Xu, J., Chen, L., Zhou, P.: Joint service caching and task offloading for mobile edge computing in dense networks. In: 2018 IEEE Conference on Computer Communications, INFOCOM 2018, Honolulu, HI, USA, 16–19 April 2018, pp. 207–215. IEEE (2018)
17. Zhao, G., Xu, H., Zhao, Y., Qiao, C., Huang, L.: Offloading tasks with dependency and service caching in mobile edge computing. IEEE Trans. Parallel Distrib. Syst. **32**(11), 2777–2792 (2021)
18. Chen, Y., Yang, Q., He, S., Shi, Z., Chen, J., Guizani, M.: FTPipeHD: a fault-tolerant pipeline-parallel distributed training approach for heterogeneous edge devices. IEEE Trans. Mob. Comput. **23**(4), 3200–3212 (2024)
19. Cai, W., Chen, H., Zhuo, Z., Wang, Z., An, N.: Flexible supervision system: a fast fault-tolerance strategy for cloud applications in cloud-edge collaborative environments. In: Liu, S., Wei, X. (eds.) NPC 2022. LNCS, vol. 13615, pp. 108–113. Springer, Cham (2022). https://doi.org/10.1007/978-3-031-21395-3_10
20. Long, T., Ma, Y., Xia, Y., Xiao, X., Peng, Q., Zhao, J.: A mobility-aware and fault-tolerant service offloading method in mobile edge computing. In: Ardagna, C.A., et al. (eds.) IEEE International Conference on Web Services, ICWS 2022, Barcelona, Spain, 10–16 July 2022, pp. 67–72. IEEE (2022)
21. Li, Y., Zhou, A., Ma, X., Wang, S.: Profit-aware edge server placement. IEEE Internet Things J. **9**(1), 55–67 (2022)

22. Guo, Y., Wang, S., Zhou, A., Xu, J., Yuan, J., Hsu, C.: User allocation-aware edge cloud placement in mobile edge computing. Softw. Pract. Exp. **50**(5), 489–502 (2020)
23. Wang, S., Guo, Y., Zhang, N., Yang, P., Zhou, A., Shen, X.: Delay-aware microservice coordination in mobile edge computing: a reinforcement learning approach. IEEE Trans. Mob. Comput. **20**(3), 939–951 (2021)

# RBLA: Rank-Based-LoRA-Aggregation for Fine-Tuning Heterogeneous Models in FLaaS

Shuaijun Chen[1]([✉])[iD], Omid Tavallaie[1,2][iD], Niousha Nazemi[1][iD], and Albert Y. Zomaya[1][iD]

[1] School of Computer Science, The University of Sydney, Camperdown, Australia
{shuaijun.chen,niousha.nazemi,albert.zomaya}@sydney.edu.au
[2] Department of Engineering Science, University of Oxford, Oxford, UK
omid.tavallaie@eng.ox.ac.uk

**Abstract.** Federated Learning (FL) is a promising privacy-aware distributed learning framework that can be deployed on various devices, such as mobile phones, desktops, and devices equipped with CPUs or GPUs. In the context of server-based Federated Learning as a Service (FLaaS), FL enables a central server to coordinate the training process across multiple devices without direct access to local data, thereby enhancing privacy and data security. Low-Rank Adaptation (LoRA) is a method that efficiently fine-tunes models by focusing on a low-dimensional subspace of the model's parameters. This approach significantly reduces computational and memory costs compared to fine-tuning all parameters from scratch. When integrated with FL, particularly in a FLaaS environment, LoRA allows for flexible and efficient deployment across diverse hardware with varying computational capabilities by adjusting the local model's rank. However, in LoRA-enabled FL, different clients may train models with varying ranks, which poses challenges for model aggregation on the server. Current methods for aggregating models of different ranks involve padding weights to a uniform shape, which can degrade the global model's performance. To address this issue, we propose Rank-Based LoRA Aggregation (RBLA), a novel model aggregation method designed for heterogeneous LoRA structures. RBLA preserves key features across models with different ranks. This paper analyzes the issues with current padding methods used to reshape models for aggregation in a FLaaS environment. Then, we introduce RBLA, a rank-based aggregation method that maintains both low-rank and high-rank features. Finally, we demonstrate the effectiveness of RBLA through comparative experiments with state-of-the-art methods.

**Keywords:** LoRA · FL · Heterogeneous Model Aggregation

## 1 Introduction

Neural Networks (NN) have become a widely applied approach in contemporary Computer Vision (CV) and Natural Language Processing (NLP). Traditionally,

Y. Zhang and L.-J. Zhang (Eds.): ICWS 2024, LNCS 15428, pp. 47–62, 2025.
https://doi.org/10.1007/978-3-031-77072-2_4

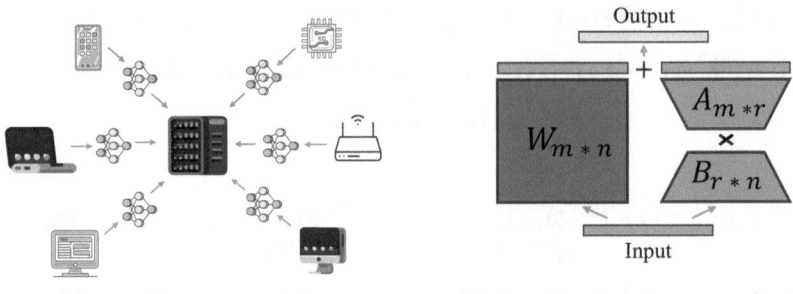

(a) FlaaS with varied devices          (b) Low-Rank Adaptation (LoRA)

**Fig. 1.** a) An application for FLaaS where devices with heterogeneous computational resources (such as smartphones, laptops, and routers) train models with different architectures and send them to a central server for aggregation (without sharing raw data). b) Reducing the dimension of the trained model in the LoRA technique by decomposing the original weight matrix into two smaller matrices to optimize computational efficiency.

model training involves collecting task-specific data and conducting centralized training in high-performance data centers. However, this centralized method raises significant privacy concerns, especially in applications dealing with sensitive data such as health information. Collecting and uploading user data to centralized servers can inherently lead to privacy breaches. To address these privacy challenges, McMahan et al. proposed Federated Learning (FL) in 2017 [24]. FL is a privacy-preserving distributed machine learning framework designed for decentralized neural network training [25]. This algorithm trains models locally on client devices (without sharing raw data), and model updates are then uploaded to a central server for aggregation. This concept has further evolved into Federated Learning as a Service (FLaaS) [7,17], shown in Fig. 1a, where federated learning capabilities are provided as a cloud-based service [2]. FLaaS simplifies the deployment process by managing the underlying infrastructure, allowing the implementation of federated learning across a diverse range of devices, including smartphones, IoT devices, and edge servers. This flexibility enables organizations to leverage privacy-preserving machine learning on a large scale without the complexities of building and maintaining their own FL systems. Despite these advantages, decentralized local model training in FL typically requires robust client device performance and communication capabilities. In practical FlaaS scenarios, significant performance variations among client devices pose challenges in deploying models with identical structures across all clients.

Recent advancements in computing power and algorithms have led to numerous applications that use large models to process vast amounts of data on mobile devices, providing responses or making decisions. Examples include ChatGPT and Tesla's autonomous driving technology. However, the inference and training processes of large models are complex and resource-intensive. Additionally, the heterogeneous nature of client devices in FL scenarios, with significant differences in performance, complicates the deployment and fine-tuning of federated large models. To address these issues, Low-Rank Adaptation (LoRA) [11] has emerged as a feasible solution. Figure 1b shows LoRA decomposes the locally deployed model into two low-rank matrices, which can then be adjusted in matrices' ranks based on the local data or device performance demands. This approach decreases both the model training cost and performance requirements and allows each client to customize the model size to its computational capacity and data characteristics. As a result, LoRA makes training and deployment more efficient.

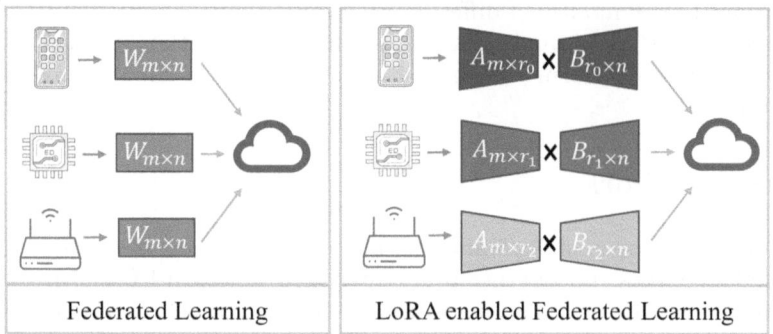

**Fig. 2.** Comparison between traditional FL and LoRA-enabled FL. The left figure shows the standard FL, where clients have full-rank $m \times n$ weight matrices. In contrast, the right figure illustrates LoRA-enabled FL, where clients send low-rank matrices (trained models) with varying ranks to reduce communication and computation costs.

Figure 2 illustrates the differences between traditional centralized training, FedAvg, and FL with LoRA. As shown in the figure, unlike traditional federated learning, FL with LoRA allows each client to customize the rank number based on its own conditions [3]. This flexibility enables the system to adapt to the diverse needs and capabilities of different clients. However, this customization introduces a challenge during the server aggregation process: matrices of different ranks cannot be directly aggregated using traditional methods. To address this, all matrices must be expanded to a uniform dimension for computation.

The current matrix expansion method primarily relies on zero-padding [3], a technique that involves padding smaller matrices with zero elements to match the dimensions of the largest matrix. While this method is straightforward to implement, it introduces significant issues. First, zero-padded matrices contain a large number of zero elements, leading to unnecessary computational overhead during the aggregation process. Second, padding with zeros can degrade model performance, as the padded zeros do not provide useful information during aggregation. Additionally, the dimensional expansion of matrices can result in a substantial increase in memory usage, which is particularly problematic for resource-constrained devices.

We propose Rank-Based Layer Aggregation (RBLA), a method designed to effectively aggregate matrices of varying ranks to address the issues posed by heterogeneous matrix ranks in FL. RBLA aims to preserve the high-dimensional features generated during the training process, mitigate the negative impacts of matrix aggregation, and enhance the global model's convergence speed. The main contributions of our work are as follows:

1. We present a toy example demonstrating weight aggregation in LoRA-enabled FL and explain the effects of zero-padding on higher-dimensional features.
2. We propose RBLA, a model aggregation method specifically designed to aggregate LoRA models of different ranks.
3. We provide a Python implementation of RBLA using the TensorFlow library and compare its performance against state-of-the-art methods across multiple datasets.

## 2   Related Work

FL is a decentralized model training method deployable on any device with computational resources and internet connectivity. In practical FL scenarios, clients often possess distinctly different local datasets [19], which may not accurately represent the overall data distribution. Additionally, client device performance is usually heterogeneous [6] due to variations in computational power, memory, and network bandwidth [23]. This heterogeneity can lead to challenges in effectively training and aggregating the global model [10,26], as some clients may contribute less due to their limited resources [21]. The non-IID nature of data can result in a global model that may not generalize effectively across all clients [35].

Various methods have been proposed to address the data non-IID problem. Collins et al. [4] proposed FedRep, which learns a shared representation across clients while allowing each to train personalized local models. Similarly, Ghosh et al. [8] proposed the IFCA, which clusters clients with similar data distributions and optimizes models within each cluster to reduce the impact of data heterogeneity. In the context of personalization, Arivazhagan et al. [1] introduced FedPer, which splits models into shared and personalized layers. FedAvg is used to train shared layers and local-update-personalized layers to obtain better end-side performance. Furthermore, to tackle client drift caused by data heterogeneity, Karimireddy et al. [13] proposed SCAFFOLD, an algorithm that uses control variates to correct client drift and achieve quicker convergence. To address the issue of device heterogeneity, Khodadadian et al. [15] tackled client communication costs by utilizing TD-learning and Q-learning to reduce communication overhead. Kumar et al. [18] applied LoRaWAN technology to FL to improve communication efficiency and robustness. Li et al. [21] proposed Fed-Prox, designed to tolerate not-completely-trained local models and use a proximal term to reduce the impact of over-fitted local models. In practical FlaaS involving multiple IoT devices, the expected local model architecture may differ among client devices due to heterogeneous hardware configurations, tasks, and personal demands [12,20], and [31]. To perform effective aggregation on a central server with models of different architectures, Wang et al. [29] proposed MaxCommon which facilitates collaborative training across various models. To further enhance the flexibility and efficiency of FL in heterogeneous environments, LoRA [11] has emerged as a promising technique. LoRA allows flexible adaptation of trainable parameters based on data quality, device performance, and other factors. Based on LoRA and FL, Yi et al. [32] proposed pFedLoRA, which incorporates LoRA in FL to increase model fine-tuning efficiency. Choi et al. proposed HetLoRA [3], which dynamically adjusts the client's rank based on the local model's quality of fit to the local data. Other approaches, such as DFLNet [34], aim to propose to improve secure authentication and model convergence in LoRA-enabled networks. LLDPC [30] enhances data transmission reliability in LoRA networks. FDLoRA [28] balances personalized and global learning for large language models (LLMs) while reducing costs, and DP-LoRA [22] ensures differential privacy in FL for LLMs with minimal communication overhead.

## 3  Problem Statement

In FL, models must have the same shape to be aggregated on the central server, and zero-padding is one of the most commonly used methods to match dimensions. However, we found that zero-padding introduces structural sparsity, which can slow down convergence. This section presents the impact of zero-padding of trained model weights on the aggregated global model. We specifically analyze how zero-padding affects the sparsity and effectiveness of weighted averaging in the aggregation of LoRA weights [3]. Consider two weight matrices $A_{p \times q}$, $B_{m \times n}$ ($pq < mn$) with corresponding aggregation weights $w_1$ and $w_2$. To aggregate models with different dimensions, matrix $A$ is padded with zeros to match the dimensions of $B$, resulting in the padded matrix $A'$ with a shape of $m \times n$. The aggregated model $C_{m \times n}$ is then computed as:

$$C = w_1 A' + w_2 B. \tag{1}$$

Here, the term 'zero-padding' introduces non-informative values that negatively impact the overall feature representation, impairing the neuron network's ability to effectively generalize target features [27]. We highlight the significance of structural sparsity and its impact on neural network capacity and learning dynamics [9,27,33], and [14], which underscores the need to avoid bringing structural sparsity during deep feature extraction when aggregating LoRA weights across different dimensions. For example, during the LoRA training process, model $A$ may fail to capture the depth features learned by model $B$ due to insufficient neurons. During aggregation, zero-padding causes the layers of matrix $A$ that are padded with zeros to dilute the depth features trained by matrix $B$, as these padded layers cannot provide the necessary non-linear transformations [27]. Consequently, zero-padding introduces invalid zero-value information, which dilutes the important depth features learned by model $B$ during the averaging process. This scenario can be illustrated as follows:

$$A' = \begin{bmatrix} a_{11} & a_{12} & a_{13} \\ a_{21} & a_{22} & a_{23} \\ 0 & 0 & 0 \end{bmatrix}, \quad B = \begin{bmatrix} b_{11} & b_{12} & b_{13} \\ b_{21} & b_{22} & b_{23} \\ b_{31} & b_{32} & b_{33} \end{bmatrix}, \quad C = \begin{bmatrix} c_{11} & c_{12} & c_{13} \\ c_{21} & c_{22} & c_{23} \\ c_{31} & c_{32} & c_{33} \end{bmatrix}. \tag{2}$$

The last row of matrix $C$ by using weighted average can be represented as:

$$C_{3,n} = \frac{w_1 \cdot a'_{3,n}}{w_1 + w_2} + \frac{w_2 \cdot b_{3,n}}{w_1 + w_2} = \frac{w_2 \cdot b_{3,n}}{w_1 + w_2}, \quad a'_{3,n} = 0_{1 \times 3}. \tag{3}$$

Equation 3 presents how zero-padding results in a loss of information by diluting the features captured by the deeper model during aggregation. Extending this scenario to $n$ weight matrices $A_1, A_2, \ldots, A_n$ with varying dimensions, let the largest matrix be of size $m \times n$. For simplicity, assume the aggregation weights are $w_1, w_2, \ldots, w_n$. For each matrix $A_i$ with dimensions $p_i \times q_i$ where $p_i q_i < mn$, zero-padding is applied to create $A'_i$, a matrix of dimensions $m \times n$.

$$A'_i = \begin{cases} A_{kj}, & 1 \le k \le p \text{ and } 1 \le j \le q, \\ 0, & \text{otherwise.} \end{cases} \tag{4}$$

For each matrix $A_i$ with dimensions $p_i \times q_i$ where $p_i q_i < mn$, we apply zero-padding to create $A'_i$ with dimensions $m \times n$ by Eq. 4. The row $C_r$ of the aggregated global model $C$ is computed using a weighted average, as below:

$$C_r = \frac{\sum_{i=1}^n w_i \cdot \delta_{i,r} \cdot \mathbf{a}_{i,r}}{\sum_{i=1}^n w_i}, \delta_{i,r} = \begin{cases} 1, & \text{if } r < n, \\ 0, & \text{otherwise.} \end{cases} \tag{5}$$

Here, $\mathbf{a}_{i,r}$ represents the $r$-th row vector of the zero-padded matrix $A'_i$, and $\delta_{i,r}$ is an indicator function that equals 1 if the $r$-th row of $A_i$ exists and 0 otherwise. This indicates that **the more zero-padded is applied to a layer, the more the original features of that layer become diluted.** Consequently, zero-padding introduces significant issues as it incorporates **a substantial number of zero values**, which dilute effective feature information during aggregation. This dilution reduces the impact of high-dimensional features learned by models with higher dimensions. These zero values, acting as invalid information in the computation, degrade the quality of the aggregated results and lead to a model populated with numerous irrelevant features. In scenarios with skewed data distributions, such as long-tailed distributions where low-rank model clients are assigned fewer classes or data, high-dimensional features learned by deeper neural networks are further diluted by shallower networks during zero-padding weighted average aggregation. This results in additional performance degradation, as zero-padding often diminishes the features from client models with smaller datasets. This issue prevents the aggregated model from fully leveraging all clients' data and features. Moreover, the **structural sparsity** introduced by zero-padding imposes invalid linear transformations, which limit the model's

**Algorithm 1.** Server Aggregation of RBLA. The server aggregates weights from all clients by accurately handling shared and unique layers using an indicator function and weighted aggregation.

---

Initialize $W_{\mathrm{agg}} \leftarrow 0$
Receive all $W_i$ from client $i$
**for** each layer $W_{\mathrm{agg},r}$ **do**
    Initialize $w_r \leftarrow 0$
    **for** each model $i = 1, 2, \ldots, N$ **do**
        **if** $\delta_{i,r} = 1$ **then**
            $W_{\mathrm{agg},r} = W_{\mathrm{agg},r} + w_i \cdot W_{i,r}$
            $w_r = w_r + w_i$
        **end if**
    **end for**
    $W_{\mathrm{agg}}.\mathrm{append}(W_{\mathrm{agg},r}/w_r)$
**end for**
$W_{\mathrm{server}} = W_{\mathrm{agg}}$
Send $W_{\mathrm{server}}$ to all clients

---

capacity to represent complex patterns and reduce its effectiveness in learning high-dimensional spaces. Additionally, structural sparsity restricts the model's generalization capability and lowers the overall performance. These factors collectively lead to a decline in accuracy and robustness, significantly impacting the model's effectiveness in practical applications.

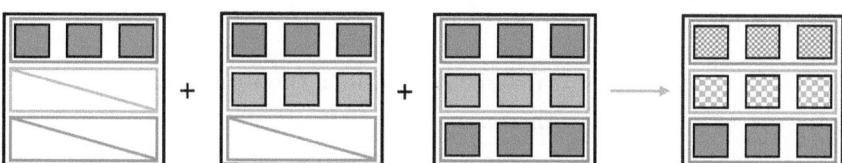

**Fig. 3.** Horizontal aggregation process for heterogeneous LoRA models: Similar to vertical aggregation, RBLA preserves the weights of shared layers and retains unique layers during the horizontal aggregation process.

## 4    RBLA

RBLA is designed to aggregate heterogeneous model weight matrices, bias matrices, and low-rank matrices of different ranks from multiple clients by re-weighting the aggregation weights. Algorithm 1 and Algorithm 2 show the procedures executed on the server and client, respectively. Considering matrix sparsity, RBLA first pads all matrices to match the dimensions of the largest LoRA matrix, filling missing entries with a neutral value. It then performs a weighted aggregation for the **existing common layer values**, either row-wise or column-wise, depending on the presence of none-values and their corresponding aggregation weights. During this procedure, RBLA calculates the aggregation weights based on the common layers, performs a weighted average for shared layers, and preserves the original value of unique stand-alone layers. Figures 4 and 3 illustrate the RBLA aggregation process for models with heterogeneous columns and rows, respectively.

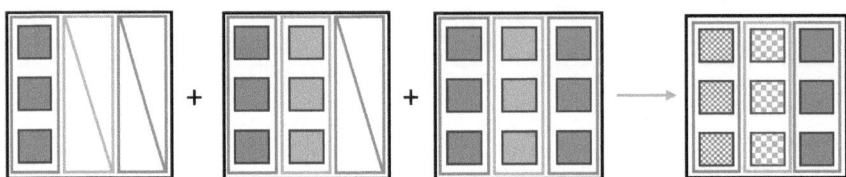

**Fig. 4.** Vertical aggregation process for heterogeneous LoRA models. Layers of the same color represent common layers. RBLA aggregation preserves the original value of unique layers and calculates a weighted average for common layers.

The detailed aggregation process of RBLA is as follows: suppose there are $N$ models indexed by $i = 1, 2, \ldots, N$, each with a weight matrix $W_i$, representing a LoRA model trained at different ranks. To aggregate these models, we use a weighted average to combine shared layers that exist across multiple weight matrices with similar structures. We also preserve unique layers that are present only in a specific matrix. To identify shared layers and unique layers, we define an indicator function $\delta_{i,r}$ as follows:

$$\delta_{i,r} = \begin{cases} 1, & \text{if matrix } \mathbf{A}_i \text{ contains the } r\text{-th layer,} \\ 0, & \text{otherwise.} \end{cases} \tag{6}$$

The aggregated weight for the $r$-th layer, $\mathbf{C}_r$, is computed as:

$$\mathbf{C}_r = \frac{\sum_{i=1}^{n} \delta_{i,r} \cdot w_i \cdot \mathbf{A}_{i,r}}{\sum_{i=1}^{n} \delta_{i,r} \cdot w_i}. \tag{7}$$

---

**Algorithm 2.** The client procedure in RBLA.

---

**Clients receive** $W_{server}$
$p, q \leftarrow$ shape of $W_i$
Extract the $p \times q$ sub-matrix from $W_{server}$
$W_i = W_{server}[0 : p, 0 : q]$
**for** $\forall e \in E$ **do**
    **for** $\forall b \in B$ **do**
        $W_i = W_i - \eta \nabla \ell(w; b)$
    **end for**
**end for**
Send $W_i$ to the server

---

In this process:

- $\mathbf{A}_{i,r}$ represents the $r$-th layer of the weight matrix for model $i$.
- $w_i$ is the weight coefficient for model $i$.
- The indicator function $\delta_{i,r}$ ensures that only the matrices containing the $r$-th layer can contribute to the aggregation.

Applying this method, we can aggregate the weights of shared layers while preserving the unique layers of each model to avoid unnecessary structural sparsity.

## 5    Experiments and Evaluation

In our study, we evaluate the effectiveness of RBLA using MLP and CNN architectures on the MNIST, FMNIST, CIFAR-10, and CINIC-10 [5] datasets, comparing its performance against two baselines: Zero-Padding (ZP) [3] and Full Fine-Tune (FFT) FedAvg [24]. The models are implemented using the Tensor-Flow library in Python, with three neural network models included. Additionally, all experiments are conducted with a **fixed seed of 42** to ensure reproducibility. All experiments within the same subfigure share the same configuration, differing only in the aggregation algorithms used.

### 5.1    Experiments Setup

In the experiment, the MNIST MLP model consists of two hidden layers with 200 neurons each, activated by ReLU, and a 10-class softmax output layer suitable for flattened $28 \times 28$ pixel images (784-dimensional vectors). The MNIST CNN model comprises two convolutional layers with 32 and 64 filters, followed by MaxPooling layers, a 512-unit fully connected layer, and a 10-class softmax output layer designed for $28 \times 28$ inputs. Both models were trained with a batch size of 64 using the SGD optimizer with a learning rate of 0.01. For the CIFAR dataset, we used a model that includes three convolutional layers: batch normalization, max pooling, dropout, and fully connected layers. The first two sets of convolutional layers have 32 and 64 filters with a $3 \times 3$ kernel size and ReLU activation, followed by pooling layers for downsampling and dropout layers for regularization. The feature maps are then flattened and passed through two fully connected layers with 512 neurons each, followed by dropout, and finally output through a 10-class softmax layer. The model that we used for the CINIC dataset has two extra dense layers with 512 neurons each compared to the CIFAR model. The optimizer for the CIFAR and CINIC experiments was set to Adam [16], and LoRA is applied only to dense layers for all experiments. Additionally, we tested two participation scenarios: one where all clients participate in each training round and another where 20% of clients are randomly selected to participate in each communication round.

## 5.2   Non-IID and Model Rank Settings

In our experiments, data is allocated to each client following two "staircase" patterns to simulate a realistic data distribution, where the label distribution within each client exhibits a long-tail "stair" pattern. These patterns reflect real-world scenarios, such as medical systems, where data from different hospitals or clinics may have **varying levels of data complexity or diversity**. For instance, some specialized hospitals might focus on specific types of diseases, while general hospitals handle a broader range of disease categories with more patients. Likewise, in sensing device systems, different devices may collect varying types and amounts of data. For example, embedded temperature control devices primarily gather temperature-related data, whereas smart devices (such as smartphones) may involve a wider variety of data, including GPS, step count, sensor data, etc. Based on this, the label distribution in each client's data in our experiment follows a long-tail distribution. Each subsequent client has an increasing number of labels with non-zero sample counts, starting from Client 1, which has samples only for Label 0. As more clients are added, they progressively add more labels, culminating in Client 10, which has a large number of samples for all labels from 0 to 9. Simultaneously, the rank ratio of the LoRA model assigned to each client is scaled based on the number of labels each client possesses, with the rank ratio increasing by 0.1 for each additional label. This approach ensures that clients with more labels are allocated higher ranks to better capture the complexity of their data, while those with fewer labels receive lower ranks.

## 5.3   Evaluation Results

**Table 1.** The minimum number of training rounds used for each method to achieve the target test accuracy for the global model in full participation experiments. N/A indicates that the corresponding aggregation strategy cannot achieve the target accuracy within 50 training rounds. All experiments in the same column are conducted under the same settings.

| Method | MNIST | | FMNIST | | CIFAR | CINIC |
|---|---|---|---|---|---|---|
| | MLP (95%) | CNN (98%) | MLP (83%) | CNN (98%) | CNN (48%) | CNN (40%) |
| ZP | N/A (94.87%) | 11 (98%) | N/A (82.87%) | 24 (97.04%) | 22 (48.73%) | 24 (40%) |
| FFT | 40 (95.04%) | 22 (98.03%) | 19 (83.04%) | N/A (91.36%) | **9** (49.16%) | 14 (40.09%) |
| RBLA | 11 (95.06%) | **4** (98.27%) | **7** (83.15%) | **7** (98.09%) | 12 (48.12%) | **12** (40.03%) |

In this section, we present the evaluation results across various datasets with different configurations. Table 1 shows the exact number of communication rounds taken for each method to reach the target test accuracy of the global model. The target accuracy was selected based on the global model accuracy at the communication round where RBLA's convergence speed significantly decreases, and this accuracy can also be reached or nearly reached by the other two methods. Figure 5, 6, 7, 8, 9, and Figure 10 show the learning curve of the global model's test accuracy to training rounds; the left sub-figure shows the result with full participants, and the right sub-figure shows the result with random client selection. As an example, the target test accuracy set for the MNIST MLP experiment is **95%**, where the convergence of RBLA significantly reduced. The maximum test accuracy of ZP can reach during training is **94.87%** (presented in the parentheses), while FFT reaches **95.04%** test accuracy in the **40th** training round, and RBLA reaches **95.06%** in the **11th** training round. **To ensure clear visual comparisons, a rolling average with a window size of 10 was applied to smooth the data,** represented by solid lines, and the dotted lines illustrate the original and unsmoothed results. The effectiveness of RBLA is assessed on the MNIST, FMNIST, and CIFAR-10 datasets using MLP and CNN models under both full participation and random selection settings. These experiments compare the performance of RBLA against zero-padding and full model fine-tuning.

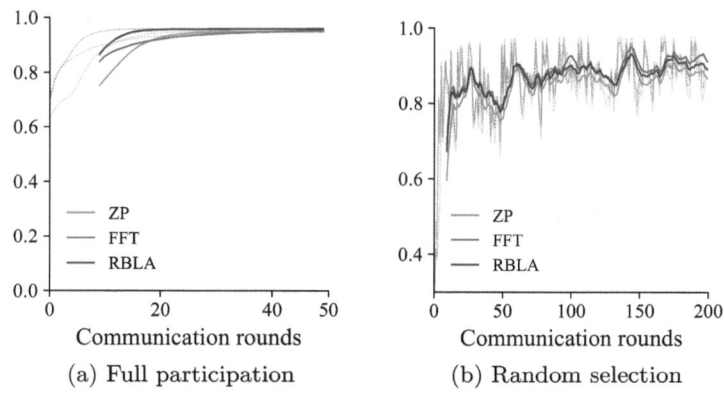

(a) Full participation                (b) Random selection

**Fig. 5.** Evaluation of RBLA for **MNIST** dataset with MLP model.

In the MNIST MLP experiments, RBLA demonstrates a superior convergence rate under the full participation setting, reaching a test accuracy of **95%** at the **11th** communication round. In contrast, zero-padding and FFT require **42** and **40 rounds**, respectively, to reach similar accuracy levels. This indicates that RBLA reduces the required training rounds by **40%** compared to zero-padding. In the random selection scenario, RBLA maintains a higher accuracy with less fluctuation throughout the training process compared to zero-padding and achieves performance close to FFT, which exhibits better variability.

Figure 6 shows the FMNIST MLP experiments, where RBLA again outperforms the other methods, reaching **80%** test accuracy by the **7th** communication round, whereas FFT achieves the same accuracy after **4 rounds**, and zero-padding fails to reach this target accuracy. This demonstrates that RBLA can reduce the number of training rounds by **36%** compared to FFT and performs significantly better than zero-padding. Figures 7 and 8 show the experimental results on CNN models using MNIST and FMNIST, respectively. In

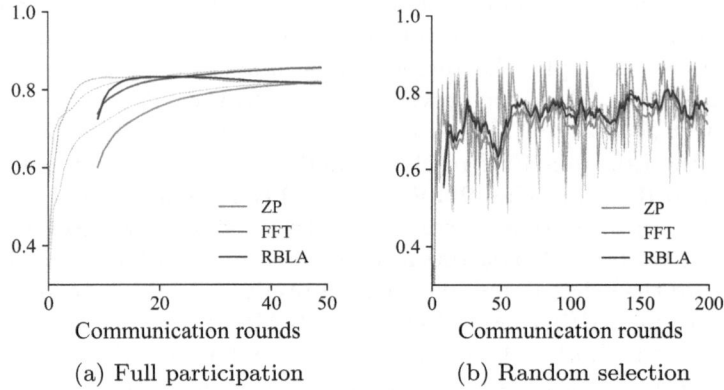

**Fig. 6.** Evaluation of RBLA for **FMNIST** dataset with MLP model.

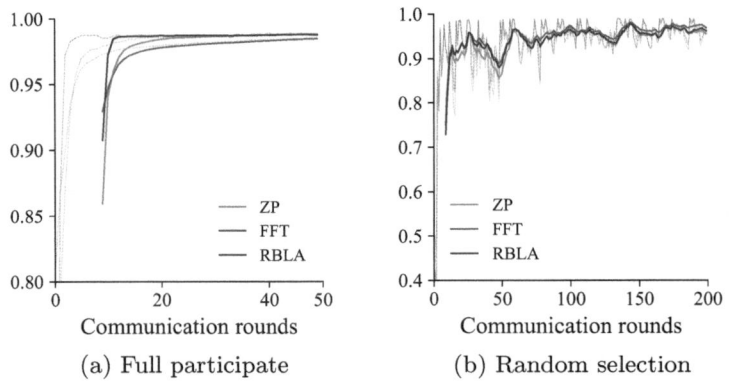

**Fig. 7.** Evaluation of RBLA for **MNIST** dataset with CNN model.

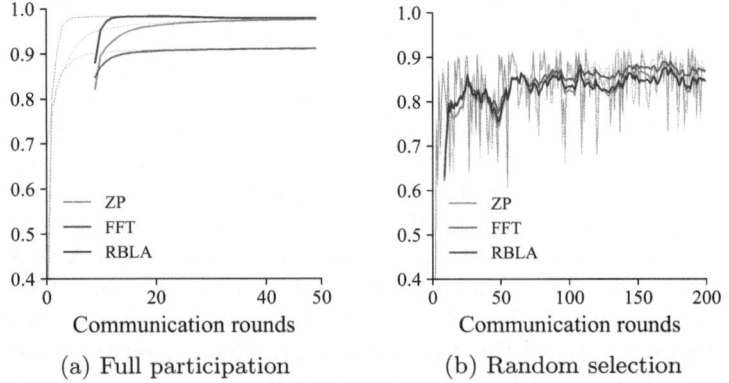

**Fig. 8.** Evaluation of RBLA for **FMNIST** dataset with CNN model.

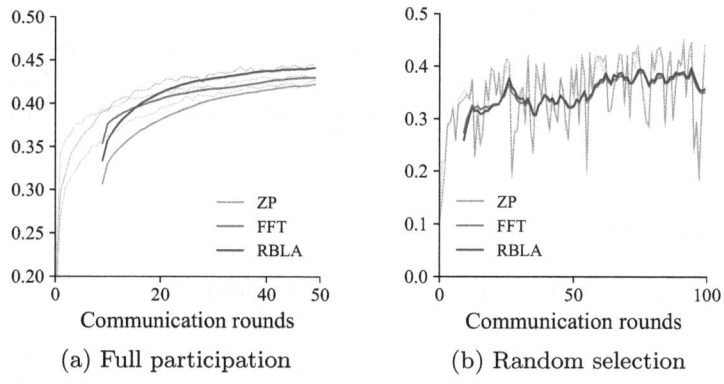

(a) Full participation    (b) Random selection

**Fig. 9.** Evaluation of RBLA for **CINIC-10** dataset with CNN model.

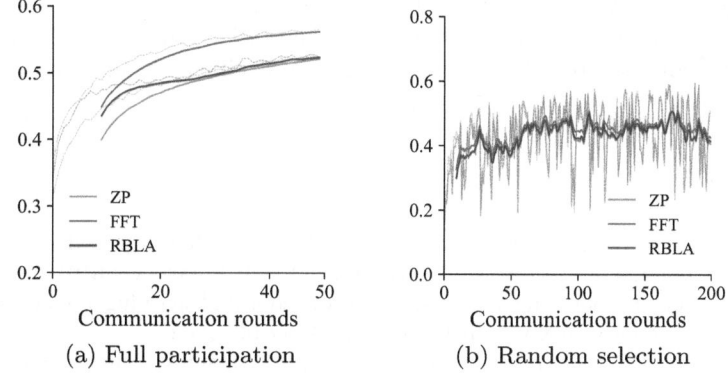

(a) Full participation    (b) Random selection

**Fig. 10.** Evaluation of RBLA for **CIFAR-10** dataset with CNN model.

both cases, the advantage of RBLA becomes even more evident. In the MNIST full participation setting, RBLA achieves **98%** test accuracy by the **4th** communication round, which is faster than FFT by **18 rounds** and faster than zero-padding by **7 rounds**. Under the random selection setting, RBLA's learning curve closely matches that of FFT and outperforms zero-padding. In the FMNIST CNN experiments, as shown in Fig. 8, RBLA shows its efficiency by achieving **98%** test accuracy of the global model at the **7th** communication round, outperforming zero-padding, which only reaches **97%** test accuracy at the **24th** communication round, while FFT fails to converge to the target accuracy. These results consistently demonstrate that RBLA converges faster and maintains higher stability across different datasets and model types. The significant reduction in training rounds and the lower fluctuation in test accuracy further confirm the effectiveness of RBLA over traditional zero-padding methods, particularly in non-IID settings. Finally, the CIFAR-10 and CINIC-10 experiments are shown in Figs. 10 and 9, respectively. RBLA gradually closes the performance gap with FFT as training rounds increase, outperforming zero-padding. While RBLA and FFT show similar convergence speeds at the beginning of training, RBLA converges more slowly after several rounds in the CIFAR-10 experiment but exhibits a faster convergence rate than both zero-padding and FFT in the CINIC-10 experiments.

## 6   Conclusion

This paper proposes RBLA, a model aggregation method specifically designed for heterogeneous LoRA models in Federated Learning as a Service (FLaaS) systems. RBLA addresses the critical challenge of preserving both low-rank and high-rank features during the aggregation process, which becomes particularly complex in scenarios with diverse client models. By leveraging FLaaS, RBLA enhances the convergence rate of the global model in non-IID scenarios with heterogeneous model structures. This improvement is effective in real-world applications with varied client device performance and skewed data distributions. The experimental results demonstrate RBLA's practicality and efficiency in practical FLaaS scenarios.

## References

1. Arivazhagan, M.G., Aggarwal, V., Singh, A.K., Choudhary, S.: Federated learning with personalization layers. arXiv preprint arXiv:1912.00818 (2019)
2. Chen, S., et al.: Boosting client selection of federated learning under device and data heterogeneity. arXiv preprint arXiv:2310.08147 (2023)
3. Cho, Y.J., Liu, L., Xu, Z., Fahrezi, A., Barnes, M., Joshi, G.: Heterogeneous LoRA for federated fine-tuning of on-device foundation models. In: International Workshop on Federated Learning in the Age of Foundation Models in Conjunction with NeurIPS 2023 (2023)
4. Collins, L., Hassani, H., Mokhtari, A., Shakkottai, S.: Exploiting shared representations for personalized federated learning. In: International Conference on Machine Learning, pp. 2089–2099. PMLR (2021)
5. Darlow, L.N., Crowley, E.J., Antoniou, A., Storkey, A.J.: Cinic-10 is not imagenet or cifar-10. arXiv preprint arXiv:1810.03505 (2018)
6. Deng, S., Zhao, H., Fang, W., Yin, J., Dustdar, S., Zomaya, A.Y.: Edge intelligence: the confluence of edge computing and artificial intelligence. IEEE Internet Things J. **7**(8), 7457–7469 (2020)
7. Gao, W., Tavallaie, O., Chen, S., Zomaya, A.: Federated learning as a service for hierarchical edge networks with heterogeneous models. arXiv preprint arXiv:2407.20573 (2024)
8. Ghosh, A., Chung, J., Yin, D., Ramchandran, K.: An efficient framework for clustered federated learning. In: Advances in Neural Information Processing Systems, vol. 33, pp. 19586–19597 (2020)
9. Goodfellow, I., Bengio, Y., Courville, A.: Deep Learning. MIT Press, Cambridge (2016)
10. Hsieh, K., Phanishayee, A., Mutlu, O., Gibbons, P.: The non-IID data quagmire of decentralized machine learning. In: ICML, pp. 4387–4398. PMLR (2020)

11. Hu, E.J., et al.: LoRA: low-rank adaptation of large language models. In: International Conference on Learning Representations (2022). https://openreview.net/forum?id=nZeVKeeFYf9

12. Kairouz, P., et al.: Advances and open problems in federated learning. Found. Trends® Mach. Learn. **14**(1–2), 1–210 (2021)

13. Karimireddy, S.P., Kale, S., Mohri, M., Reddi, S., Stich, S., Suresh, A.T.: Scaffold: stochastic controlled averaging for federated learning. In: International Conference on Machine Learning, pp. 5132–5143. PMLR (2020)

14. Kawaguchi, K., Kaelbling, L.P., Bengio, Y.: Generalization in deep learning. arXiv preprint arXiv:1710.05468 **1**(8) (2017)

15. Khodadadian, S., Sharma, P., Joshi, G., Maguluri, S.T.: Federated reinforcement learning: linear speedup under markovian sampling. In: International Conference on Machine Learning, pp. 10997–11057. PMLR (2022)

16. Kingma, D.P., Ba, J.: Adam: a method for stochastic optimization. In: 3rd International Conference on Learning Representations (ICLR) (2015). https://arxiv.org/abs/1412.6980

17. Kourtellis, N., Katevas, K., Perino, D.: Flaas: federated learning as a service. In: Proceedings of the 1st Workshop on Distributed Machine Learning, pp. 7–13 (2020)

18. Kumar, R., Mishra, R., Gupta, H.P.: A federated learning approach with imperfect labels in LoRA-based transportation systems. IEEE Trans. Intell. Transp. Syst. **24**(11), 13099–13107 (2023)

19. Li, Q., Diao, Y., Chen, Q., He, B.: Federated learning on non-IID data silos: an experimental study. In: 2022 IEEE 38th International Conference on Data Engineering (ICDE), pp. 965–978 (2022). https://doi.org/10.1109/ICDE53745.2022.00077

20. Li, T., Sahu, A.K., Talwalkar, A., Smith, V.: Federated learning: challenges, methods, and future directions. IEEE Signal Process. Mag. **37**(3), 50–60 (2020). https://doi.org/10.1109/MSP.2020.2975749

21. Li, T., Sahu, A.K., Zaheer, M., Sanjabi, M., Talwalkar, A., Smith, V.: Federated optimization in heterogeneous networks. Proc. Mach. Learn. Syst. **2**, 429–450 (2020)

22. Liu, X.Y., et al.: Differentially private low-rank adaptation of large language model using federated learning. ACM Trans. Manag. Inf. Syst. (2024). https://doi.org/10.1145/3682068

23. Liu, Y., Dong, Y., Wang, H., Jiang, H., Xu, Q.: Distributed fog computing and federated-learning-enabled secure aggregation for IoT devices. IEEE Internet Things J. **9**(21), 21025–21037 (2022)

24. McMahan, B., Moore, E., Ramage, D., Hampson, S., Arcas, B.A.: Communication-efficient learning of deep networks from decentralized data. In: Proceedings of the 20th International Conference on Artificial Intelligence and Statistics, vol. 54, pp. 1273–1282. PMLR (2017)

25. Nazemi, N., et al.: Access-FL: agile communication and computation for efficient secure aggregation in stable federated learning networks. arXiv preprint arXiv:2409.01722 (2024)

26. Nazemi, N., Tavallaie, O., Chen, S., Zomaya, A.Y., Holz, R.: Boosting communication efficiency of federated learning's secure aggregation. arXiv preprint arXiv:2405.01144 (2024)

27. Neyshabur, B., Bhojanapalli, S., McAllester, D., Srebro, N.: Exploring generalization in deep learning. In: Advances in Neural Information Processing Systems, vol. 30 (2017)

28. Qi, J., Luan, Z., Huang, S., Fung, C., Yang, H., Qian, D.: FDLoRA: personalized federated learning of large language model via dual LoRA tuning. arXiv preprint arXiv:2406.07925 (2024)
29. Wang, K., et al.: Flexifed: personalized federated learning for edge clients with heterogeneous model architectures. In: Proceedings of the ACM Web Conference 2023, pp. 2979–2990 (2023)
30. Yang, K., Du, W.: A low-density parity-check coding scheme for LoRA networking. ACM Trans. Sens. Netw. (2024)
31. Ye, M., Fang, X., Du, B., Yuen, P.C., Tao, D.: Heterogeneous federated learning: state-of-the-art and research challenges. ACM Comput. Surv. 56(3), 1–44 (2023)
32. Yi, L., Yu, H., Wang, G., Liu, X.: Fedlora: model-heterogeneous personalized federated learning with LoRA tuning. arXiv preprint arXiv:2310.13283 (2023)
33. Zhang, C., Bengio, S., Hardt, M., Recht, B., Vinyals, O.: Understanding deep learning requires rethinking generalization. Commun. ACM 64(3), 107–115 (2021)
34. Zhang, T., Xu, D., Ren, P., Yu, K., Guizani, M.: DFLNet: deep federated learning network with privacy preserving for vehicular LoRA nodes fingerprinting. IEEE Trans. Veh. Technol. (2023)
35. Zhao, Y., Li, M., Lai, L., Suda, N., Civin, D., Chandra, V.: Federated learning with non-IID data. arXiv preprint arXiv:1806.00582 (2018)

# User Preference-Informed and Mobility-Aware Caching in a Cooperative MEC Environment

Guanglin Guo[1], Jiafeng Feng[2], Yunni Xia[1(✉)], Ke Zhang[2], Zhaoguang Ding[2], Xingli Zhong[1], Xifeng Xu[1], and Jinpeng Li[1]

[1] College of Computer Science, Chongqing University, Chongqing, China
**xiayunni@hotmail.com**
[2] China Huadian Corporation Ltd., Guangdong Company, Guangzhou 510620, China

**Abstract.** As massive data is generated by Internet of Things (IoT) devices, user-end devices, which are usually resource and storage-poor, are required to implement computation-intensive functionalities. Mobile Edge Computing (MEC) is a significant technological convergence that has the potential to fill the gap and extent the computation and storage capacities of user-end devices by decentralization of required resources and contents near users and at the edge. Cooperative caching upon edge servers is becoming popular in this direction. Since cached content may not always align with user requests, potentially impacting the perceived quality of service, a key challenge is to develop an intelligent mechanism that efficiently pre-caches content based on the preferences of mobile users to ensure a high cache hit rate. For this purpose, in this paper, we propose a User Preference-informed and Mobility-aware method for cooperative MEC caching (MCL_CPC). The proposed method predicts future user preferences and destinations, clusters users accordingly, and caches content according to the clusters. Extensive experiments demonstrate that our proposed method outperforms its peers in terms of hit rate, content delivery latency, and cache utilization.

**Keywords:** Edge Computing · Cooperative Caching · User Preferences · Mobility-aware Clustering

## 1 Introduction

With the rapid growth of the Internet and the widespread adoption of smart devices, global data volume has exploded, leading to escalating demands for network traffic and data processing. Traditional centralized data centers are under immense pressure and struggle to efficiently meet the increasing demands for low latency and high bandwidth from users. Emerging applications such as Internet of Things (IoT), Virtual Reality (VR), Augmented Reality (AR), and others impose stricter requirements on real-time performance and reliability, posing challenges to existing network architectures [1]. In this context, Edge Computing has emerged as a crucial technology. Edge Computing shifts data processing and storage capabilities from central data centers to network edge nodes closer to data sources and users. As a vital component of Edge Computing, edge caching plays a significant role in enhancing user experience, optimizing network resource utilization, and improving overall system performance.

Due to limited caching capacity and vast amounts of data requests, proactively caching content during non-peak periods becomes critically important. Cooperative caching in a proactive manner enables more effective caching of valuable content into edge servers (MECs). Nevertheless, it remains a great challenge to decide effective content caching schemes due to the fact that in reality content requests can be highly unevenly distributed when a small portion of content is requested by a large number of requesters. Cooperative caching effectively addresses this challenge by allowing servers to collaboratively share content [2].

Recently, various works suggest that preference information of mobile users can be exploited as well in deciding and optimizing the content caching schemes. The logic behind is simply that requests of users can be driven by preference of accessing potentially interested content. This is usually achieved by analyzing the historical check-in records at different content.

Previous research often overlooks both user similarity and mobility, or considers only one of these factors without integrating them to optimize caching efficiency. This paper aims to propose an effective cooperative caching strategy in MEC with mobile users featuring varying content preferences. We introduce a user preference-informed and mobility-aware cooperative caching method:

1. We first propose a Merge and Split Clustering (MSC) algorithm to bound the number and the distances of BSs within a cooperative BS cluster.
2. We employ a Spectral Clustering model to cluster users based on their preferences and group users accordingly. We propose a greedy allocation strategy to assign the clustered user groups to servers.
3. We predict user preference and the sequence of base stations requested by users by using a Self-Attentive Sequential Recommendation (SASRec) model.
4. We conduct extensive simulations by using real-world datasets. Results indicate that our approach outperforms existing methods across multiple performance metrics.

## 2   Related Work

Recently, extensive research efforts are paid to mobile and distributed content caching technologies [3]. For instance, Li *et al.* [4] introduce various types of cellular networks, including macro cells, Het Nets, D2D networks, C-RAN, and F-RAN, and examine their capabilities under both non-caching and caching-enabled modes. Shanmugam *et al.* [5] propose a caching mechanism for each assisting node to reduce expected download latency. Piao *et al.* [6] focus on the results of edge caching in RAN, examining caching strategies at deployment locations such as BSs and mobile devices and integrating them.

Cooperative caching is a promising solution to the above problems [7]. Kazez *et al.* [8] propose an optimal caching scheme to enhance content diversity and hit rates in D2D networks by clustering assisting nodes. Wang *et al.* [9] propose a region-based cooperative content caching and distribution scheme and develop a heuristic cooperative content caching strategy. Chien *et al.* [10] propose a Q-learning-based cooperative caching mechanism to minimize latency and backhaul pressure. Wang *et al.* [11] smoothly combine incremental dynamic clustering with the contextual MAB paradigm for real-time online recommendation. Ren *et al.* [12] propose a hierarchical cooperative caching strategy based on user distribution characteristics and MEC locations. Tran *et al.* [13] propose a low-complexity heuristic caching management strategy and design the cache-aware request scheduling (CARS) algorithm to online optimize the trade-off between content download rate and content delivery latency.

Zhang *et al.* [14] propose a content popularity prediction method based on temporal convolutional neural networks and a dynamic programming caching strategy in cooperative caching. Song *et al.* [15] propose a multimodal transformer popularity prediction model and a dynamic cache-based population prediction algorithm. Guan *et al.* [16] propose a new preference learning-based cache admission strategy, PrefCache, for video content edge caching. Tsigkari *et al.* [17] proposes joint optimization of caching and recommendation in generic caching networks to maximize Quality of Experience (QoE). Lee *et al.* [18] study probabilistic modeling and parameterization of personal preferences for video content in wireless caching networks to represent user content preferences more accurately.

# 3   System Models and Problem Formulation

## 3.1   System Model

Our method clusters BSs according to their geographic coordinates. Figure 1 illustrates the cooperative caching environment for one of the clustered BS groups. Users request content by sending requests to BSs, which then forward the requests to specific MECs. If the MEC doesn't cache the content, it requests the content from neighboring MECs or further from the cloud. Due to capacity limitations, edge servers can only cache part of the content, while cloud servers are usually considered to be limitless. The set of MECs is $E = \{e_1, e_2, \ldots, e_{ne}\}$, that of all users $U = \{u_1, u_2, \ldots, u_{nu}\}$, that of requested content $C = \{c_1, c_2, \ldots, c_{nc}\}$ and the set of clustered user groups $L = \{l_1, l_2, \ldots, l_{nl}\}$. $ra_i$ indicates the service radius of $e_i$, $s_i$ the size of $c_i$, and $es_i$ the cache capacity of $e_i$.

## 3.2   Caching Model

Limited space makes it impossible to cache all content. $d_{i,j}(t)$ indicates whether $e_i$ has cached $c_j$ at time $t$. The total volume of cached content is bounded by the cache capacity of the server:

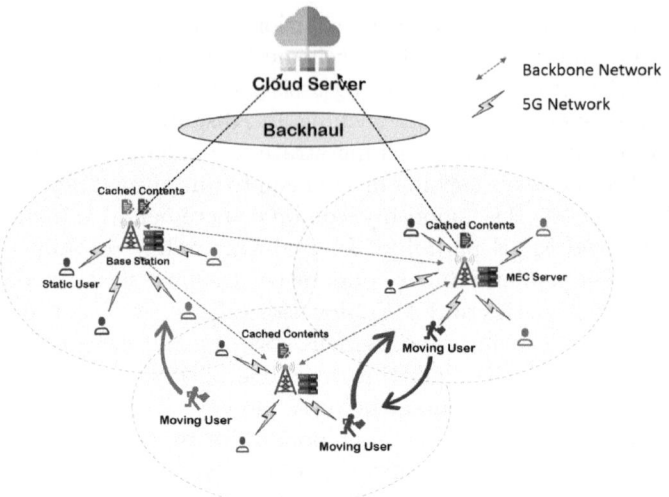

**Fig. 1.** Cooperative cache environment

$$\sum_{j=0}^{nc} d_{i,j}(t) \cdot s_j \leq es_i \tag{1}$$

The objective is thus to cache as much content as possible with the capacity constraint. It should be avoided as well for multiple servers in close proximity to each other to cache the same content due to the fact that such content can be shared according to a cooperative caching mechanism for capacity saving. $dn_{i,j}(t)$ indicates whether $e_i$'s neighboring server caches $c_j$ at time t.

$$dn_{i,j}(t) = \begin{cases} 1, & (\exists e_p \in N_i, d_{p,j}(t) = 1) \\ 0, & otherwise \end{cases} \tag{2}$$

The amount of space wasted by $e_i$ at time $t$ when content sharing is unsuccessful is thus $w_i(t)$:

$$w_i(t) = \sum_{j=0}^{nc} d_{i,j}(t) \cdot dn_{i,j}(t) \tag{3}$$

### 3.3 Transmission Model

Communication latency is mainly decided by on transmission delay.

$$tc_{i,j,k}(t) = \begin{cases} \frac{s_k}{teu_{j,i}}, & if\ d_{j,k}(t) = 1 \\ \frac{s_k}{teu_{j,i}} + \frac{s_k}{tee_{j,p}}, & if\ d_{j,k}(t) = 0 \wedge dn_{p,j}(t) = 1 \\ \frac{s_k}{tee_{j,p}} + lrc, & otherwise \end{cases} \tag{4}$$

where $d_{j,k}(t)$ indicates whether $c_k$ can be found on $e_j$ at time $t$, $dn_{p,j}(t)$ whether $c_j$ can be found on the neighboring server of $e_p$ at time $t$, $s_k$ the size of $c_k$, $tee_{j,p}$ the transmission rate when $e_p$ transmits data to $e_j$, $teu_{j,i}$ the transmission rate when $e_i$ transmits data to $e_j$ and $lrc$ the latency of delivering data from the cloud server.

## 3.4    Problem Formulation

A request is considered to be met by a cache hit when the requested content is found on the local server or a neighbouring server. The number of requests with a cache hit at a given moment:

$$h(t) = \sum_{i=0}^{nu}\sum_{j=0}^{ne}\sum_{k=0}^{nc} r_{i,j,k}(t)\,(d_{j,k}(t) \vee dn_{j,k}(t)) \tag{5}$$

The number of requests at time $t$ is:

$$nr(t) = \sum_{i=0}^{nu}\sum_{j=0}^{ne}\sum_{k=0}^{nc} r_{i,j,k}(t) \tag{6}$$

The transmission delay following a cache hit is thus:

$$tcu(t) = \sum_{i=0}^{nu}\sum_{j=0}^{ne}\sum_{k=0}^{nc} r_{i,j,k}(t) \cdot tc_{i,j,k}(t) \tag{7}$$

The optimization objectives is thus:

1. to maximize the global cache hit rate.
2. to minimise the average latency of content delivery.
3. to minimise the amount of wasted space.

$$Max: \frac{\sum_{t=0}^{t^{max}} h(t)}{\sum_{t=0}^{t^{max}} nr(t)} \tag{8}$$

$$Min: \frac{\sum_{t=0}^{t^{max}} tcu(t)}{\sum_{t=0}^{t^{max}} nr(t)} \tag{9}$$

$$Min: \sum_{t=0}^{t^{max}}\sum_{i=0}^{ne} w_i(t) \tag{10}$$

**C1.** $\quad \sum_{j=0}^{nc} d_{i,j}(t) \cdot s_j \leq es_i, \quad \forall i, \forall t$

**C2.** $\quad \sqrt{(dis_{i,j})^2} < ra_j, \quad \forall i, \forall j$

C1 indicates that the size of the content cached by the edge server is bounded by the capacity of the server. C2 indicates that the user must be within the service range of the base station. The cooperative cache placement problem, as shown in (8–10), is proven to be NP-hard [19].

# 4   Cooperative Caching Based on Mobility-Aware Clustering

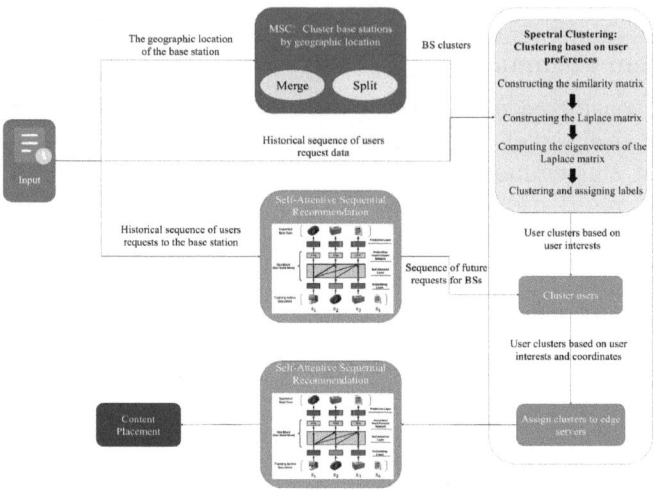

**Fig. 2.** MCL_CPC process

This section presents our proposed cooperative caching algorithm. It first takes the geographic coordinates of BSs as inputs to obtain base station clusters. Then, it takes the base station clusters and the historical sequences of user content requests as input for spectral clustering, incorporating user mobility to obtain user clusters. Finally, a greedy strategy is employed to allocate user clusters to MECs and perform pre-caching. Figure 2 shows the algorithm process of MCL_CPC.

Since the distribution of base stations remains constant over an extended period, the execution speed of the MCL_CPC algorithm is primarily determined by the clustering and allocation processes. The time complexity of the clustering process is $O(\mu^3)$, where $\mu$ represents the number of users involved in clustering. The time complexity of the allocation process is $O(\chi\rho)$, where $\chi$ and $\rho$ represent the number of user clusters and base stations, respectively. Over a time period $T$, this process is executed $T/w$ times. Therefore, the overall time complexity of the algorithm can be expressed as $O((\mu^3 + \chi\rho) \times (T/w))$, where $w$ is the size of the clustering window.

## 4.1   Clustering of Base Stations Based on Geographic Location

The distance between users and MECs should not be too far; otherwise, the content transmission will require forwarding through multiple base stations, causing greater latency. To reasonably divide the cooperative caching area, this paper

---

**Algorithm 1.** Merge and Split Clustering

---

1: **Input:** $B = \{b_1, b_2, \ldots, b_n\}$ ▷ Set of BSs
2: **Input:** $d^{max}$, $n^{max}$
3: **Initialize** $b_i \in B$ as a single cluster $bl_i, BL = \{bl_1, bl_2 \ldots, bl_n\}$
4: Set *convergence* = false
5: **while** not *convergence* **do**
6:    *convergence* = true
7:    **for** each pair of clusters $(bl_i, bl_j)$ in $BL$ **do**
8:       **if** distance$(bl_i, bl_j) < d^{max}$ **then**
9:          Merge $bl_i$ and $bl_j$ into a new cluster $bl_k$
10:          Update distance list with $bl_k$
11:          Remove $bl_i$ and $bl_j$ from $BL$
12:          Add $bl_k$ to $BL$
13:          *convergence* = false
14:       **end if**
15:    **end for**
16:    **for** each cluster $bl_k$ in $BL$ **do**
17:       **if** max_distance$(bl_k) > d^{max}$ or $|bl_k| > n^{max}$ **then**
18:          **if** max_distance$(bl_k) > d^{max}$ **then**
19:             Split $bl_k$ based on distance criteria
20:          **else**
21:             Split $bl_k$ based on size criteria
22:          **end if**
23:          *convergence* = false
24:       **end if**
25:    **end for**
26: **end while**
27: **return** $BL$ ▷ Set of base station clusters

---

proposes a clustering algorithm based on merging and splitting. Merging is to gather base stations in close geographical proximity into one network, while splitting does the opposite. These two operations ensure that the network structure of cooperative caching is within an appropriate range and increase the number of base stations that can directly communicate as much as possible to minimize communication delay. The specific steps of the algorithm are detailed in Algorithm 1.

## 4.2  Clustering Users Based on User Preference

The philosophy behind preference-informed clustering is that users with similar preferences exhibit similar request patterns and are likely to request the same content. When users with similar preferences request the same MEC, the server only needs to cache one copy of the content.

Users' content preferences change over time and thus we employ an adjustable time window-based mechanism. Over time, previous clustering results become invalid, requiring re-clustering at the start of a set time window. Since user preferences follow a Zipf distribution, a small amount of high-request content

---

**Algorithm 2.** Clustering of Users

1: **Input:** $U = \{u_1, u_2, \ldots, u_n\}$, $C = \{c_1, c_2, \ldots, c_m\}$, $BL = \{bl_1, bl_2, \ldots, bl_k\}$
2: **Initialize** $P(u_i, c_j)$: Number of requests by user $u_i$ for content $c_j$, $Loc(u_i)$: Location
   of user $u_i$
3: **for** each user $u_i$ in $U$ **do**
4:     $Pref(u_i) \leftarrow$ Top 30% of $C$ based on $P(u_i, c_j)$
5: **end for**
6: **for** each pair of users $(u_i, u_j)$ in $U$ **do**
7:     $A \leftarrow Pref(u_i)$
8:     $B \leftarrow Pref(u_j)$
9:     $Sim(u_i, u_j) \leftarrow \frac{|A \cap B|}{|A \cup B|}$
10: **end for**
11: $InitialUserClusters \leftarrow$ Apply spectral cluster
12: $L \leftarrow \{\}$
13: **for** each cluster $Cluster$ in $InitialUserClusters$ **do**
14:     $TempClusters \leftarrow \{\}$
15:     **for** each user $u_i$ in $Cluster$ **do**
16:         $bl_i \leftarrow Loc(u_i)$
17:         $TempClusters[bl_i] \leftarrow TempClusters[bl_i] \cup \{u_i\}$
18:     **end for**
19:     **for** each subcluster $SubCluster$ in $TempClusters$ **do**
20:         $L \leftarrow L \cup SubCluster$
21:     **end for**
22: **end for**
23: **return** $L$

---

suffice to represent their preferences. After calculating the number of requests for each content, the content is sorted in a descending order by request volume. The top 30% of the requested content indicates the user's preferred content set. User similarity is expressed a using a Jaccard coefficient as shown in (11).

$$\text{Sim}(u_i, u_j) = \frac{|A \cap B|}{|A \cup B|} \qquad (11)$$

where $A$ and $B$ respectively represent the preferred content sets of $u_i$ and $u_j$.

The clustering process is based on a spectral clustering model, which are widely acknowledged to be with low computational complexity and high effectiveness for dealing with sparse data [20]. The quality of the clustering is evaluated by a loss function defined as the sum of squared differences between each sample in the cluster and other samples:

$$\text{Loss} = \sum_{i=1}^{nl} \frac{1}{|l_i|} \sum_{u_a \in l_i, u_b \in l_i} \left(1 - \frac{|A \cap B|}{|A \cup B|}\right)^2 \qquad (12)$$

The clustering objects are users in multiple cooperative caching environments. First, users are clustered based on their preferences, and then further grouped according to the BS clusters requested by the users. Specifically, users who request the same BS cluster and share similar preferences should be classified into the same user cluster. This method not only considers the similarity of user preferences but also integrates the geographical information of users. The specific steps of the algorithm are detailed in Algorithm 2.

### 4.3   Assigning User Clusters to Edge Servers

Assuming that MECs are identical except for their geographical location. Based on the principle that more capable BSs should handle more requests, this paper calculates the number of BSs each base station can communicate with directly, as well as the number it can communicate with strictly through two hops. If no MEC within the two-hop range cache the content, the request is forwarded to the cloud server. The ability of $e_i$ to exchange data with other BSs (i.e., service capability) is defined as: $ser_i = |N_i| + 0.5Y_i$, where $Y_i$ indicates the set of BSs that $e_i$ can communicate with strictly through two hops. Our method predicts future request quantities based on the number of recent user requests, sorts user clusters in descending order by request volume, and assigns user clusters with high request volumes to BSs with strong service capabilities. However, it is also necessary to consider load balancing and the average distance to the user cluster. Therefore, this paper proposes the base station allocation weight calculation formula:

$$we_{i,j} = ser_j - \frac{1}{|l_i|} \sum_{k \in l_i} dis_{k,j} - ld_j \tag{13}$$

where $ld_j$ indicates the number of requests processed by $e_j$ within the most recent clustering window. The specific steps of the algorithm are detailed in Algorithm 3.

### 4.4   Content and Mobility Prediction

User preference based algorithms require more computational resources since they predict for individual users, and servers often need to serve many users simultaneously, especially during peak periods. Compared to user preference-based algorithms, content popularity-based algorithms require fewer computational resources as they use aggregated request data from user groups, enabling a single service to cater to multiple users. To serve more users during peak periods, our method adjusts the prediction strategy based on the load pressure of the base stations. When the load pressure is high, we use content popularity-based prediction; otherwise, we use user preference-based prediction. The diversity of user preferences often results in poor performance for content-based predictions. To address this, our method takes the request sequences of user clusters as input. The similarity of preferences within user clusters mitigates the impact of heterogeneous user preferences, thereby enhancing prediction accuracy and cache hit rates.

**Algorithm 3.** User Cluster Assignment

1: **Input:** $U = \{u_1, u_2, \ldots, u_n\}$, $B = \{b_1, b_2, \ldots, b_k\}$
2: **Initialize** $Req(l_i)$: Historical number of requests by user clusters, $Loc(u_i)$: Location of user $u_i$
3: **for** each base station $b_i$ in $B$ **do** Calculate $N_i$ and $Y_i$
4:     $ser_i \leftarrow |N_i| + 0.5 \times |Y_i|$
5:     Normalize($ser(i)$), Normalize($ld_i$)
6: **end for**
7: **for each** user cluster $l_j$ **in** $Req$ **and each** base station $b_i$ **in** $B$ **do**
8:     Normalize($AvgDist(b_i, l_j)$)
9:     $we_{i,j} \leftarrow ser_i - AvgDist(b_i, l_j) - ld_i$
10: **end for**
11: $Allocation \leftarrow \{\}$
12: $SortedClusters \leftarrow$ Sort($Req$) by requests in descending order
13: **for** each user cluster $l_j$ in $SortedClusters$ **do**
14:     $BestBS \leftarrow \arg \max_{b_i \in BS} we_{i,j}$
15:     $Allocation[BestBS] \leftarrow Allocation[BestBS] \cup \{l_j\}$
16: **end for**
17: **return** $Allocation$

Unlike traditional trajectory prediction methods that rely on latitude and longitude coordinates and often waste computational and storage resources due to trajectory deviations, this paper abandons conventional coordinate input and uses the user's historical base station cluster sequences as input. When a user's base station cluster changes, the user is assigned to the most similar user cluster within the new cooperative caching environment. Simultaneously, the user is removed from the original cluster. If a user cluster exceeds the size limit after assignment, it is split into two equally sized clusters. This step prevents too many users from overloading the same MEC to reduce the load on the base station.

## 5  Performance Evaluation

### 5.1  Experiment Setting

We employ the Shanghai Telecom and lastfm-dataset-1K dataset to simulate an MEC environment with multiple ESs capable of caching content. The Lastfm-1K dataset comprises 19,098,852 records, including user ID, timestamp, artist ID, artist name, track ID, and track name, featuring 107,295 artists and 1K users. The Telecom Dataset is provided by Shanghai Telecom, containing over 7.2 million records, documenting how 9,481 mobile phones accessed the internet through 3,233 BSs over a period of six months. Parameters. System parameters are given in Table 1.

In the lastfm-dataset-1K dataset, we calculate the preferences of contents according to their corresponding requesting frequencies with the 300 most active users. The Telecom Dataset includes the latitude and longitude coordinates of

**Table 1.** Experimental parameters

| Parameters | Values |
| --- | --- |
| Number of requests | 4524116 |
| Number of users | 300 |
| Number of BSs | 27 |
| Number of Cooperative Caching Clusters | 3 |
| Delay between Bss | 20 ms |
| BS to user delay | 15 ms |
| Delay in getting data from the cloud by the BS | 80 ms |
| Server cache size | 50–300 |

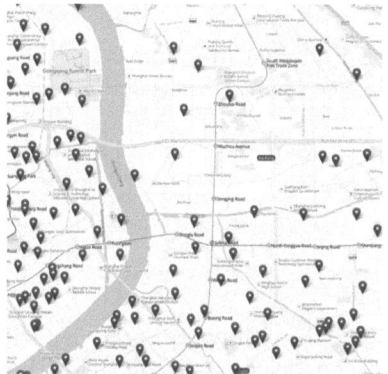

**Fig. 3.** Distribution of the Shanghai Base Station Dataset

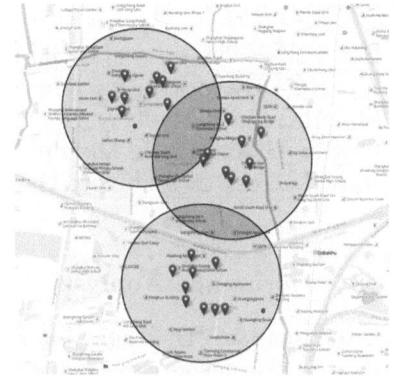

**Fig. 4.** Cooperative Caching Environment Selected in this paper

each user's requests to BSs at different time points. Figure 3 shows the geographical distribution of the Shanghai Base Station Dataset, and Fig. 4 depicts the three cooperative caching areas selected for this experiment. For simplicity, we assume that contents have the same size. The cache size of the server is expressed as the number of contents it can cache.

## 5.2   Baseline Algorithms and Metrics

We compare our method with the following existing methods:

**Nearest Match (NM):** This is the simplest nearest match algorithm, where user requests are directed to the nearest BS without considering cooperative caching.
**Cooperative Cache (CC):** This operates in a cooperative caching environment, where user requests are directed to the nearest BS to demonstrate the positive impact of cooperative caching.

**Clustered Cooperative Cache (CL_CC):** Building upon CC, this algorithm clusters users based on their interest preferences to demonstrate the positive impact of clustering.

**Motion-aware Clustered Cooperative Cache (MCL_CC):** Extending CL_CC, this algorithm incorporates mobility prediction to demonstrate the positive impact of mobility awareness.

**BA1** [19]: This algorithm utilizes a combination of Long Short-Term Memory (LSTM) and Temporal Pattern Attention (TPA) techniques to extract traffic features and predict future content popularity.

**BA2** [21]: This algorithm predicts user preferences based on user behavior and clusters users according to the predicted preferences.

To evaluate the performance of our proposed algorithm, we use the following metrics:

**Hit Rate:** The ratio of cache hits to the total number of requests.

**Average Response Latency:** The time elapsed from the moment a request is made until it is responded to.

**Cache Utilization:** The ratio of the average number of different contents cached across all servers to the total cache capacity.

### 5.3 Performance Analysis

Figure 5 compares the cache hit rates of different algorithms as cache capacity varies. As the cache capacity increases, the cache hit rates of all algorithms improve. Our proposed algorithm, MCL_CPC, achieves the best performance under all scenarios, with average improvements in cache hit rates of 15.42%, 13.28%, and 10.43% compared to CL_CC, BA1, and BA2, respectively.

Figure 6 compares the average content delivery latency of different algorithms as cache capacity varies. As the cache capacity increases, the average content delivery latency of all algorithms decreases. Compared to CL_CC, BA1, and BA2, MCL_CPC reduces the average content delivery latency by 43.11%, 32.26%, and 18.43%, respectively.

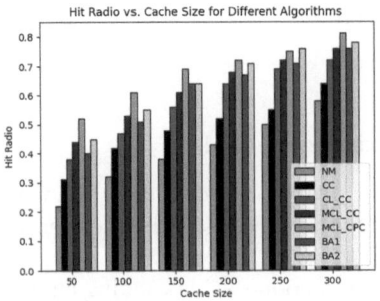

**Fig. 5.** Impact of Cache Capacity on Cache Hit Ratio

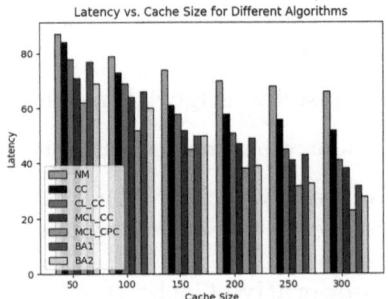

**Fig. 6.** Impact of Cache Capacity on Content Delivery Latency

Table 2 compares the cache utilization rates of different algorithms as cache capacity varies. Algorithms that incorporate user clustering (CL_CC, MCL_CC, MCL_CPC, BA2) generally exhibit higher average cache utilization rates compared to those that do not utilize clustering (NM, CC, BA1). When the cache capacity is 300, the average cache utilization rate of clustering algorithms outperforms that of non-clustering algorithms by 15.42%. Furthermore, as the cache capacity increases, the performance gap between the two types of algorithms continues to widen.

**Table 2.** Impact of Cache Capacity on Cache Utilisation

| Algorithm | Cache Utilisation | | | | | |
| --- | --- | --- | --- | --- | --- | --- |
| | es = 50 | es = 100 | es = 150 | es = 200 | es = 250 | es = 300 |
| NM | 0.86 | 0.84 | 0.81 | 0.77 | 0.72 | 0.68 |
| CC | 0.88 | 0.86 | 0.83 | 0.78 | 0.73 | 0.69 |
| CL_CC | 0.95 | 0.93 | 0.92 | 0.91 | 0.88 | 0.84 |
| MCL_CC | 0.94 | 0.92 | 0.89 | 0.88 | 0.86 | 0.83 |
| **MCL_CPC** | **0.96** | **0.95** | **0.93** | **0.90** | **0.87** | **0.86** |
| BA1 | 0.91 | 0.89 | 0.86 | 0.81 | 0.78 | 0.71 |
| BA2 | 0.95 | 0.94 | 0.94 | 0.91 | 0.86 | 0.86 |

Figures 7 and 8 demonstrate that as the number of BSs increases, all algorithms exhibit significant improvements in hit rate and content delivery latency. The performance growth rate of algorithms in cooperative caching environments is notably higher than that of the NM algorithm. The performance growth rate of content delivery latency decreases with the increasing number of BSs, due to the base station service capacity exceeding the user request capacity, resulting in performance surplus. Therefore, appropriately setting the number of BSs in a clustered base station group can effectively balance resource consumption and performance improvement.

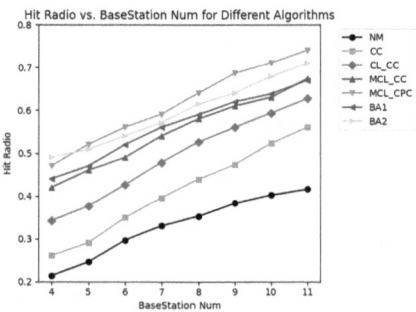

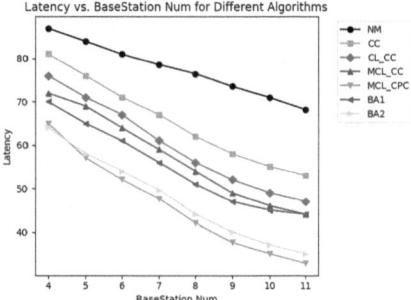

**Fig. 7.** The impact of the number of BSs on cache hit rate

**Fig. 8.** The impact of the number of BSs on content delivery latency

## 6 Conclusion

In this work, we propose a User Preference-informed and Mobility-aware method for cooperative MEC caching (MCL_CPC) to improve cache hit rates and reduce content delivery latency. This method clusters BSs and users based on geographic location, mobility, and interest preferences, respectively. An efficient greedy strategy is proposed to allocate user clusters to BSs. By synthesizing interest preference prediction model and request base station sequence prediction model, this method captures the dynamic changes in user activities and preferences to achieve content pre-caching. Experimental results demonstrate that this method outperforms traditional algorithms on multiple metrics.

## References

1. Shi, W., Cao, J., Zhang, Q., Li, Y., Lanyu, X.: Edge computing: vision and challenges. IEEE Internet Things J. **3**(5), 637–646 (2016)
2. Kuppusamy, P., Thirunavukkarasu, K., Kalaavathi, B.: A review of cooperative caching strategies in mobile ad hoc networks. Int. J. Comput. Appl. **29**(11), 22–26 (2011)
3. Safavat, S., Sapavath, N.N., Rawat, D.B.: Recent advances in mobile edge computing and content caching. Digit. Commun. Netw. **6**(2), 189–194 (2020)
4. Li, L., Zhao, G., Blum, R.S.: A survey of caching techniques in cellular networks: research issues and challenges in content placement and delivery strategies. IEEE Commun. Surv. Tutor. **20**(3), 1710–1732 (2018)
5. Shanmugam, K., Golrezaei, N., Dimakis, A.G., Molisch, A.F., Caire, G.: Femtocaching: wireless content delivery through distributed caching helpers. IEEE Trans. Inf. Theory **59**(12), 8402–8413 (2013)
6. Piao, Z., Peng, M., Liu, Y., Daneshmand, M.: Recent advances of edge cache in radio access networks for Internet of Things: techniques, performances, and challenges. IEEE Internet Things J. **6**(1), 1010–1028 (2018)
7. Glass, S., Mahgoub, I., Rathod, M.: Leveraging manet-based cooperative cache discovery techniques in VANETs: a survey and analysis. IEEE Commun. Surv. Tutor. **19**(4), 2640–2661 (2017)
8. Kazez, A.C., Girici, T.: Clustering-based device-to-device cache placement. Ad Hoc Netw. **84**, 170–177 (2019)
9. Wang, Y., Zhang, W., Ma, J., Jin, Q.: ADCB: adaptive dynamic clustering of bandits for online recommendation system. Neural Process. Lett. **55**(2), 1155–1172 (2023)
10. Chien, W.-C., Weng, H.-Y., Lai, C.-F.: Q-learning based collaborative cache allocation in mobile edge computing. Futur. Gener. Comput. Syst. **102**, 603–610 (2020)
11. Wang, S., Guo, Y., Zhang, N., Yang, P., Zhou, A., Shen, X.: Delay-aware microservice coordination in mobile edge computing: a reinforcement learning approach. IEEE Trans. Mob. Comput. **20**(3), 939–951 (2019)
12. Ren, D., Gui, X., Lu, W., An, J., Dai, H., Liang, X.: GHCC: grouping-based and hierarchical collaborative caching for mobile edge computing. In: 2018 16th International Symposium on Modeling and Optimization in Mobile, Ad Hoc, and Wireless Networks (WiOpt), pp. 1–6. IEEE (2018)

13. Tran, T.X., Le, D.V., Yue, G., Pompili, D.: Cooperative hierarchical caching and request scheduling in a cloud radio access network. IEEE Trans. Mob. Comput. **17**(12), 2729–2743 (2018)
14. Zhang, X., Qi, Z., Min, G., Miao, W., Fan, Q., Ma, Z.: Cooperative edge caching based on temporal convolutional networks. IEEE Trans. Parallel Distrib. Syst. **33**(9), 2093–2105 (2021)
15. Song, Z., Cao, R., Niu, B., Gu, J., Li, C.: A hybrid active and passive cache method based on deep learning in edge computing. In: Tari, Z., Li, K., Wu, H. (eds.) ICA3PP 2023. LNCS, vol. 14490, pp. 148–159. Springer, Singapore (2024). https://doi.org/10.1007/978-981-97-0859-8_9
16. Guan, Y., Zhang, X., Guo, Z.: PrefCache: edge cache admission with user preference learning for video content distribution. IEEE Trans. Circuits Syst. Video Technol. **31**(4), 1618–1631 (2020)
17. Tsigkari, D., Spyropoulos, T.: User-centric optimization of caching and recommendations in edge cache networks. In: 2020 IEEE 21st International Symposium on A World of Wireless, Mobile and Multimedia Networks (WoWMoM), pp. 244–253. IEEE (2020)
18. Lee, M.-C., Molisch, A.F., Sastry, N., Raman, A.: Individual preference probability modeling and parameterization for video content in wireless caching networks. IEEE/ACM Trans. Netw. **27**(2), 676–690 (2019)
19. Yi, B., Li, F., Zhang, Y., Wang, X.: TPA based content popularity prediction for caching and routing in edge-cloud cooperative network. In: 2021 IEEE Global Communications Conference (GLOBECOM), pp. 1–6. IEEE (2021)
20. Ng, A., Jordan, M., Weiss, Y.: On spectral clustering: analysis and an algorithm. In: Advances in Neural Information Processing Systems, vol. 14 (2001)
21. Somesula, M.K., Rout, R.R., Somayajulu, D.V.L.N.: Greedy cooperative cache placement for mobile edge networks with user preferences prediction and adaptive clustering. Ad Hoc Netw. **140**, 103051 (2023)

# Personalized Mobility-Aware Caching Strategies in Multi-access Edge Computing

Kunyin Guo[1], Han Zhao[1(✉)], Yunni Xia[1], Yunye Wan[1], Long Yang[2],
Jiafeng Feng[3], Yang Yu[4], and Ke Zhang[5]

[1] College of Computer Science, Chongqing University, Chongqing 400030, China
unicornzh@163.com
[2] College of Digital Industry, Jiangxi Normal University, Shangrao 334000, China
[3] China Huadian Corporation Ltd Guangdong Company, Guangzhou 510620, China
[4] Guodian Nanjing Automation Co., Ltd., Nanjing 210032, China
[5] China Huadian Corporation, Beijing 100031, China

**Abstract.** Although Multi-Access Edge Computing (MEC) has evolved into a key technology for provisioning mobility-oriented and delay-sensitive applications, the storage and computing power limitations of user-end MEC devices still present a significant challenge in guaranteeing low latency in content delivery. When the requested content is out of the caching scope of local devices, effectively caching user-requested content with low cost and high hit rate has become a widely acknowledged research hotspot. Traditional caching strategies inadequately address the challenges posed by mobility and runtime variations in content popularity. In this work, we propose a personalized mobility-aware caching method (MAPHC) that synthesizes a content suitability prediction algorithm (CSPA) for identifying the caching needs of edge servers and a multi-agent deep reinforcement learning model for dynamically adjusting user mobility-aware caching strategies. Simulation results clearly demonstrate that MAPHC outperforms its peers across multiple performance metrics.

**Keywords:** Multi-access edge computing · Multi-agent deep reinforcement learning · Mobility-aware · Cooperative caching

## 1 Introduction

With the swift advancement of the Internet of Things (IoT) [1], applications that are computationally demanding and sensitive to latency, such as Augmented Reality/Virtual Reality (AR/VR) [2] and Facial Recognition (FR), are growing exponentially. However, the limitations of smart mobile devices in computing and storage make it challenging to fully support these applications. To tackle this challenge, caching data closer to the user at the edge has emerged as an effective solution. Multi-Access Edge Computing (MEC) [3], a promising technology,

Y. Zhang and L.-J. Zhang (Eds.): ICWS 2024, LNCS 15428, pp. 78–92, 2025.
https://doi.org/10.1007/978-3-031-77072-2_6

reduces data transmission latency and network congestion by distributing computing and storage at the network edge, thereby enhancing user experience and application performance.

Despite MEC's ability to provide low-latency, high-speed services, the limited storage capacity of edge servers makes it difficult to meet the caching demands of all content [4]. Therefore, accurately predicting users' interests and preferences for personalized caching becomes crucial.

This study presents a mobility-aware caching strategy called MAPHC, utilizing multi-agent deep reinforcement learning tailored for MEC environments. The approach focuses on minimizing request latency and enhancing cache hit rates, ultimately improving the user experience. The key contributions of this paper include:

(1) Proposing a content suitability prediction algorithm (CSPA) based on user preferences to dynamically predict the content most likely to be requested by users.
(2) Utilizing multi-agent deep reinforcement learning to define states, actions, and reward functions, and determine the optimal cooperative caching strategy to minimize content transmission latency.
(3) The proposed method's effectiveness is validated through simulation experiments.

The paper is structured as follows: Sect. 2 reviews related work, Sect. 3 outlines the system model, Sect. 4 states the problem, Sect. 5 introduces the caching strategy, Sect. 6 analyzes experimental results, and Sect. 7 discusses conclusions and future research directions.

## 2    Related Work

With the widespread use of mobile devices and the surge in data traffic, content caching technology has gained significant attention in MEC environments [5]. Content caching, by pre-storing data and content at the network edge, significantly reduces data transmission latency, alleviates network congestion, and decreases reliance on central cloud servers. By locally caching popular content, edge servers can quickly respond to user requests, further reducing latency and network load [6].

Many studies have explored content caching from various perspectives. Zhong et al. [7] developed a multi-objective artificial bee colony algorithm for task offloading and cache placement in multi-MEC server systems, aiming to maximize cache hit rates and minimize latency. Wang et al. [8] proposed a joint optimization method for content caching, recommendation, and transmission in NOMA networks to reduce system latency. Personalized caching has attracted attention, with Malik et al. [9] introducing a preference learning framework that uses efficient algorithms like greedy algorithms to optimize cache allocation. Yu et al. [10] focused on group preferences and content popularity to create effective content placement strategies through collaborative caching.

Mobility-aware caching technology optimizes content caching decisions by considering user mobility patterns and location changes. For example, Li et al. [11] proposed a mobility-aware content caching and user association framework for ultra-dense MEC networks, aiming to optimize network performance by minimizing system costs. Wei et al. [12] proposed a cache placement scheme with short response times by predicting users' target locations and applying this prediction to the caching decision algorithm.

Reinforcement learning (RL) methods, like Q-learning [13], have proven effective in tackling the scale and complexity of MEC caching problems. These algorithms learn optimal strategies by interacting with the environment, making them well-suited for dynamic MEC caching decisions. Wang et al. [14] proposed a caching strategy based on Newton's cooling law, focusing on time- and energy-intensive content and modeling cooperative caching as a multi-objective optimization problem, leading to the development of a distributed multi-node cooperative caching (DCCC) algorithm. However, these approaches have limitations in accounting for user mobility. Zhong et al. [15] developed an RL-based caching strategy to improve cache efficiency and reduce latency, though it did not consider mobility patterns. Multi-agent deep reinforcement learning is particularly effective for complex decision-making scenarios [16], making it ideal for MEC environments where edge nodes collaborate to optimize caching strategies. This approach addresses dynamic user behavior and mobility by continuously optimizing caching through interactions with the environment.

Based on the above literature analysis, this paper proposes a Personalized Mobility-Aware Caching Algorithm based on multi-agent deep reinforcement learning in an MEC environment.

## 3    System Models

### 3.1    System Model of Mobility-Aware Caching

Figure 1 illustrates the MEC system model based on a three-layer architecture. It includes edge servers with cloud capabilities and base stations (BS) near smart mobile devices (SMDs) [17]. The top layer is the cloud center with high-performance servers and large storage. The middle layer includes base stations integrated with edge servers for data storage, caching, and computing, with caching capabilities constrained by the available storage capacity. The bottom layer includes mobile users who exchange data with edge servers via wireless connections for real-time processing. Mobile users connect to one MEC server and communicate with one base station at a time. Edge servers connect to cloud servers via backhaul links for large-scale processing when needed.

We assume that "base station" and "edge server" are synonymous. The set of base stations is BS $= \{bs_1, bs_2, \ldots, bs_i, \ldots, bs_m\}$ and that of users User $= \{u_1, u_2, \ldots, u_j, \ldots, u_n\}$. The cloud server acts as the content source. Assuming content requests are independent, each user requests unique content at any time slot, and their location remains fixed within that slot. Content requests are sent to the nearest base station. If available locally, the base station transmits the content. If not, it retrieves the content from neighboring base stations or forwards it to the cloud center.

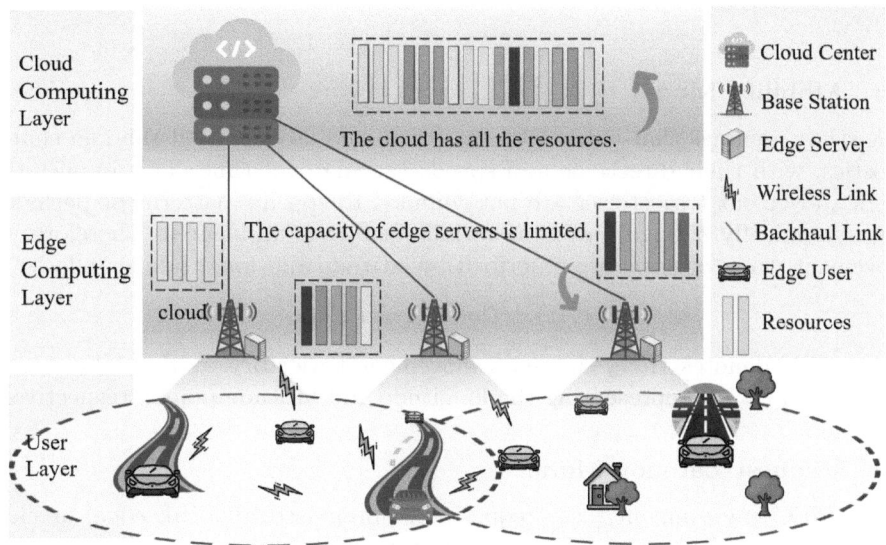

**Fig. 1.** System Model.

## 3.2 Caching Management Model

Edge servers are limited by storage and computing resources, making selective content caching essential for maintaining high-quality service. Consider a time period divided into $t_{\max}$ time slots, denoted as $\{t_0, t_1, \ldots, t_h, \ldots, t_{\max}\}$, where each slot represents a fixed-length interval. For each time slot $t_h$, $\mathrm{cs}_{i,k}(t_h)$ denotes a boolean indicator of whether the $k$-th content is in the cache of edge server $bs_i$ at time slot $t_h$:

$$\mathrm{cs}_{i,k}(t_h) = \begin{cases} 1, & \text{if the } k\text{-th content is cached at } bs_i \text{ at time slot } t_h \\ 0, & \text{otherwise} \end{cases} \tag{1}$$

The size of the $k$-th content is $d_k$. Therefore, the total size of the cached content at base station $bs_i$ is limited by its capacity $sc_i$:

$$\sum_{k=1}^{total} cs_{i,k}(t_h) \cdot d_k \leq sc_i \qquad (2)$$

where $d_k$ denotes the size of the $k$-th content, and $total$ is the number of content types.

## 3.3   Mobility Model

The study assumes that the movements of mobile users exhibit random characteristics, with their directions and speeds varying over time. This implies that users' movement trajectories are not confined to specific patterns or paths but can dynamically change based on various factors or influences. Therefore, the movement paths of users are described by latitude and longitude as follows:

$$l_j(t) = (lon_j(t), lat_j(t)) \qquad (3)$$

where $l_j(t)$ denotes the $j$-th user's movement trajectory at time slot $t$, with $lon_j(t)$ and $lat_j(t)$ representing the longitude and latitude points, respectively.

## 3.4   Request Latency Model

In an MEC environment, user requests are processed at local, edge, or cloud servers. Request latency consists of computation and transmission latency. Computation latency is the processing time, while transmission latency is the data transfer time. If local devices can't meet demands, requests go to edge servers. If edge servers can't handle them, requests are sent to cloud servers with greater capacity.

(1) Due to the varying processing capabilities of local devices, edge servers, and cloud servers, the computational efficiency at each layer directly impacts the overall response time.

1. Local computation latency ($tl$):

$$tl(t) = \sum_{j=1}^{n} \frac{wl_j(t) \cdot brq_j(t)}{cl} \qquad (4)$$

   where $wl_j(t)$ denotes the requests made by user $u_j$ to the local device during time slot $t$, $brq_j(t)$ refers to the size of the content requested by $u_j$, and $cl$ represents the processing capability of the local device.
2. Edge server computation latency ($tn$):

$$tn(t) = \sum_{i=1}^{m} \sum_{j=1}^{n} \frac{w_{i,j}(t) \cdot brq_j(t)}{cb_i} \qquad (5)$$

   where $w_{i,j}(t)$ denotes the requests made by user $u_j$ to base station $bs_i$ at $t$, and $cb_i$ represents the processing capability of base station $bs_i$.

3. Cloud server computation latency $(tc)$:

$$tc(t) = \sum_{j=1}^{n} \frac{wc_j(t) \cdot brq_j(t)}{cc} \tag{6}$$

where $wc_j(t)$ represents the requests sent by user $u_j$ to the cloud server during time slot $t$, and $cc$ signifies the processing capability of the cloud server.

Therefore, the total computational overhead is given by:

$$tt(t) = wld \cdot tl(t) + wes \cdot tn(t) + wcs \cdot tc(t) \tag{7}$$

$$wld + wes + wcs = 1 \tag{8}$$

where $wld$, $wes$, and $wcs$ represent the weights of the computation times for the local devices, edge servers, and cloud servers, respectively.

The varying locations of local devices, edge, and cloud servers in the network lead to differences in data transmission efficiency, which significantly affect overall response time.

1. Local transmission latency $(tdl)$:
   If the locally cached content meets the user's request, the transmission latency is considered zero:

   $$tdl(t) = 0 \tag{9}$$

2. Edge server transmission latency $(tdn)$:
   If the locally cached content does not meet the user's request, but the nearby edge server can provide the requested content, the transmission latency is defined as:

   $$tdn(t) = \sum_{i=1}^{m} \sum_{j=1}^{n} \frac{w_{i,j}(t) \cdot brq_j(t) \cdot \theta_{w1}}{R_{i,j}(t)} \tag{10}$$

   where $\theta_{w1}$ denotes the ratio of the data volume of user $u_j$'s request $w_{i,j}(t)$ to the data volume returned by base station $bs_i$ during time slot $t$. The data transmission rate $R_{i,j}(t)$ from user $u_j$ to base station $bs_i$ within time slot $t$ is determined by the channel gain $G_{i,j}(t)$, Gaussian white noise $\sigma^2$, and transmission power $P_{i,j}(t)$. The expression for $R_{i,j}(t)$ is given as follows:

   $$R_{i,j}(t) = v \log_2 \left( 1 + \frac{G_{i,j}(t) \cdot P_{i,j}(t)}{\sigma^2} \right) \tag{11}$$

3. Cloud server transmission latency $(tdc)$:
   If neither the local cache nor nearby base stations have the requested content, the request is sent to the cloud server. The transmission latency from the cloud server to the user via the backhaul link is given by:

   $$tdc(t) = \sum_{i=1}^{m} \sum_{j=1}^{n} \frac{wc_j(t) \cdot brq_j(t) \cdot \theta_{w2}}{Rc} \tag{12}$$

where $Rc$ denotes the backhaul link transmission rate between the cloud and base stations, and $\theta_{w2}$ represents the ratio of the data volume of user $u_j$'s request $wc_j(t)$ to the data returned by the cloud server during time slot $t$.

Therefore, the total delay overhead can be expressed as:

$$td(t) = wdl \cdot tdl(t) + wdn \cdot tdn(t) + wdc \cdot tdc(t) \tag{13}$$

$$wdl + wdn + wdc = 1 \tag{14}$$

where $wdl$, $wdn$, and $wdc$ represent the weights of the transmission latency for the local devices, base stations, and cloud servers, respectively.

## 4    Problem Formalization

The content caching problem is framed around specific objectives and constraints. This paper aims to minimize request latency while respecting each MEC server's time and capacity constraints, ensuring efficient content delivery. Accordingly, the problem is formally defined as follows:

$$\text{F1:} \quad \min \frac{1}{m} \frac{1}{n} \sum_{i=1}^{m} \sum_{j=1}^{n} (wt \cdot tt(t) + wd \cdot td(t)) \tag{15}$$

$$wt + wd = 1 \tag{16}$$

$$\text{C1:} \quad \sum_{j=1}^{n} w_{i,j}(t) \cdot brq_j(t) \leq sc_i, \quad \forall j \in [1, n] \tag{17}$$

$$\text{C2:} \quad td(t) \leq td_{\max}(t) \tag{18}$$

$$\text{C3:} \quad 0 < d_j \leq d_{\max}, \quad \forall j \in [1, n] \tag{19}$$

where $wt$ and $wd$ represent the weights assigned to the computation overhead $tt(t)$ and delay overhead $td(t)$, respectively, with $wt + wd = 1$. Constraint C1 ensures that the content requested by users stays within the edge server's storage capacity. Constraint C2 guarantees that the total processing and transmission latency remains below the maximum permissible limit. Constraint C3 confirms that the user-requested service does not surpass the maximum service range.

## 5    Implementation of Mobility-Aware Caching Algorithm

### 5.1    User Preference-Based Content Prediction Algorithm

While highly popular content is frequently requested, relying solely on this criterion for caching decisions overlooks specific user needs. In a dynamic environment, accurately predicting and pre-caching content of potential interest helps edge servers better meet user demands, reduce latency, and improve cache hit rates. This study proposes a content suitability prediction algorithm based on user preferences to better match individual needs, as outlined in Algorithm 1.

First, during the time period $T$, the base stations collect users' content access history, recorded as $N$ accesses. Let $t_h$ be a time slot. The access history includes all types of content users browse, watch, or read, obtained from server logs. Let the content accessed during $t_h$ be denoted as $f_k$, where $k$ represents the content category. The request count for content $f_k$ at $t_h$ is $R_{f_k}(t_h)$, and the user's preference for this content is $P_{f_k}(t_h)$. The higher the preference, the greater the user's interest. The calculation formula is as follows:

$$P_{f_k}(t_h) = \frac{R_{f_k}(t_h)}{\sum_k R_{f_k}(t_h)} \tag{20}$$

To further analyze, the obtained content preferences, represented as the set $\{P_{f_k}(t_0), P_{f_k}(t_1), \ldots, P_{f_k}(t_h), \ldots, P_{f_k}(t_{max})\}$, are input into a single exponential smoothing prediction model. This model forecasts the user's preference for content $f_k$ in the next time slot $t_{h+1}$, denoted as $\hat{P}_{fk}(t_{h+1})$, reflecting potential user behavior trends. The predicted preference $\hat{P}_{fk}(t_{h+1})$ essentially indicates the user's relative interest in various content types in the next time slot, helping identify the predicted content $\hat{f}_k(t_{h+1})$ that the user might find interesting.

To measure the suitability and similarity between the content accessed in consecutive time slots ($t_h$ and $t_{h+1}$) and the predicted content $\hat{f}_k(t_{h+1})$, we define the content feature fitness $S_k$, calculated as follows:

$$S_k = \sqrt{\sum_k \theta_k \left( \widehat{\mathrm{Cha}}_k(t_{h+1}) - \mathrm{Cha}_k(t_h) \right)^2} \tag{21}$$

where $\theta_k$ represents the weights of content features, $\mathrm{Cha}_k(t_h)$ denotes the feature value of content $f_k(t_h)$ accessed by the user in time slot $t_h$, and $\widehat{\mathrm{Cha}}_k(t_{h+1})$ is the predicted feature value of $\hat{f}_k(t_{h+1})$ based on preference $\hat{P}_{fk}(t_{h+1})$.

The user's preference for the predicted content in the next time slot $t_{h+1}$, denoted as $P_{f_k}(t_{h+1})$, is calculated using the content feature fitness $S_k$ as follows:

$$P_{f_k}(t_{h+1}) = \frac{\sum_k S_k P_{f_k}(t_h)}{N} \tag{22}$$

---

**Algorithm 1:** CSPA Algorithm

---

**Require:** User content access history, time period $T = \{t_0, t_1, \ldots, t_{max}\}$,
and content types $F = \{f_0, f_1, \ldots, f_{total}\}$.

**Ensure:** Set of content with high user preference

1: **while** $h + 1 < max$ **do**
2:    **for** each $k < total$ **do**
3:       Calculate the number of requests for content $f_k$ during time slot $t_h$;
4:       Calculate content preference $P_{f_k}(t_h)$;
5:       Represent the obtained content preferences as the set
       $\{P_{f_k}(t_0), P_{f_k}(t_1), \ldots, P_{f_k}(t_h), \ldots, P_{f_k}(t_{max})\}$;
6:    **end for**
7:    $h = h + 1$;
8:    Use the single exponential smoothing prediction model to forecast the
     user preference for content $f_k$ in the next time slot $t_{h+1}$, denoted as
     $\hat{P}_{f_k}(t_{h+1})$;
9:    **while** each $k < total$ **do**
10:       Calculate content feature fitness $S_k$;
11:       Calculate the user preference for the predicted content in the next
       time slot $P_{f_k}(t_{h+1})$;
12:    **end while**
13:    During the time period $T$, define the calculated high preference
     content as the preference content set $Pcs$;
14: **end while**
15: **return** Preference content set $Pcs$

---

### 5.2 Multi-agent Mobility-Aware Content Caching Algorithm

To effectively decide which high-preference content to cache, this paper utilizes
a MARL algorithm that leverages the Actor-Critic (AC) architecture [18]. The
edge server first uses the CSPA algorithm to analyze mobile users' requests and
filter high-preference content. This information is passed to the Actor network
$\mu(s|\theta^\mu)$, which formulates the optimal caching strategy $a$ based on the state $s$
and parameters $\theta^\mu$. The system receives rewards $r$, transitions to a new state $s'$
based on feedback, and updates the Actor network's parameters using the Critic
network $Q(s, a|\theta^Q)$ to optimize future decisions [19]. The detailed implementa-
tion process can be referred to in Algorithm 2.

In this study, we define the state, action, and reward as follows:

State: At time slot $t$, the state of the edge caching server is denoted as $s^t = \{s_1^t, s_2^t, \cdots, s_m^t\}$. Each agent operates on a specific edge server, interacting
and competing with others to optimize its strategy.

Action: The action set $a_v^t = \{a_{vs}^t, a_{vf}^t\}$ includes decisions made by agent $v$
based on the observed state, where $a_{vs}^t$ involves caching content, and $a_{vf}^t$
involves discarding it.

Reward: The reward function $r_v^t$ quantifies the benefit agent $v$ receives for
choosing a specific action in the current state. Agents adjust their actions to

minimize content retrieval latency. If an action meets the criteria, the reward increases. The reward function is defined as follows:

$$r_v^t = \begin{cases} e^{-\frac{1}{m}\frac{1}{n}\sum_{i=1}^{m}\sum_{j=1}^{n}(wt\cdot tt(t)+wd\cdot td(t))} & a_{vs}^t \\ -1 & a_{vf}^t \end{cases} \tag{23}$$

The computational complexity of the $MAPHC$ algorithm plays an important role in determining its scalability in multi-agent systems. This complexity is influenced by the number of neurons and layers in the Actor and Critic networks, as well as the input and output sizes. For the Actor network, the complexity is $O(d_s \times h_{1,1} + \sum_{m=1}^{w_1-1} h_{1,m} \times h_{1,m+1} + h_{1,w_1} \times \iota)$, where $d_s$ is the input size, $h_{1,m}$ is the number of neurons in each hidden layer, and $\iota$ is the output size. The Critic network has a similar complexity. In a system with $n$ agents, the overall complexity is proportional to $n$, as each agent requires its own Actor and Critic networks.

---

**Algorithm 2:** MAPHC Algorithm

---

**Require:** Number of episodes $X$, number of iterations $iter$, learning rates $\delta_a$ and $\delta_c$, discount factor $\gamma$, preference content set $Pcs$
**Ensure:** Optimal caching strategy
1: Initialize the actor network parameters $\theta^\mu$, critic network parameters $\theta^Q$, and their corresponding target network parameters $\theta^{\mu'}$ and $\theta^{Q'}$ for each agent $v$
2: **for** episode $= 1$ to $X$ **do**
3:     **for** t $= 1$ to $iter$ **do**
4:         Each agent obtains state $s_v^t$ from the environment based on $Pcs$
5:         Each agent selects action $a_v^t$ based on the current policy $\mu\left(s_v^t|\theta^\mu\right)$
6:         Execute $a_v^t$ and obtain reward $r_v^t$ and new state $s_v^{t+1}$
7:         Store $\left(s_v^t, a_v^t, r_v^t, s_v^{t+1}\right)$ in replay buffer
8:         Randomly select a batch of $A$ samples from the replay buffer
9:         Compute target $y = r + \gamma Q(s', \mu\left(s'|\theta^{\mu'}\right)|\theta^{Q'})$
10:        Compute loss $\mathcal{L} = \frac{1}{A}\sum\left(y - Q\left(s, a|\theta^Q\right)\right)^2$
11:        Update $\theta^Q$ via gradient descent $\theta^Q - \delta_c\nabla_{\theta^Q}\mathcal{L}$
12:        Compute policy gradient
            $\nabla_{\theta^\mu}J \approx \frac{1}{A}\sum\nabla_a Q(s,a|\theta^Q)|_{a=\mu(s)}\nabla_{\theta^\mu}\mu\left(s|\theta^\mu\right)$ and update $\theta^\mu$
13:        Soft update target network parameters $\theta^{Q'}$ and $\theta^{\mu'}$
14:     **end for**
15: **end for**
16: **return** Optimal caching strategy

---

## 6   Experimental Simulation Results Analysis

The experiment combines the Shanghai Telecom dataset [20] with the Movielens 1M [21] dataset to simulate mobile user content requests and mobility behaviors.The Shanghai dataset contains over 7.2 million content access records and mobility data from 9481 users across 3233 edge sites over six months, capturing user behaviors and movement patterns. By integrating Movielens rating data, we align content preferences with these trajectories, simulating user interests in movies or videos across different locations and times. Figure 2 shows each edge node in central Shanghai (blue icons) and the travel trajectory of a taxi on a particular day (green lines).

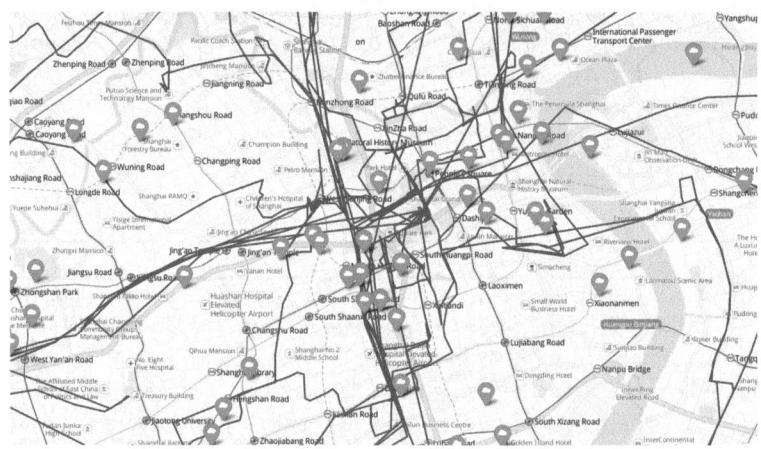

**Fig. 2.** Combined Display of Edge Nodes and a Taxi's One-Day Trajectory in Central Shanghai.

## 6.1 Comparative Algorithms

MAPHC was evaluated against several algorithms: Thompson Sampling (TS) [22], which balances exploration and exploitation but can converge slowly in complex environments and struggles to adapt to dynamic user preferences; Random Selection Algorithm (RSA) [23], a non-adaptive strategy that randomly selects actions, leading to poor performance due to its lack of optimization, resulting in low cache hit rates and high latency; Greedy Algorithm (GA) [24], which prioritizes immediate gains but often gets stuck in local optima, failing to adapt to long-term request changes; and Wang *et al.*'s Distributed Cooperative Caching (DCCC) [14], which, while collaborative, incurs high computational and communication costs and does not fully address user mobility challenges.

## 6.2 Performance Analysis

During the performance analysis, we configured an environment in which each base station, equipped with an edge server, stores diverse content according to its caching strategy to test mobile users' responses to content requests. As shown

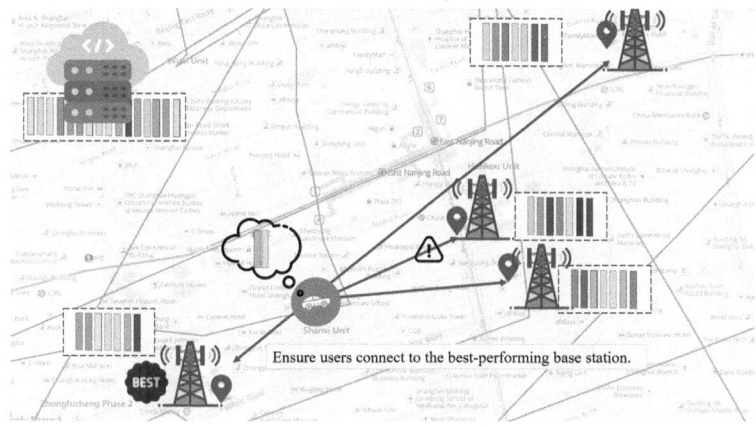

Ensure users connect to the best-performing base station.

**Fig. 3.** Edge User Content Request Scenarios.

in Fig. 3, different types of content are distinguished by various colors, with each color representing the content type cached by different edge servers.

Figure 4 shows the hit rates of different caching strategies as cache capacity increases. While all strategies improve with larger capacities, MAPHC consistently outperforms them. It achieves 9.2%, 21.7%, 37.5%, and 14.3% higher hit rates than DCCC, TS, RSA, and GA, respectively. At a capacity of 500, MAPHC's hit rate approaches 70%, while DCCC's is around 50%. MAPHC's advantage comes from its content suitability prediction and multi-agent deep reinforcement learning, enabling dynamic cache adjustments based on real-time user behavior.

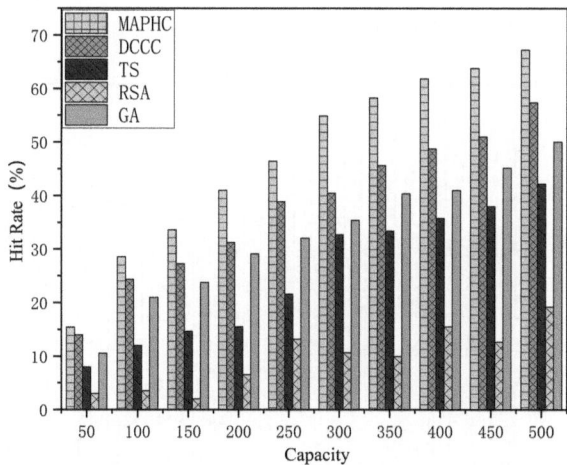

**Fig. 4.** Cache Hit Rates across Different Capacities.

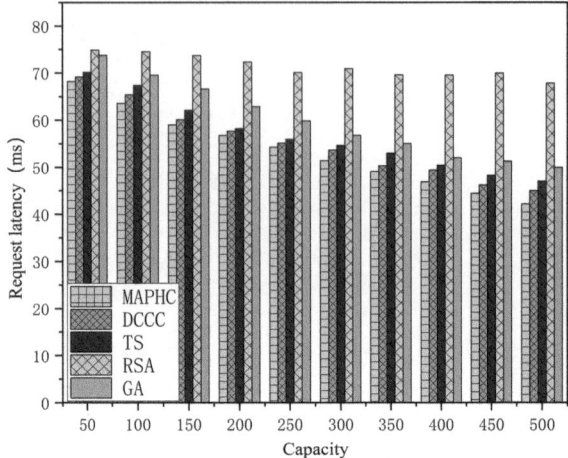

**Fig. 5.** Request Latency under Varying Cache Capacities.

Figure 5 illustrates the request latency performance of different caching strategies under varying cache capacities. The results show that MAPHC consistently achieves lower latency across all capacities, with a significant reduction in latency compared to TS and RSA, particularly at a capacity of 500. This is attributed to MAPHC's ability to dynamically predict user preferences and cache the corresponding content at edge nodes, thereby effectively reducing request latency.

Figure 6 shows the cache hit rate performance of MAPHC and DCCC over 30 rounds of experiments. MAPHC consistently outperforms DCCC, maintaining a hit rate above 50% throughout, while DCCC shows more fluctuation, indicating instability. As the rounds progress, MAPHC exhibits greater stability and adaptability in its hit rate compared to DCCC.

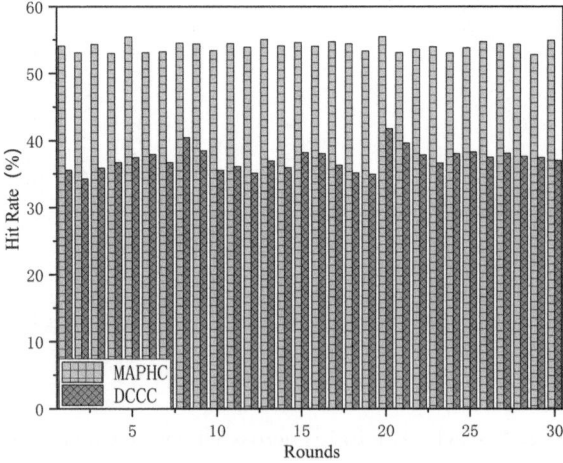

**Fig. 6.** Comparison of Hit Rates with Varying Rounds under Equal Capacity

# 7    Conclusion and Future Works

This paper introduces the MAPHC algorithm for mobility-aware caching in MEC environments. The main advantage of MAPHC lies in its User Preference-based Content Suitability Prediction Algorithm (CSPA), which adapts to varying user content preferences. Using a Multi-Agent Deep Reinforcement Learning framework, each edge server independently optimizes its caching strategy. Simulations with real-world datasets show that MAPHC improves cache hit rates and reduces latency compared to other algorithms.

In the future, we plan to conduct larger-scale experiments by increasing the number of users and edge servers, and evaluate the performance of MAPHC using different datasets to further validate its adaptability and robustness. Additionally, we will thoroughly investigate the security of edge caching to address potential vulnerabilities to attacks and failures.

**Acknowledgments.** This work was supported by the National Natural Science Foundation of China under Grant No. 62162036 and the Sichuan Provincial Natural Science Foundation under Grant No. 2024NSFTD0008.

**Conflicts of Interest.** The authors declare that there are no conflicts of interest regarding the publication of this paper.

# References

1. Li, S., Da Xu, L., Zhao, S.: 5G Internet of Things: a survey. J. Ind. Inf. Integr. **10**, 1–9 (2018)
2. Zarantonello, L., Schmitt, B.H.: Experiential AR/VR: a consumer and service framework and research agenda. J. Serv. Manag. **34**(1), 34–55 (2023)
3. Mao, Y., You, C., Zhang, J., Huang, K., Letaief, K.B.: A survey on mobile edge computing: the communication perspective. IEEE Commun. Surv. Tutor. **19**(4), 2322–2358 (2017)
4. Reiss-Mirzaei, M., Ghobaei-Arani, M., Esmaeili, L.: A review on the edge caching mechanisms in the mobile edge computing: a social-aware perspective. Internet of Things **22**, 100690 (2023)
5. Xue, Z., Liu, C., Liao, C., Han, G., Sheng, Z.: Joint service caching and computation offloading scheme based on deep reinforcement learning in vehicular edge computing systems. IEEE Trans. Veh. Technol. **72**(5), 6709–6722 (2023)
6. Zhou, H., Wang, Z., Zheng, H., He, S., Dong, M.: Cost minimization-oriented computation offloading and service caching in mobile cloud-edge computing: an A3C-based approach. IEEE Trans. Netw. Sci. Eng. **10**(3), 1326–1338 (2023)
7. Li, Y.M., et al.: Collaborative content caching and task offloading in multi-access edge computing. IEEE Trans. Veh. Technol. **72**(4), 5367–5372 (2022)
8. Fu, Y.R., Zhang, Y., Zhu, Q., Chen, M.Z., Quek, T.Q.S.: Joint content caching, recommendation, and transmission optimization for next generation multiple access networks. IEEE J. Sel. Areas Commun. **40**(5), 1600–1614 (2022)
9. Malik, A., Kim, J., Kim, K.S., Shin, W.Y.: A personalized preference learning framework for caching in mobile networks. IEEE Trans. Mob. Comput. **20**(6), 2124–2139 (2021)

10. Yu, Y., Schneider, U., Yang, S., et al.: Evaluating the GPCC Full Data Daily Analysis Version 2018 through ETCCDI indices and comparison with station observations over mainland of China. Theor. Appl. Climatol. **142**, 835–845 (2020)
11. Li, H., et al.: Mobility-aware content caching and user association for ultra-dense mobile edge computing networks. In: Proceedings IEEE Global Communications Conference (GLOBECOM), pp. 1–6 (2020)
12. Wei, H., Luo, H., Sun, Y.: Mobility-aware service caching in mobile edge computing for Internet of Things. Sensors **20**(3), 610 (2020)
13. Wang, Z., Hu, J., Min, G., et al.: Agile cache replacement in edge computing via offline-online deep reinforcement learning. IEEE Trans. Parallel Distrib. Syst. **35**(4), 663–674 (2024)
14. Wang, T., et al.: Towards intelligent adaptive edge caching using deep reinforcement learning. IEEE Trans. Mob. Comput. (2024)
15. Zhong, C., Gursoy, M.C., Velipasalar, S.: Deep reinforcement learning-based edge caching in wireless networks. IEEE Trans. Cogn. Commun. Netw. **6**(1), 48–61 (2020)
16. Lee, H., Jeong, J.: Multi-agent deep reinforcement learning (MADRL) meets multi-user MIMO systems. In: 2021 IEEE Global Communications Conference (GLOBECOM), pp. 1–6. IEEE (2021)
17. Hirsch, M., Mateos, C., Zunino, A.: Augmenting computing capabilities at the edge by jointly exploiting mobile devices: a survey. Futur. Gener. Comput. Syst. **88**, 644–662 (2018)
18. Zhang, K., Yang, Z., Başar, T.: Multi-agent reinforcement learning: a selective overview of theories and algorithms. In: Vamvoudakis, K.G., Wan, Y., Lewis, F.L., Cansever, D. (eds.) Handbook of Reinforcement Learning and Control. SSDC, vol. 325, pp. 321–384. Springer, Cham (2021). https://doi.org/10.1007/978-3-030-60990-0_12
19. Nie, Y., Zhao, J., Gao, F., Yu, F.R.: Semi-distributed resource management in UAV-aided MEC systems: a multi-agent federated reinforcement learning approach. IEEE Trans. Veh. Technol. **70**(12), 13162–13173 (2021)
20. Tian, S., Deng, X., Chen, P., et al.: A dynamic task offloading algorithm based on greedy matching in vehicle network. Ad Hoc Netw. **123**, 102639 (2021)
21. Harper, F.M., Konstan, J.A.: The movielens datasets: history and context. ACM Trans. Interact. Intell. Syst. (TiiS) **5**(4), 1–19 (2015)
22. Liu, J.: Comprehensive exploration and implementation of multi-armed bandit algorithms across various domains. Highlights Sci. Eng. Technol. **94**, 230–235 (2024)
23. Xiao, H., Zhao, J., Pei, Q., et al.: Vehicle selection and resource optimization for federated learning in vehicular edge computing. IEEE Trans. Intell. Transp. Syst. **23**(8), 11073–11087 (2021)
24. Chen, J., Xing, H., Lin, X., et al.: Joint resource allocation and cache placement for location-aware multi-user mobile-edge computing. IEEE Internet Things J. **9**(24), 25698–25714 (2022)

# Workflow Task Offloading Upon MEC: A Novel Mobility-Aware and Clustering-Based Approach

Tenghui Wang[1], Jiafeng Feng[2], Yong Ma[3(✉)], Yunni Xia[1(✉)], Yang Yu[4], Yumin Dong[5], Xifeng Xu[1], Jinpeng Li[1], Han Zhao[1], and Mengxuan Dai[1]

[1] College of Computer Science, Chongqing University, Chongqing 400030, China
xiayunni@hotmail.com
[2] China Huadian Corporation Ltd. Guangdong Company, Guangzhou 510620, China
[3] School of Computer and Information Engineering, Jiangxi Normal University, Nanchang 330022, Jiangxi, China
may@jxnu.edu.cn
[4] Guodian Nanjing Automation Co., Ltd., Nanjing 210032, China
[5] College of Computer and Information Science, Chongqing Normal University, Chongqing 401331, China

**Abstract.** The widespread deployment of intelligent Internet of Things (IoT) devices brings strict latency demands on complex workload patterns such as workflows. In such scenarios, tremendous data is generated and processed in accordance with specific service chains. Mobile Edge Computing (MEC) has proven its feasibility in reducing the traffic in the core network and relieving cloud datacenters of fragmented computational demands. However, existing solutions to multi-workflow scheduling and offloading in MEC are still limited due to the fact that they usually make task dispatching decisions prior to real execution, making it difficult to cope with the dynamicity of the environment and the mobility of users. To address this challenge, we developed a novel computation offloading strategy by synthesizing a Harris Hawks Optimization-based particle filter trajectory prediction algorithm for forecasting future user locations, a clustering-based multi-workflow merging algorithm for identifying redundant tasks and a Lyapunov optimization-based DQN algorithm for yielding computation offloading schedules. Simulation results clearly show that method beats traditional ones across multiple performance metrics.

**Keywords:** MEC · multi-workflow computation offloading · trajectory prediction · multi-workflow merging · Lyapunov optimization · DQN

Y. Ma and Y. Xia—This work was supported by the grants from Sichuan Provincial Natural Science Foundation under Grant No. 2024NSFTD0008.

Y. Zhang and L.-J. Zhang (Eds.): ICWS 2024, LNCS 15428, pp. 93–107, 2025.
https://doi.org/10.1007/978-3-031-77072-2_7

# 1   Introduction

With the continuous development of Big Data, the Internet of Things (IoT), and 5G technology, mobile devices (MDs) have become indispensable components of daily life [1,2]. Concurrently, there has been a sharp increase in the number of compute-intensive real-time, organized in terms of business processes or work-flows, applications generated based on mobile devices (MDs). However, limited computing power and battery capacity make executing complex workflows on mobile devices slow and inefficient. Mobile Cloud Computing (MCC) addresses this by offloading tasks to the cloud, bridging the gap between device limitations and the need for timely processing [3]. Nevertheless, the MCC faces challenges with large-scale data, including high latency, bandwidth limitations, and data privacy concerns. The centralized nature of cloud computing increases latency and costs, reducing service quality and failing to meet real-time needs effectively [4,5]. To address these issues, Mobile Edge Computing (MEC), an emerging computing paradigm, has been proposed and widely applied.

Existing research on workflow computation offloading in MEC often relies on static assumptions, overlooking user mobility, which can lead to inefficiencies like increased latency and costs. Addressing user mobility in offloading decisions is crucial. Moreover, many studies skip preliminary workflow analysis, leading to poor resource utilization and redundant computations. This lack of optimization results in non-optimal task allocation, increased execution time, and performance degradation, particularly in large-scale applications.

To address the aforementioned issue, We propose a multi-workflow offloading strategy using a Harris Hawks optimization-based particle filter for dynamic task allocation, enhancing flexibility, reducing latency and costs. Additionally, we introduce a clustering-based workflow merging algorithm to optimize structure, reduce redundant computations, and improve resource utilization. Finally, a Lyapunov optimization-based DQN algorithm minimizes average cost and latency under long-term constraints.

# 2   Related Work

Computation offloading in Mobile Edge Computing (MEC) for multiple work-flows is a key research area. This chapter reviews recent advances, highlighting key approaches, innovations, and limitations:

Wang *et al.* proposed a dynamic multi-workflow offloading method with soft deadlines, improving efficiency through cooperative partial offloading, though flexibility with burst tasks remains a challenge [6].

Pan *et al.* proposed a multi-objective clustering evolutionary algorithm to optimize the offloading of multiple workflows. This algorithm significantly enhances the performance and efficiency of multi-workflow computation offloading through multi-objective optimization and clustering evolution methods. The main innovation lies in combining multi-objective optimization with clustering evolution, effectively balancing different optimization goals. However, the algorithm has high computational complexity when dealing with large-scale workflows [7].

Fu *et al.* investigated the problem of minimizing total energy consumption in multi-user multi-workflow MEC systems and proposed an offloading and scheduling scheme. By comprehensively considering energy consumption and computational efficiency, they introduced a novel energy optimization method. The innovation lies in the joint optimization of multiple users and multiple workflows, significantly reducing total energy consumption. However, the scalability of this scheme in large-scale user environments still needs improvement [8].

Kuang *et al.* proposed a multi-workflow scheduling framework encompassing the IoT layer, MEC layer, and cloud computing layer, aimed at reducing the execution time of multiple workflows. This framework employs an adversarial-based ocean predator algorithm, significantly enhancing scheduling efficiency through optimized resource allocation. The innovation lies in introducing a novel algorithm for resource optimization, but its robustness in handling dynamic environments still requires further investigation [9].

Sun *et al.* investigated the multi-workflow computation offloading problem in resource-constrained IIoT environments involving local computing, edge computing, and remote service platforms. They proposed a multi-objective optimization algorithm that optimizes overall computational efficiency through the rational allocation of different computing resources. The innovation lies in the application of a multi-objective optimization model, but its performance improvement for highly complex computational tasks still needs to be validated [10].

Considering that existing research lacks consideration of user mobility in computation offloading decisions and lacks analysis and processing of multiple workflows before offloading, we have designed a computation offloading strategy. This strategy targets user mobility scenarios and performs an analysis of the structure and content of multiple workflows to merge them. Finally, it completes the computation offloading of multiple workflows under long-term cost constraints.

## 3 System Model and Problem Formulation

### 3.1 System Model

As illustrated in Fig. 1, the system comprises a three-tier MEC environment involving user-end mobile devices, edge devices (in terms of base stations and edge servers), and a remote cloud. Each base station is equipped with an edge server, denoted as $ED = \{ed_1, ed_2, \ldots, ed_m\}$. The set of user-end mobile devices is $MD = \{md_1, md_2, \ldots, md_n\}$. The mobile devices connect to $ED$ via a 5G network, while $ED$ and the remote cloud are interconnected through a backbone network.

The $j$-th edge device is described by a tuple $ed_j = (cap_j, proc_j, LE_j, rad_j)$, where $cap_j$ represents its processing capacity, $proc_j$ its processing cost, $LE_j$ its set of the two-dimensional coordinates and $rad_j$ its the coverage radius.

The $l$-th mobile device can be described by the tuple $md_l = (LE_l, v_l, cap_l, proc_l)$, where $LE_l$ represents its set of two-dimensional coordinates, $v_l$ its movement speed, $cap_l$ its processing capacity and $proc_l$ its processing cost.

Key symbols and parameters are enumerated in Table 1.

**Table 1.** Main Symbols and Definitions

| Symbol | Definition |
|---|---|
| $w_k$ | The $k$-th workflow, represented as a tuple $(T_k, E_k)$, where $T_k$ is the set of tasks and $E_k$ is the set of dependencies between tasks |
| $t_{i,k}$ | The $i$-th task in the $k$-th workflow |
| $PR_{i,k}$ | The set of predecessor tasks for task $t_i$ in the $k$-th workflow |
| $SU_{i,k}$ | The set of successor tasks for task $t_i$ in the $k$-th workflow |
| $vs_k$ | Virtual start node for workflows with multiple starting tasks of the $k$-th workflow |
| $ve_k$ | Virtual end node for workflows with multiple ending tasks of the $k$-th workflow |
| $et_{i,k}$ | Execution time of task $t_i$ in the $k$-th workflow |
| $est_{i,k}$ | The earliest start time of task $t_i$ in the $k$-th workflow |
| $eft_{i,k}$ | The earliest finish time of task $t_i$ in the $k$-th workflow |
| $ft_{i,k}$ | Finishing time of task $t_i$ in the $k$-th workflow |
| $cp_{i,k}$ | Computation price for executing task $t_i$ in the $k$-th workflow |
| $tc_k$ | Total cost of workflow $k$ |

### 3.2   Multi-workflow Model

In an MEC environment, workflows are typically described using directed acyclic graphs (DAGs). A workflow can be represented by the tuple $w_k = (T_k, E_k)$, where $k$ denotes the $k$-th workflow $(1 \leq k \leq K)$ and $K$ represents the total number of workflows. Each workflow consists of several nodes, with $T_k = \{t_{1,k}, t_{2,k}, \ldots, t_{m,k}\}$ representing the set of tasks formed by these nodes and $E = \{e_{i_1,k,i_2,k} | t_{i_1,k}, t_{i_2,k} \in T_k\}$ representing the dependency relationships and data transmission directions between different tasks in the workflow. A subtask $t_{i,k}$ in the $k$-th workflow can be defined by the tuple $t_{i,k} = \{PR_{i,k}, SU_{i,k}, dc_{i,k}, o_{i,k}\}$, where the set of predecessor nodes of subtask $t_{i,k}$ is denoted as $PR_{i,k}$, and the set of successor nodes of subtask $t_{i,k}$ is denoted as $SU_{i,k}$. The term $dc_{i,k}$ represents the execution data cost of task $t_{i,k}$, and $o_{i,k}$ indicates whether the task has completed computation offloading.

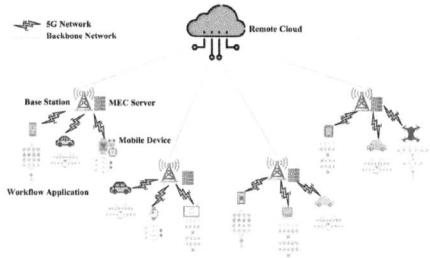

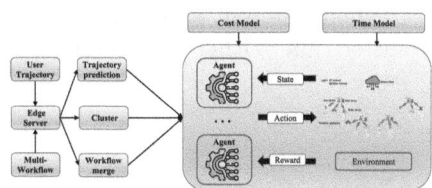

**Fig. 1.** MEC System Model.        **Fig. 2.** Algorithmic framework for computing offloading strategies.

### 3.3 Communication Model

In the three-tier MEC environment comprising user-end mobile devices, edge devices, and the remote cloud, wireless access transmission is primarily used for communication between different layers. We model the communication scenario using the Rayleigh fading channel model. It is assumed that a channel scheduler can dynamically allocate independent sub-channels for each $MD$ in the MEC environment to avoid communication interference between sub-channels [11].

In the current MEC environment, the transmission rates for communication between $MD$ and $ED$ is:

$$rme = bme \log_2 \left( 1 + \frac{pmd|hme|^2 dme^{-\alpha}}{\sigma^2} \right) \qquad (1)$$

where $bme$ is the bandwidth allocated to the communication links between $MD$ and $ED$. $pmd$ denotes the transmission power of the mobile device. $hme$ denotes the Rayleigh fading coefficients for the communication links between $MD$ and $ED$. $dme$ denote the physical distances between $MD$ and $ED$. $\alpha$ denotes the path loss exponent and $\sigma^2$ the noise power.

Consequently, we have

$$tme = dame/rme \qquad (2)$$

where $tme$ represents the transmission dely, $dame$ represents the data size for communication from $MD$ to $ED$.

### 3.4 Time Consumption Model

When completing a workflow, it is essential to focus on three aspects of time consumption: task execution time, task transmission time, task waiting time.

For a task $t_{i,k}$, when it is submitted to a specific device, the task execution time:

$$et_{i,k} = \frac{exd_{i,k}}{cap_j} \qquad (3)$$

where $exd_{i,k}$ represents its execution data size and $cap_j$ the processing capability of edge device $ed_j$.

When different tasks are offloaded to the same edge device they have zero transfer time. Otherwise, the transmission rate between edge devices is:

$$r = b \log_2 \left( 1 + \frac{ped|h|^2 d^{-\alpha}}{\sigma^2} \right) \tag{4}$$

where $b$ is the bandwidth between edge devices, $ped$ the transmission power of the edge devices, $h$ the Rayleigh fading coefficient for the communication link and $d$ the physical distance. $\alpha$ denotes the path loss exponent and $\sigma^2$ the noise power.

Therefore, the task transmission time is:

$$ct_{i_1,k_1,i_2,k_2} = \frac{d_{i_1,k_1,i_2,k_2}}{r} \tag{5}$$

where $d_{i_1,k_1,i_2,k_2}$ is transmission data from task $t_{i_1,k_1}$ to $t_{i_2,k_2}$.

The latest completion time $est_{i,k}$ for all predecessor tasks of task $t_{i,k}$ is:

$$\max_{t_{i_2,k} \in PR_{i_1,k}} \{eft_{i_2,k} + ct_{i_1,k,i_2,k}\} \tag{6}$$

$$eft_{i_2,k} = est_{i_2,k} + et_{i_2,k} \tag{7}$$

where $t_{i_2,k} \in PR_{i_1,k}$ indicates the predecessor tasks that must be completed before task $t_{i_1,k}$, $PR_{i_1,k}$ denotes the set of parent tasks of $t_{i_1,k}$, $eft_{i_2,k}$ denotes the earliest finish time of task $t_{i_2,k}$, which is the sum of the latest finish time of the predecessor tasks and the execution time.

Therefore, the waiting time for task $t_{i_1,k}$ is:

$$est_{i_1,k} = \begin{cases} 0 & if \quad PR_{i_1,k} \quad is \quad none \\ \max_{t_{i_2,k} \in PR_{i_1,k}} \{eft_{i_2,k} + ct_{i_1,k,i_2,k}\} & else \end{cases} \tag{8}$$

In summary, the completion time of task $t_{i_1,k}$ depends on it is whether executed locally or offloaded to an edge device:

$$ft_{i_1,k} = \begin{cases} et_{i_1,k} + est_{i_1,k} + tme & if \quad Executed \quad Locally \\ et_{i_1,k} + ct_{i_1,k,i_2,k} + est_{i_1,k} + tme & else \end{cases} \tag{9}$$

### 3.5  Cost Consumption Model

In MEC, when offloading multiple workflows, two types of costs are typically considered [12]: computation cost and communication cost. In the calculation of communication costs, we assume that the communication cost between tasks offloaded to the same mobile device can be neglected. For workflow $k$, the total cost calculation is as follows:

$$tc_k = \sum_{i,k \in T_k} et_{i,k} * cp_{i,k} + \sum_{i_1,k \in T_k} \sum_{i_2,k \in SU_{i_1,k}} (ct_{i_1,k,i_2,k} * bp + tme * bp) \tag{10}$$

where $et_{i,k}$ represents the execution time of task $t_{i,k}$, $cp_{i,k}$ the cost of executing task $t_{i,k}$ and $T_k$ the set of all tasks. Where $ct_{i_1,k,i_2,k}$ is the transmission time between different tasks, $bp$ the bandwidth price between different computing devices and $tme$ the transmission time for offloading tasks to the edge device.

### 3.6 Problem Formulation

The optimization objectives of this paper are the execution time and cost of multiple workflows. We aim to minimize the completion time of computational tasks, as well as the computation and communication costs of the server, through a novel computation offloading scheduling algorithm.

We use $w_k$ to represent the workflow $k$ of $MD$, $K$ is the total number of all workflows, where each workflow consists of several subtasks. The task set of workflow $k$ is denoted as $T_k$. The execution time of each task in workflow $k$ is represented as $ft_{i,k}$. start$(t_{i,k})$represents the start time of task $t_{i,k}$, and finish$(t_{i,k})$represents the finish time of task $t_{i,k}$. Define the variable $o_{i,k,j}$ to indicate whether task $t_{i,k}$ is assigned to edge device $ed_j$.

The problem is formulated as follows:

$$min \quad f_1 = \sum_{k \in K} \sum_{i,k \in T_k} ft_{i,k} \tag{11}$$

$$min \quad f_2 = \sum_{k \in K} tc_k \tag{12}$$

s.t.

$$\lim_{K \to \infty} \frac{1}{K} \sum_{k=1}^{K} tc_k \leq qm \tag{13}$$

$$ft_{i,k} \geq 0, tc_k \geq 0 \tag{14}$$

$$\forall t_{i,k} \in T_k, \forall t_{i_2,k} \in PR_{i_1,k}, \quad start(t_{i_1,k}) \geq finish(t_{i_2,k}) \tag{15}$$

$$o_{i,k,j} = \begin{cases} 1 & if \quad t_{i,k} \quad belongs \quad to \quad ed_j \\ 0 & else \end{cases} \tag{16}$$

The constraints are as follows:

The long-term cost constraint for the mobile user requires that the average cost does not exceed the limit $qm$. Each task $t_{i,k}$ must be executed only after all its predecessor tasks $PR_{i,k}$ have been completed. Each task $t_{i,k}$ can only be assigned to one edge device $ed_j$.

## 4    Proposed Algorithm

In this section, we detail the framework and algorithms we developed for multi-workflow computation offloading. Using a Harris Hawks optimization-based particle filter, we predict user trajectories, considering mobility and updating periodically to account for uncertainties. After predicting locations, a globally optimized K-means clustering algorithm groups users into clusters based on density, enabling workflows within the same cluster to be merged. To efficiently merge workflows, we designed a greedy strategy-based algorithm that identifies and combines redundant parts, optimizing structure and reducing computation and transmission overhead. Finally, a DQN algorithm based on Lyapunov optimization is used to complete the offloading process. The Fig. 2 shows the framework of our proposed solution.

### 4.1    Trajectory Prediction Algorithm Based on Harris Hawks Optimization and Particle Filter

In trajectory prediction, we enhance the Particle Filter (PF) by integrating the Harris Hawks Optimization (HHO) algorithm to mitigate particle degradation. By incorporating an improved HHO hunting strategy into particle updates, this method increases particle diversity and distribution, thereby improving the accuracy and robustness of trajectory prediction.

The steps of particle filtering with the Harris Hawks Optimization (HHO) model are as follows:

- Initializing Eagle Position:
  Hawks' positions and fitness are initialized:

$$h \sim \mathcal{U}(lb, ub), \quad fi = f(h, tp) \tag{17}$$

- Updating Eagle Position:
  Hawks move based on a probability-driven strategy:

$$h_{(t+1)} = h_{\text{best}} + r \cdot |h_{\text{best}} - h_{(t)}| \quad \text{if } r_1 < 0.5 \tag{18}$$

$$h_{(t+1)} = h_{(t)} + r \cdot |h_{\text{best}} - h_{(t)}| \quad \text{if } r_1 \geq 0.5 \tag{19}$$

- Updating Optimal Position:
  The globally optimal position and fitness are updated if improved:

$$\text{if } fi_{(t+1)} < fi_{\text{best}}, \quad h_{\text{best}} = h_{(t+1)}, \quad fi_{\text{best}} = fi_{(t+1)} \tag{20}$$

The overall description of the algorithm combining particle filtering and HHO is in Algorithm 1:

---

**Algorithm 1:** Particle Filter with HHO Optimization

---

1 **Initialize** *particles $p \sim \mathcal{U}(lb, ub)$ and weights $we = \frac{1}{N}$;*
2 **for** *each time step $t$* **do**
3      **for each** *particle* Predict particle state: $p_{(t+1)} = p_{(t)} + \mathcal{N}(0, \sigma^2)$;
4      Apply HHO to optimize particle positions;
5      **Initialize** *hawks $h \sim \mathcal{U}(lb, ub)$*;
6      Evaluate fitness of hawks $fi = f(h, z_{(t+1)})$;
7      Find best hawk: $h_{\text{best}} = \arg\min fi$;
8      **for** *each iteration $e$* **do**
9          **for each** *hawk* **if** $r_1 < 0.5$ Update position: $h_{(e+1)} = h_{\text{best}} + r \cdot |h_{\text{best}} - h_{(e)}|$;
10          **else** *Update position:* $h_{(e+1)} = h_{(e)} + r \cdot |h_{\text{best}} - h_{(e)}|$;
11          Evaluate fitness: $fi_{(e+1)} = f(h_{(e+1)}, z_{(t+1)})$;
12          **if** $fi_{(e+1)} < F_{best}$ Update best hawk: $h_{\text{best}} = h_{(e+1)}$;
13          Update best fitness: $fi_{\text{best}} = fi_{(e+1)}$;
14      Replace particles with optimized hawks: $p_{(t+1)} = h_{\text{best}}$;
15      Store the best particle position;
16 **return** *predictions*

---

## 4.2 Cluster-Based Multi-workflow Consolidation Algorithm

- Globally Optimized K-Means Clustering Algorithm Based on Sample Density: Use the Gaussian model to estimate the estimated density of each cluster center. Assume the cluster radius $rc$ is the distance from the cluster center to the farthest sample point in the cluster. Select a circle with center $z_v$ and radius $r = rc \times ra$ as the sample region for statistics. The estimated density $de$ is:

$$de = 2\phi(3\sigma \times ra) - 1 \qquad (21)$$

where $\phi$ is the standard normal distribution function and $\sigma$ the standard deviation of the data.

Calculate the actual density $ade$ for each cluster center:

$$ade = \frac{\sum_{x_u \in clu_v} \psi(d(x_u, z_v), r)}{|clu_v|} \qquad (22)$$

$$\psi(d(x_u, z_v), r) = \begin{cases} 1, & \text{if } d(x_u, z_v) < r, \\ 0 & \text{otherwise} \end{cases} \qquad (23)$$

where $x_u$ is each sample point, $z_v$ each cluster center, $|clu_v|$ the number of sample points in cluster $clu_v$.

Determine whether there exists a cluster center whose actual density $ade$ is less than the estimated density $de$. If such a center exists, identify the cluster center $z_v$ with the maximum difference between actual and estimated density. Randomly select several sample points $x_u$ in cluster $clu_v$ and calculate their densities $cde$. If there exists a sample point with $cde > de$, then select the sample point $x_u$ with the highest density as the new cluster center $z_v$.

- Determining the Merge Target:
  First, each user can submit a request in terms of multiple tasks organized according to a workflow. Within a cluster, we encounter multiple workflows. The goal is to select workflows with the highest functionality and structural significance for merging.
  Merging Value $V(w_k)$ is defined as the weighted sum of functionality and structurality:

$$V(w_k) = \alpha F(w_k) + \beta S(w_k) \tag{24}$$

  where $\alpha$ and $\beta$ are the weight coefficients for functionality and structurality, respectively. The functionality $F(w_k)$ can be expressed as a weighted sum function of the node attributes in the $k$-th workflow $w_k$, the structurality $S(w_k)$ can be expressed as a weighted sum function of the edges in the workflow $w_k$.

- Performing Merge Operation
  Define the set of overlapping nodes as $T_{k,\text{overlap}}$, satisfying:

$$T_{k,\text{overlap}} = \bigcap_{i=1}^{N} T_k \tag{25}$$

  Create a new workflow $\hat{w}_k$, starting by inserting all overlapping nodes $T_{k,\text{overlap}}$:

$$\hat{w}_k = \{T_{k,\text{overlap}}, E_{k,\text{virtual}}\} \tag{26}$$

  where $E_{k,\text{virtual}}$ is the set of virtual edges connecting the overlapping nodes to maintain the structural integrity of the workflow.
  Based on the connection relationship of each edge, insert the non-overlapping nodes and edges from each workflow in sequence:

$$\hat{w}_k = \hat{w}_k \cup \{\bigcup_{i=1}^{N}(T_k - T_{k,\text{overlap}}), \bigcup_{i=1}^{N}(E_k - E_{k,\text{overlap}})\} \tag{27}$$

  Then we remove the virtual edge set $E_{k,\text{virtual}}$. For any original node $t_k \in T_{k,\text{new}}$ that previously had no predecessor but now has one after merging, add a virtual start node $vs_k$ to indicate that this is a workflow branch. For any original node $t_k \in T_{k,\text{new}}$ that previously had no successor but now has one after merging, add a virtual end node $ve_k$ to indicate that this is a workflow branch. Finally, the merged new workflow set can be represented as $\hat{W}$.

Based on the above description, we provide the detailed steps of the Cluster-Based Multi-Workflow Consolidation Algorithm (CMWCA) in Algorithm 2.

### 4.3  Multi-objective and Multi-workflow Offloading with Lyapunov Optimization-Based DQN

We consider the computation offloading problem of multiple workflows as a Markov Decision Process (MDP). This process mainly consists of states, actions, and rewards, and our agent is defined as the edge server.

---

**Algorithm 2:** Cluster-Based Multi-Workflow Consolidation Algorithm (CMWCA)

---

**1 while** *not converged* **do**

**2**     **foreach** *sample point* $x_u$ **do**

**3**        Assign $x_u$ to the nearest cluster center $z_v$ based on Euclidean distance.

**4**     **foreach** *cluster* $clu_v$ **do**

**5**        Update centroid $\mu_v$ based on the current cluster members. Calculate estimated density $de$ and actual density $ade$.

**6**     **if** *exists* $z_v$ *with* $ade < de$ **then**

**7**        Update cluster center $z_v$ by selecting the sample point with the highest density $cde$.

**8**     **if** *centroid change* $< \epsilon$ **then**

**9**        break

**10 foreach** *cluster* $clu_v$ **do**

**11**     Select top $h$ workflows with the highest merging value $V(w_k) = \alpha F(w_k) + \beta S(w_k)$. Create new workflow $\hat{w}_k$ by merging overlapping nodes $T_{\text{overlap}}$ and adding non-overlapping nodes and edges. Remove virtual edges and add virtual start/end nodes where necessary.

**12 return** *consolidated workflow set* $\hat{\mathcal{W}}$;

---

---

**Algorithm 3:** MDP-Based Multi-Workflow Offloading with Lyapunov Optimization

---

**1 while** *not converged* **do**

**2**     Observe current state $s_t$, select action $a_t$ using $\epsilon$-greedy policy;

**3**     Execute action $a_t$, observe reward $r_t$ and next state $s_{t+1}$;

**4**     Update cost queue:

$$cq(t+1) = cq(t) + \sum_{es} \text{cost}_{es}\text{new}(t) - \sum_{es} \text{cost}_{es}\text{finish}(t)$$

    Store transition $(s_t, a_t, r_t, s_{t+1})$;

**5**     **if** *time to update* **then**

**6**        Sample mini-batch from $buf$, calculate target $y_i$ and perform gradient descent on $L_i(\theta)$;

**7**        Update target network $\theta^-$;

**8 foreach** *episode* **do**

**9**     Initialize state $s_0$;

**10**     **while** *not terminal* **do**

**11**        Choose action $a_t$ from policy $\pi(s_t)$;

**12**        Execute action $a_t$, observe reward $r_t$ and next state $s_{t+1}$;

**13**        Store transition $(s_t, a_t, r_t, s_{t+1})$ ;

**14**        Update state $s_t = s_{t+1}$;

**15 return** *optimized policy* $\pi$;

---

We define the state space as:

$$S = \{(L_1, L_2, \ldots, L_l) \mid L_l = (t_{l1}, t_{l2}, \ldots, t_{l|L_l|})\} \tag{28}$$

The action space $A$ includes the operations of assigning tasks to edge servers. Suppose we have $N$ edge servers, each action $a \in A$ can be represented as:

$$a = (a_1, a_2, \ldots, a_N) \tag{29}$$

We use Lyapunov optimization to establish constraint queues for cost resources. At time slot $t$, the cost queue $cq(t)$ is calculated as:

$$cq(t+1) = cq(t) + \sum_{es \in ES} \text{cost}_{es}\text{new}(t) - \sum_{es \in ES} \text{cost}_{es}\text{finish}(t) \tag{30}$$

where $\text{cost}_{es}\text{new}(t)$ is the cost of newly added unscheduled servers at time $t$ and $\text{cost}_{es}\text{finish}(t)$ the cost of servers that completed scheduled tasks at time $t$.

The cost load state of each server can be represented as $cq_n(t)$, where $n$ denotes the server index and $t$ the time slot. Thus, we can represent the cost load state of the entire system as $CQ(t)$, which is formulated as follows:

$$CQ(t) = \{cq_1(t), cq_2(t), \ldots, cq_N(t)\} \tag{31}$$

Thus, we define the total Lyapunov function of the system as:

$$Lya(t) = \frac{1}{2}CQ(t)^2 \tag{32}$$

The formula $cq(t+1)$ represents the backlog state of the cost queue in the system. We can maintain the stability of cost resources by incorporating the Lyapunov drift into the reward function of the DQN. The Lyapunov drift is defined as follows:

$$\Delta(CQ(t)) = Lya(t+1) - Lya(t) \tag{33}$$

Next, we define the reward function of the DQN as follows:

$$R_{\text{time}} = \left[\frac{ft_i - \left(\sum_{k \in K}\sum_{i \in T}(ft_i\text{new} - FT_i\text{old})\right)}{ft_i}\right]^3 \tag{34}$$

$$R_{\text{cost}} = \left[\frac{\text{cost}_{\text{worst}} - ft_i \cdot cp_i}{\text{cost}_{\text{worst}} - \text{cost}_{\text{best}}}\right]^3 + \Delta(CQ(t)) \tag{35}$$

The ultimate goal of our algorithm is to achieve joint optimization of delay and cost in a multi-agent environment. The Lyapunov-based DQN algorithm is described in Algorithm 3.

# 5    Performance Evaluation

## 5.1    Simulation Setup

In the simulation, we use telecom base station and taxi datasets from Shanghai. Base stations have resource-rich edge servers for computation offloading, while taxis are equipped with cellular and GPS modules for network connectivity and trajectory tracking, making these datasets ideal for validation.

We simulate workflow generation on the FogWorkflowSim platform, using mobile trajectory data for prediction tasks. Workflow data sizes range from 10-500MB, with processing speeds from $5 \times 10^6$ to $1 \times 10^7$ kB/s for mobile users and $3 \times 10^7$ to $5 \times 10^7$ kB/s for edge servers. The bandwidth is 10 MHz, transmission power is 250 mW, and path loss exponent is 3. Computation and communication costs vary with task size.

In the scenario, users send offloading requests after ten minutes. We assign different workflow applications to mobile users, each in different areas with 7 edge devices handling tasks.

## 5.2    Result

Figure 3 illustrates the performance of our prediction algorithm. Circular trajectories represent actual user movements, while triangular trajectories show our predictions, demonstrating a high overall fit and accurate trajectory prediction. The results indicate an average MAE of 0.0016, MSE of 0.0001, and an average deviation distance of 93.27 m. This level of accuracy is deemed acceptable in an MEC environment, with minimal impact on subsequent computation offloading strategies.

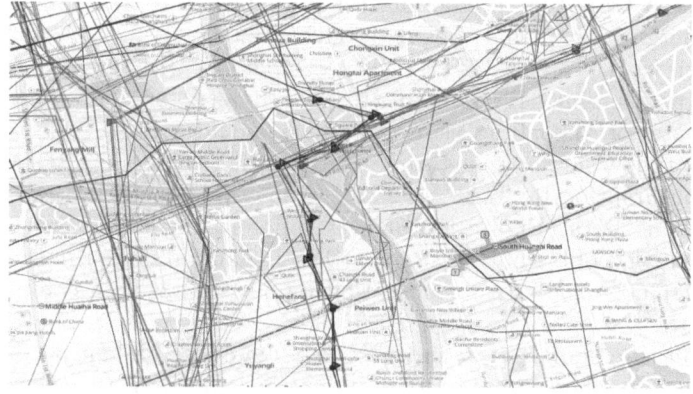

**Fig. 3.** Comparison of real and predicted trajectories.

Based on the density, mobile users are divided into four different areas. Figure 4 and Fig. 5 shows the changes in the number of workflows and tasks in

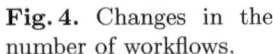

**Fig. 4.** Changes in the number of workflows.

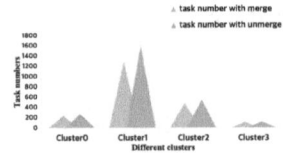

**Fig. 5.** Changes in the number of tasks.

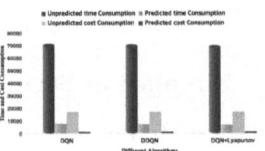

**Fig. 6.** Comparison of forecasting or not.

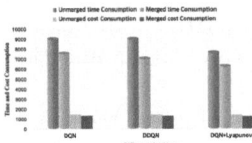

**Fig. 7.** Comparison of merging or not.

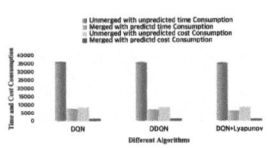

**Fig. 8.** Comparison of forecasting and merging or not.

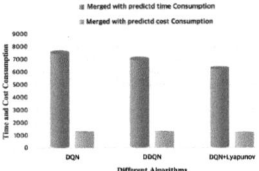

**Fig. 9.** Comparison of algorithms.

different clusters after workflow merging. It can be seen that we have effectively reduced the number of workflows and tasks, saving time and cost for subsequent computation offloading.

Figure 6 shows the three algorithms(DQN, DDQN and DQN+Lyapunov) with trajectory prediction save time consumption by 89.17%/89.83%/90.81% and cost consumption by 92.29%/92.37%/92.67% in comparison with the algorithms without trajectory prediction. Figure 7 shows the three algorithms with workflow merging save time consumption by 16.06%/21.72%/17.51% and cost consumption by 9.04%/8.51%/11.47% in comparison with the algorithms without workflow merging. Figure 8 shows the three algorithms with our complete computation offloading strategy, which includes both trajectory prediction and workflow merging save time consumption by 89.39%/90.00%/90.98% and cost consumption by 92.35%/92.35%/92.35% in comparison with the algorithms without both. Figure 9 compares different algorithms with our complete computation offloading strategy. DQN+Lyapunov saves time consumption by 16.62%/10.60% and cost consumption by 5.31%/4.31% in comparison with DQN/DDQN.

Our algorithm effectively reduces latency and cost. While it is currently limited to scenarios where users send computation offloading requests in advance and where there are mergeable tasks across multiple workflows, it is foreseeable that as the time difference between offloading requests increases, the benefits of mobile trajectory prediction will grow. Additionally, increasing the number of merge points in multiple workflows is likely to further reduce latency and cost.

# 6    Conclusion

In this paper, we propose a novel approach to mobility-aware and predictive multi-workflow offloading in a MEC environment. By employing a user mobility prediction model, a mechanism for merging duplicate workflow tasks, and a dynamic computation task allocation strategy built upon a DQN algorithm with a Lyapunov optimization, the proposed framework is capable of achieving high workflow execution efficiency and resource utilization. We conduct extensive numerical analysis based on real-worlds datasets as well and demonstrate the our approach outperforms its peers across multiple metrics.

# References

1. Qi, L., et al.: Finding all you need: web APIs recommendation in web of things through keywords search. IEEE Trans. Comput. Soc. Syst. **6**(5), 1063–1072 (2019)
2. Xu, X., Liu, Q., Zhang, X., Zhang, J., Qi, L., Dou, W.: A blockchain-powered crowdsourcing method with privacy preservation in mobile environment. IEEE Trans. Comput. Soc. Syst. **6**(6), 1407–1419 (2019)
3. Dinh, H.T., Lee, C., Niyato, D., Wang, P.: A survey of mobile cloud computing: architecture, applications, and approaches. Wirel. Commun. Mob. Comput. **13**(18), 1587–1611 (2013)
4. Gao, H., Kuang, L., Yin, Y., Guo, B., Dou, K.: Mining consuming behaviors with temporal evolution for personalized recommendation in mobile marketing apps. Mob. Netw. Appl. **25**, 1233–1248 (2020)
5. Zhang, Y., et al.: Covering-based web service quality prediction via neighborhood-aware matrix factorization. IEEE Trans. Serv. Comput. **14**(5), 1333–1344 (2019)
6. Wang, J.: Dynamic multiworkflow offloading and scheduling under soft deadlines in the cloud-edge environment. IEEE Syst. J. **17**(2), 2077–2088 (2023)
7. Pan, L., Liu, X., Jia, Z., Xu, J., Li, X.: A multi-objective clustering evolutionary algorithm for multi-workflow computation offloading in mobile edge computing. IEEE Trans. Cloud Comput. **11**(2), 1334–1351 (2021)
8. Fu, S., Ding, C., Jiang, P.: Computational offloading of service workflow in mobile edge computing. Information **13**(7), 348 (2022)
9. Kuang, F., Xu, Z., Masdari, M.: Multi-workflow scheduling and resource provisioning in mobile edge computing using opposition-based marine-predator algorithm. Pervasive Mob. Comput. **87**, 101715 (2022)
10. Sun, B.S., Huang, H., Chai, Z.Y., Zhao, Y.J., Kang, H.S.: Multi-objective optimization algorithm for multi-workflow computation offloading in resource-limited IIoT. Swarm Evol. Comput. **89**, 101646 (2024)
11. Jiang, W., Feng, G., Qin, S., Yum, T.S.P., Cao, G.: Multi-agent reinforcement learning for efficient content caching in mobile D2D networks. IEEE Trans. Wireless Commun. **18**(3), 1610–1622 (2019)
12. Mousavi Nik, S.S., Naghibzadeh, M., Sedaghat, Y.: Task replication to improve the reliability of running workflows on the cloud. Clust. Comput. **24**(1), 343–359 (2021)

# PLNCaE: Advanced Framework for Preprocessed Lightweight Neural Networks in Brain Tumor Classification and Explanation

Quy Thanh Lu, Thuan Van Tran, and Triet Minh Nguyen$^{(\boxtimes)}$

FPT University, Can Tho, Vietnam
`trietnm3@fe.edu.vn`

**Abstract.** The brain is one of the most complicated parts of the human body. However, the impact of radiation rays from natural to artificial has a huge effect on human health. In particular, it is a cause of hundreds of fatal diseases in humans. One of these is a brain tumor, which is an overgrowth of abnormal cells in the brain or near it. In this research, the Magnetic Resonance Imaging (MRI) dataset was combined from three sources, including Figshare, SARTAJ, and Br35H. Besides, the PLNCaE (Prepro-LiteNeuro Classification and Explanation) framework was proposed with preprocessing progress by removing the extra margins and combining layers to generate a lightweight Convolutional Neural Network (CNN) model. Moreover, SHapley Additive exPlanations (SHAP) were employed to explain the model's predictions in the outcome. Through various experiments, the suggested model reached an impressive test accuracy score of 97.58% in classifying four classes, including normal, pituitary, glioma, and meningioma. In binary classification, the result achieved the highest accuracy of 99.02% between normal and abnormal images.

**Keywords:** Brain tumor · Classification · Lightweight · Convolutional Neural Network (CNN) · SHapley Additive exPlanations (SHAP)

## 1 Introduction

Neoplasms within the brain or tissues surrounding it, meaning the abnormal development of new cells, is a problem that has not been solved. Several papers have been conducted with the purpose of raising awareness in the community [1–4]. Reporting in [5], the United States recorded 86,030 deaths resulting from malignant brain and central nervous system tumors between the years 2016 and 2020, which is approximately 17,206 deaths per year. This corresponds to the mortality rate which was about 4.42 deaths per 100,000 of the population each year. The same is also true in China where the level of breast cancer is equally alarming. Data of [6] from 2003 to 2013 show that there were 10,391 cases of brain tumors. Nevertheless, the National Brain Tumor Registry of China has revealed a rise during the past few years with approximately 12,768 new cases

Y. Zhang and L.-J. Zhang (Eds.): ICWS 2024, LNCS 15428, pp. 108–122, 2025.
https://doi.org/10.1007/978-3-031-77072-2_8

per year between 2019 and 2020, which is nearly ten times more than previous decade. These statistics call for further study and well-coordinated measures in dealing with this difficult disease.

Computer science has been advanced to help experts in this problem. In addition, theories as transfer learning and fine-tuning are also considered to be typical for the given field [7]. To explain about transfer learning, it is an aspect of the machine learning technique where a trained model is used or retrained for another related task [8]. It is very suitable when labeled data for the target task is limited, expensive, or difficult to obtain. Fine-tuning is a process of reusing the previously learned model in order to improve the performance on the new task [9]. However, current available pre-train models have a number of parameters that are extremely huge. The larger parameters of neural networks for natural language processing mean more negative impacts. This results in the need for a lightweight CNN model which provides for the detailed compounding of the model depth and width including, but not limited to generalizability and deployability. Additionally, an explanation process is also necessary for providing transparency and insight into the basic factors producing the results of the model [10], which enables experts to gain a deeper understanding of the inside function of the model and identify which features are driving specific predictions.

The contributions of this paper are as follows:

- By using the ability of CNN, this research created a lite model with 1.09 million parameters and 20 layers, which is lower than other pre-trained models 3 to 20 times in parameters and 4 to 8 times in layers dense. This helps to drop costs, overfitting, and difficulties in training and optimization progress.
- After several experiments, the proposed model reached a surprise in the accuracy of 97.87% in classifying four classes and gained from 98.08% to 99.20% in two classes. Thus, this demonstrates the proposed model still produces a high accuracy even using lower resources. Furthermore, The results of these trials demonstrate the utility of the PLNCaE architecture and point to its potential applications in the real world.
- Throughout scenarios, preprocessing was applied to ensure data quality and enhance the performance of machine learning models by making the data more suitable for analysis. The study indicated cropping the image truly increases performance scores and decreases calculation size.
- SHAP was utilized to quantify the impact of each feature on model predictions, aiding in understanding model behavior, feature importance analysis, and debugging. In this proposed framework, SHAP demonstrated insightful explanations without unnecessary chatter.

The research paper includes five primary sections. First, it begins with an introduction segment. Next to related works, it presents a prolonged discussion of literature concerning this theme. The third segment implements the process where is specified the method used, where the specific procedures are indicated. In section four the experiments are given in a way to explain the experiment along with the procedures involved and the results gained. Lastly, the last part is the synthesis of results and perspectives of the limit and further works.

## 2  Related Works

Chetana Srinivas et al. [11] used transfer learning with pre-trained CNN architectures in VGG16, Inception-v3, and ResNet50 models to achieve up to 96% accuracy in binary classification. They noted that VGG16, with its 138 million hyperparameters, had the best performance on trained and tested datasets. Jaeyong Kang et al. [12] proposed an ensemble of deep features and machine learning classifiers, achieving 98.83% accuracy in binary classification and 93.72% in four-class classification. Furthermore, CNN with other techniques such as transfer learning and fine-tuning was also present in several papers in [13–15]. As a result, it showed great promise in brain tumor classification with an average accuracy from 90.41% to 96.94%. However, Related models demand significant computational power and memory with an extremely of parameters. Thus, this can limit its performance on new, unseen data. In addition, a lack of feature extraction which is an important technique for enhancing the interpretability of deep learning models created a big drawback for some papers. Because it is a crucial side of medical applications where understanding the reasoning behind diagnoses is vital. As a result, the proposed model is necessary for filling these issues by applying recent advances to create a lightweight model combined with a feature extraction method.

Vision Transformers (ViT) are a recent innovation in computer vision that has shown remarkable performance in various image classification tasks, including MRI brain tumor classification. For example, Sudhakar Tummala [16] ensembled four ViT models and achieved 97.71% testing accuracy. Xiaoli Zhou et al. [17] proposed an adaptive sparse interaction ResNet-ViT dual-branch network to achieve 95.24% accuracy in four-class classification. Abdullah A. Asiri et al. [18] introduced FT-ViT which fine-tunes the ViT model for improved accuracy and faster inference times and reached 98.13% accuracy. However, ViT typically requires large computational resources, which can be a limiting factor in real-world medical imaging applications. While sources and report high accuracy scores using ViT, the computational cost of deploying such models in real-world clinical settings is a significant consideration. Thus, this research emphasis on a lightweight CNN addresses this concern, aiming for efficiency without compromising accuracy. The proposed also combines CNN and ViT architectures, aiming to leverage the strengths of both. This approach aligns with the growing trend of hybrid architectures in deep learning, which seek to combine the strengths of different model types for improved performance.

## 3  Methods

This research presents the 9-step framework as illustrated in Fig. 1. The specifics of each stage are indicated below:

1. Input Data: The dataset utilized in this study is a combination of three distinct datasets: Figshare, SARTAJ, and Br35H.

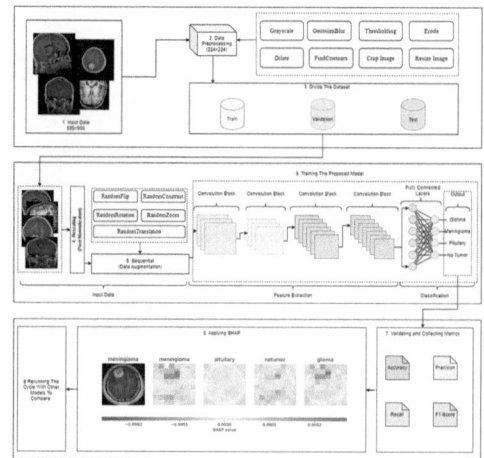

**Fig. 1.** The Prepro-LiteNeuro Classification and Explanation (PLNCaE) framework was combined with multiple steps from input images to classify images and explain the results

2. Data Preprocessing: Data preprocessing includes several important steps to prepare the MRI images for model training. Initially, unnecessary margins are removed to focus on the region of interest. Following this, resized was applied for the original to create a standard image

3. Divide the Dataset: The dataset is divided using an 8-1-1 ratio. This division strategy ensures that the model has 80 percent for training, 10 percent for validation, and 10 percent for testing.

4. Rescaling: Pixel normalization is applied to scale the pixel values into a regular range.

5. Data Augmentation: In this study, various augmentation methods such as random flipping, rotation, contrast adjustment, zooming, and translation are applied to the images.

6. Training the Proposed Model: The proposed model is a lightweight CNN designed specifically for the classification of breast cancer MRI images. This CNN comprises 20 layers and has a total of 1.09 million parameters.

7. Validating and Collecting Performance: The performance of the trained model is evaluated using a variety of metrics based on correct and incorrect image prediction rates.

8. Applying SHAP: SHAP is utilized to express the contribution to important areas of the model.

9. Rerunning the cycle with other models to compare: To ensure the robustness and generalizability of the findings, the entire process is repeated using various other models.

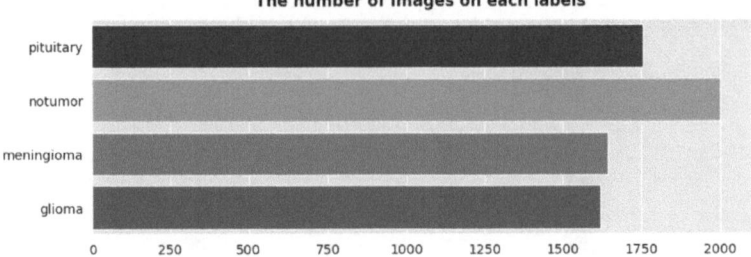

**Fig. 2.** The distribution between four classes including glioma, meningioma, pituitary, and no tumor

### 3.1   Dataset

This dataset is an amalgamation of three distinct sources: the Figshare [19], SARTAJ [20], and Br35H [21] datasets. It is designed for the classification of brain MRI images into four categories: glioma, meningioma, pituitary tumors, and no tumor. The dataset comprises a total of 7023 images, as indicated in Fig. 2, and is distributed as follows: 2000 images without tumors, 1757 images of pituitary tumors, 1621 images of gliomas, and 1645 images of meningiomas. This diverse and extensive collection supports the development of machine learning models to accurately classify these brain tumors, which is crucial for early detection and treatment.

### 3.2   Data Preprocessing

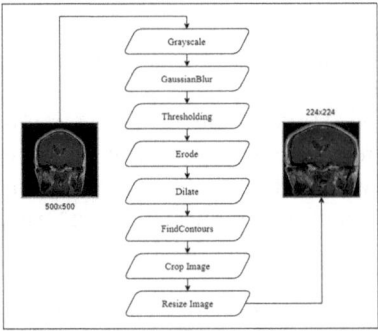

**Fig. 3.** The image preprocessing process include 8 steps of the proposed framework

The preprocessing journey includes various steps indicated in Fig. 3 the process steps commence with converting the images to grayscale and finish with cropping the image to the standard input dimensions required by the neural network. In summary, The incorporation of multiple strategies in the preprocessing pipeline for MRI images in brain tumor classification not only standardizes the data but also improves the robustness and effectiveness of classification algorithms. Thus, MRI images are standardized, noise-reduced, and focused on the brain region.

### 3.3  Training the Lightweight Model

The proposed lightweight CNN model called NeuroCNNLite is designed for the efficient classification of brain tumors within MRI images while maintaining a low parameter count. With approximately 1.09 million parameters, this model showcases a streamlined architecture that balances computational efficiency with high-performance classification capabilities. The architecture in Fig. 4 begins with input preprocessing layers including rescaling and data augmentation, which normalize the pixel values of MRI images and enhance the diversity of the training dataset, respectively. Subsequently, a series of convolutional layers interspersed with max-pooling operations to extract hierarchical features from the input images. Following the convolutional layers, the feature maps undergo flattening before being fed into fully connected layers for classification. Despite its limited layers and parameters, the NeuroCNNLite model demonstrates robust performance in accurately identifying and classifying brain tumors in MRI images.

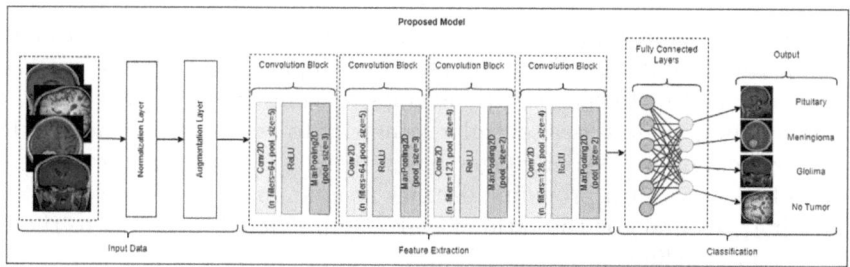

**Fig. 4.** Configuration of internal layers in the structure of NeuroCNNLite model

### 3.4  Applying SHapley Additive ExPlanations (SHAP)

The interpretation of MRI images often requires specialized expertise and can be subject to interobserver variability. Thus, SHapley Additive exPlanations (SHAP) can visualize the output and resolve this problem [22,23]. Mathematically, the Shapley value for feature $j$ in the context of a prediction $f(x)$ is defined as (Fig. 5):

$$\phi_j(f, x) = \sum_{S \subseteq \{1, ..., M\} \setminus \{j\}} \frac{|S|!(M - |S| - 1)!}{M!} [f(S \cup \{j\}) - f(S)] \qquad (1)$$

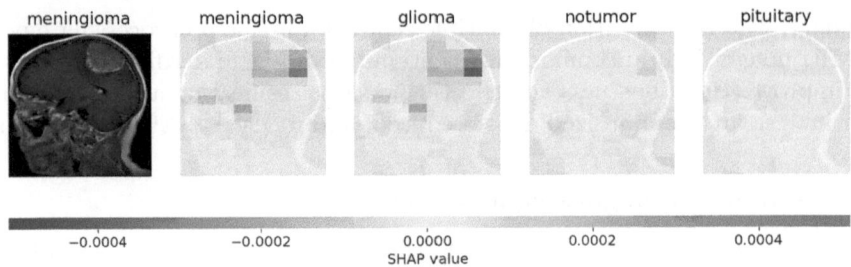

meningioma      meningioma      glioma      notumor      pituitary

−0.0004          −0.0002          0.0000          0.0002          0.0004
SHAP value

**Fig. 5.** The result of applying SHAP for model explanation

In Eq. 1, $M$ is the total number of features, $S$ represents a subset of features excluding $j$, and $f(S)$ denotes the model prediction given the subset $S$. The integration of SHAP into brain tumor classification pipelines holds promise for enhancing diagnostic accuracy and clinical decision support.

## 4   Experiments

### 4.1   Performance and Metrics

The performance of classifying brain tumors from MRI images was trained using NVIDIA TESLA P100 GPUs with 16 GB of memory. The neural network was trained using the Adam optimizer, which is known for its adaptive learning rate and momentum properties. Early stopping was employed to mitigate overfitting, ceasing training after 15 epochs without improvement. Besides, the evaluation of machine learning models uses several key metrics to assess performance in brain tumor classification from MRI images. These metrics include accuracy, precision, recall, and F1 score each providing distinct insights into the effectiveness of the model. First, Accuracy is the ratio of correctly predicted instances to the total instances and is defined as:

$$Accuracy = \frac{Tp + Tn}{Tp + Tn + Fp + Fn} \tag{2}$$

Equation 2 provides a general measure of the classifier's performance, particularly useful when the classes are balanced. Next, Precision or positive predictive value quantifies the accuracy of the positive predictions and is given by Eq. 3

$$Precision = \frac{Tp}{Tp + Fp} \tag{3}$$

This metric is critical in the context of brain tumor classification, where minimizing false positives is essential to avoid unnecessary alarms. In addition, Recall also known as sensitivity or true positive rate measures the classifier's ability to correctly identify positive instances and is expressed in Eq. 4:

$$Recall = \frac{Tp}{Tp + Fn} \tag{4}$$

In medical imaging, recall is vital as it ensures that most of the actual tumors are correctly detected, minimizing the chances of missing a diagnosis. In Eq. 5, F1 Score is the harmonic mean of precision and recall providing a single metric that balances both concerns:

$$F1 = 2 \times \frac{Precision \times Recall}{Precision + Recall} \tag{5}$$

**Table 1.** The comparison between experimental models in the architecture

| Model Name | Number of Parameters (Millions) | Number of Layers | Output Features Map |
|---|---|---|---|
| ResNet50 | 23.6 | 177 layers | $7 \times 7 \times 2048$ |
| DenseNet169 | 12.65 | 597 layers | $7 \times 7 \times 1664$ |
| Xception | 20.87 | 134 layers | $7 \times 7 \times 2048$ |
| MobileNet | 3.23 | 88 layers | $7 \times 7 \times 1024$ |
| **Proposed Model** | **1.09** | **20 layers** | $\mathbf{3 \times 3 \times 128}$ |

This score is particularly useful in cases where there is an uneven class distribution. Before going to scenarios, Table 1 presents a comparison of various neural network architectures based on their number of parameters, number of layers, and output feature maps. Among the models listed, the most intriguing aspect of this comparison lies in the proposed model, which diverges notably from its counterparts.

### 4.2 Scenario 1: The Results of Classifying Brain Tumors in Four Classes: No Tumor, Pituitary, Glioma, Meningioma

Table 2 provides a comprehensive comparison of experimental performance across different phases including transfer learning and fine-tuning, for four distinct classes: no tumor, pituitary, glioma, and meningioma. Among the architectures, the most striking results emerge from the proposed model, which is trained from scratch. With an impressive validation accuracy of 98.01% and a test accuracy of 97.58%, it outperforms all other models in both phases.

Overall, the NeuroCNNLite model presents a compelling alternative, showcasing superior performance in brain tumor classification tasks. In addition, an example training and validation progress curve in the loss and accuracy values of the suggested model during fine-tuning is displayed in Fig. 6. An upward trend in learning behavior is seen in the training and validation sets in the picture. Besides, Fig. 7 illustrates the confusion matrix which represents the percentage of correct and incorrect between four classes.

**Table 2.** The comparison in results of experiment models for four classes including no tumor, pituitary, glioma, and meningioma

| Model | Phase | Accuracy | | Other metrics | | |
|---|---|---|---|---|---|---|
| | | Validation | Test | Precision | Recall | F1 |
| ResNet50 | Transfer Learning | 96.44% | 92.18% | 92.25% | 92.18% | 92.21% |
| | Fine Tuning | 97.72% | 96.73% | 96.80% | 96.73% | 96.74% |
| DenseNet169 | Transfer Learning | 87.46% | 79.80% | 85.49% | 79.80% | 79.94% |
| | Fine Tuning | 97.44% | 96.87% | 96.89% | 96.87% | 96.88% |
| Xception | Transfer Learning | 86.04% | 85.63% | 86.43% | 85.63% | 85.68% |
| | Fine Tuning | 96.72% | 95.45% | 95.62% | 95.45% | 95.49% |
| MobileNet | Transfer Learning | 85.90% | 83.64% | 86.20% | 83.64% | 83.33% |
| | Fine Tuning | 93.87% | 94.31% | 94.35% | 94.31% | 94.33% |
| **Proposed Model** | **Train From Scratch** | **98.01%** | **97.58%** | **97.61%** | **97.58%** | **97.59%** |

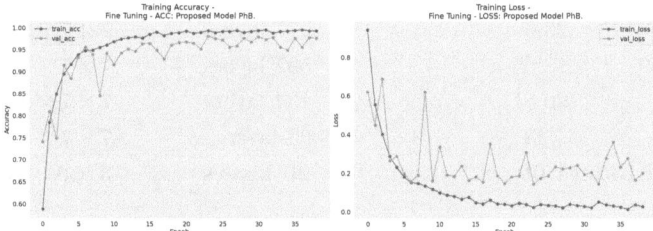

**Fig. 6.** The line graph indicates training accuracy and loss of the proposed model in four classes: no tumor, pituitary, glioma, meningioma

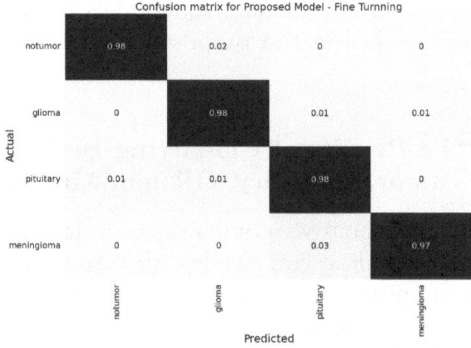

**Fig. 7.** The confusion matrix of the proposed model in four classes: no tumor, pituitary, glioma, meningioma

### 4.3    Scenario 2: The Results of Classifying Brain Tumors in Two Classes: No Tumor, Pituitary

**Table 3.** The comparison in results of experiment models for two classes including no tumor and pituitary

| Model | Phase | Accuracy | | Other metrics | | |
|---|---|---|---|---|---|---|
| | | Validation | Test | Precision | Recall | F1 |
| ResNet50 | Transfer Learning | 100.00% | 97.61% | 97.68% | 97.61% | 97.61% |
| | Fine Tuning | 100.00% | 99.20% | 99.20% | 99.20% | 99.20% |
| DenseNet169 | Transfer Learning | 99.73% | 98.40% | 98.41% | 98.40% | 98.40% |
| | Fine Tuning | 99.73% | 99.47% | 99.47% | 99.47% | 99.47% |
| Xception | Transfer Learning | 53.19% | 53.19% | 28.29% | 53.19% | 36.94% |
| | Fine Tuning | 100.00% | 98.40% | 98.43% | 98.40% | 98.41% |
| MobileNet | Transfer Learning | 99.47% | 98.67% | 98.68% | 98.67% | 98.67% |
| | Fine Tuning | 100.00% | 99.20% | 99.20% | 99.20% | 99.20% |
| **Proposed Model** | **Train From Scratch** | **99.73%** | **99.20%** | **99.20%** | **99.20%** | **99.20%** |

Table 3 presents a comparative analysis of various experiment models for classifying images into two categories: no tumor and pituitary. Notably, the custom model achieved competitive results comparable to the best-performing models, with an accuracy of 99.73% in the validation dataset and 99.20% in the test dataset. While transfer learning proved beneficial for most models, the Proposed Model stood out for its exceptional performance despite being trained from scratch.

### 4.4    Scenario 3: The Results of Classifying Brain Tumors in Two Classes: No Tumor, Glioma

Table 4 presents a comparative analysis of various experiment models aimed at classifying images into no tumor and glioma categories. Noteworthy is the performance of the NeuroCNNLite Model. Despite lacking pre-trained weights, it achieved commendable results with an accuracy of 99.45% on the validation dataset and 98.90% on the test dataset. This underscores the efficacy of the Proposed Model as a viable alternative, particularly in scenarios where leveraging pre-trained models may not be feasible or preferred.

### 4.5    Scenario 4: The Results of Classifying Brain Tumors in Two Classes: No Tumor, Meningioma

In Table 5, our model displayed strong performance with a validation accuracy of 99.45% and a test accuracy of 98.08%. Despite not utilizing pre-trained models,

**Table 4.** The comparison in results of experiment models for two classes including no tumor and glioma

| Model | Phase | Accuracy | | Other metrics | | |
|---|---|---|---|---|---|---|
| | | Validation | Test | Precision | Recall | F1 |
| ResNet50 | Transfer Learning | 99.72% | 99.45% | 99.45% | 99.45% | 99.45% |
| | Fine Tuning | 99.72% | 99.45% | 99.45% | 99.45% | 99.45% |
| DenseNet169 | Transfer Learning | 99.17% | 98.35% | 98.35% | 98.35% | 98.35% |
| | Fine Tuning | 100.00% | 100.00% | 100.00% | 100.00% | 100.00% |
| Xception | Transfer Learning | 97.79% | 97.52% | 97.65% | 97.52% | 97.53% |
| | Fine Tuning | 100.00% | 99.72% | 99.73% | 99.72% | 99.72% |
| MobileNet | Transfer Learning | 98.90% | 98.62% | 98.62% | 98.62% | 98.62% |
| | Fine Tuning | 100.00% | 100.00% | 100.00% | 100.00% | 100.00% |
| **Proposed Model** | **Train From Scratch** | **99.45%** | **98.90%** | **98.90%** | **98.90%** | **98.90%** |

**Table 5.** The comparison in results of experiment models for two classes including no tumor and meningioma

| Model | Phase | Accuracy | | Other metrics | | |
|---|---|---|---|---|---|---|
| | | Validation | Test | Precision | Recall | F1 |
| ResNet50 | Transfer Learning | 99.45% | 98.63% | 98.67% | 98.63% | 98.63% |
| | Fine Tuning | 99.72% | 99.45% | 99.45% | 99.45% | 99.45% |
| DenseNet169 | Transfer Learning | 98.63% | 96.71% | 96.77% | 96.71% | 96.72% |
| | Fine Tuning | 98.90% | 96.44% | 96.52% | 96.44% | 96.44% |
| Xception | Transfer Learning | 96.43% | 96.44% | 96.46% | 96.44% | 96.44% |
| | Fine Tuning | 97.25% | 97.26% | 97.27% | 97.26% | 97.26% |
| MobileNet | Transfer Learning | 98.63% | 96.71% | 96.74% | 96.71% | 96.72% |
| | Fine Tuning | 98.35% | 96.71% | 96.72% | 96.71% | 96.71% |
| **Proposed Model** | **Train From Scratch** | **99.45%** | **98.08%** | **98.08%** | **98.08%** | **98.08%** |

its metrics (i.e., Precision, Recall, and F1 score) all stand at 98.08%. Comparing this with Scenario 2 and Scenario 3, the proposed model consistently performs well across different classifications (i.e., pituitary, glioma, meningioma). While models like ResNet50 and DenseNet169 generally show high performance, the NeuroCNN Lite's ability to achieve competitive results without pre-training highlights its potential as an effective alternative in image classification tasks, demonstrating flexibility and independence from existing architectures.

### 4.6 Scenario 5: The Results of Classifying Brain Tumors in Three Classes: Pituitary, Glioma, Meningioma

Table 6 presents a comparison of various experimental models for classifying images into three classes: pituitary, glioma, and meningioma. Our model achieved an impressive accuracy of 98.61% during validation and 98.01% on the test set.

Its Precision, Recall, and F1 scores are all around 98.01%, reflecting robust and consistent performance across all metrics. The custom model consistently outperforms other models, demonstrating its effectiveness and flexibility in more complex scenarios.

**Table 6.** The comparison in results of experiment models for three classes including pituitary, glioma, and meningioma

| Model | Phase | Accuracy | | Other metrics | | |
|---|---|---|---|---|---|---|
| | | Validation | Test | Precision | Recall | F1 |
| ResNet50 | Transfer Learning | 95.02% | 94.23% | 94.28% | 94.23% | 94.24% |
| | Fine Tuning | 94.62% | 93.64% | 93.70% | 93.64% | 93.57% |
| DenseNet169 | Transfer Learning | 88.25% | 88.47% | 88.34% | 88.47% | 88.32% |
| | Fine Tuning | 88.05% | 89.66% | 89.60% | 89.66% | 89.58% |
| Xception | Transfer Learning | 87.05% | 85.69% | 85.62% | 85.69% | 85.55% |
| | Fine Tuning | 87.45% | 87.08% | 87.09% | 87.08% | 86.84% |
| MobileNet | Transfer Learning | 89.64% | 86.48% | 86.49% | 86.48% | 86.49% |
| | Fine Tuning | 90.24% | 86.68% | 86.61% | 86.68% | 86.63% |
| **Proposed Model** | **Train From Scratch** | **98.61%** | **98.01%** | **98.03%** | **98.01%** | **98.01%** |

## 4.7 Results and Comparison

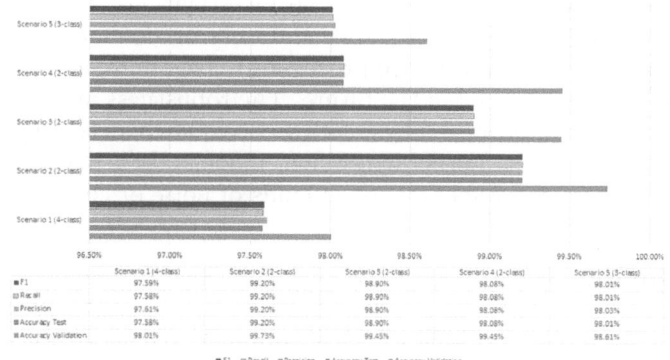

**Fig. 8.** The result of comparison over scenarios

Figure 8 compares the performance metrics for different scenarios of classifying brain tumors using a lightweight CNN model with approximately 1.09 million parameters and 20 layers. Each scenario represents a different classification task based on the number of tumor classes considered. In addition, the purpose of comparing the proposed PLNCaE framework with other state-of-the-art methods in Table 7 is two-fold. Firstly, to benchmark its performance against existing approaches in image classification. Secondly, it highlights the advantages in terms of efficiency, accuracy, and resource utilization. Through such comparisons, researchers can assess the effectiveness and competitiveness of the PLNCaE pipeline in applications.

**Table 7.** Comparison with other state-of-the-art methods in CNN and ViT architecture

| Reference | Other methods | Parameters (Million) | Classes | Accuracy | Year |
|---|---|---|---|---|---|
| Chetana Srinivas et al. [11] | VGG16 | 138 | 2 | 96% | 2022 |
| Jaeyong Kang et al. [12] | Ensemble CNN | ~ 63 | 2 and 4 | 98.83% and 93.72% | 2021 |
| Shahriar Hossain et al. [13] | IVX16 | ~ 185 | 3 | 96.94% | 2023 |
| Osman özkaraca et al. [14] | DenseNet, VGG16, and basic CNN | – | 4 | 93.76% | 2023 |
| Sahan M. Vijithananda et al. [15] | Custom CNN | – | 2 | 90.41% | 2022 |
| Francisco Javier Díaz-Pernas et al. [16] | Multiscale CNN | 2.8 | 3 | 97.30% | 2021 |
| Sudhakar Tummala [17] | Ensemble ViT | – | 3 | 97.71% | 2022 |
| Abdullah A. Asiri et al. [18] | FT-ViT | – | 4 | 98.13% | 2023 |
| **Proposed Model** | | **1.09** | **2** | **98.08% to 99.20%** | **2024** |
| | | | **3** | **98.01%** | |
| | | | **4** | **97.87%** | |

### 4.8    Limitation and Future Works

There are a few issues with the PLNCaE model that may be investigated, even if it has been successful in attaining high accuracy rates. MRI image classification problems have been the main focus of the investigations. It is unknown how well the model performs in more varied datasets or domains (such as multi-class classifications or natural image processing). Therefore, additional research on this topic may be required in the future. The robustness and accuracy of the model might further be improved by creating ensemble models or hybrid systems that combine PLNCaE with other lightweight models. By using this method, the model could be more resistant to various kinds of noise or changes in the data.

## 5    Conclusion

In conclusion, this study introduces a novel approach to image classification using a lightweight CNN architecture called PLNCaE, which features a significantly reduced parameter count and layer density compared to existing pre-trained models. Through various experiments, the proposed PLNCaE model achieved remarkable classification accuracies, surpassing 97.87% in four-class classification tasks and ranging from 98.08% to 99.20% in two-class scenarios. Additionally, the NeuroCNNLite model reached a test accuracy of 98.01% in classifying tumor images. These results underscore the efficacy of the PLNCaE framework, demonstrating its potential for real-world applications while requiring fewer computational resources. The integration of preprocessing techniques, such as image cropping, significantly enhances data quality and machine-learning model performance. Moreover, the adoption of SHAP facilitates insightful feature importance analysis and model behavior understanding. Overall, the findings in this paper pave the way for further exploration and refinement of lightweight ensemble model architectures for efficient and accurate image classification tasks.

**Acknowlegement.** We would like to extend our heartfelt gratitude to Huong Hoang Luong, Phuc Tan Huynh and Hao Van Tran for his invaluable contributions to this project. His dedication, expertise, and unwavering support have been instrumental in its success.

**Availability of Data, Code, and Material.** Code and dataset for this research is published on the repository link at (https://github.com/luthanhquy/brain-tumor-mri-2024) and (https://www.kaggle.com/datasets/masoudnickparvar/brain-tumor-mri-dataset).

# References

1. Price, M., et al.: Childhood, adolescent, and adult primary brain and central nervous system tumor statistics for practicing healthcare providers in neuro-oncology, CBTRUS 2015–2019. Neuro-Oncol. Pract. **11**(1), 5–25 (2024)
2. Mondia, M.W.L., Espiritu, A.I., Jamora, R.D.G.: Brain tumor infodemiology: worldwide online health-seeking behavior using google trends and Wikipedia pageviews. Front. Oncol. **12**, 855534 (2022)
3. Schüz, J., Pirie, K., Reeves, G.K., Floud, S., Beral, V., Collaborators, M.W.S.: Cellular telephone use and the risk of brain tumors: update of the UK million women study. JNCI: J. Natl. Cancer Inst. **114**(5), 704–711 (2022)
4. Riano, I., Bravo, P., Bravo, L.E., Garcia, L.S., Collazos, P., Carrascal, E.: Incidence, mortality, and survival trends of primary CNS tumors in Cali, Colombia, from 1962 to 2019. JCO global oncology **6**, 1712–1720 (2020)
5. Ostrom, Q.T., et al.: CBTRUS statistical report: primary brain and other central nervous system tumors diagnosed in the united states in 2016-2020. Neuro-Oncol. **25**(Supplement_4), iv1–iv99 (2023)
6. Xiao, D., et al.: National brain tumour registry of china (NBTRC) statistical report of primary brain tumours diagnosed in china in years 2019–2020. Lancet Regional Health–Western Pac. **34** (2023)
7. Nguyen, H.T., et al.: Brain tumors detection on MRI images with k-means clustering and residual networks. In: Bădică, C., Treur, J., Benslimane, D., Hnatkowska, B., Krótkiewicz, M. (eds.) ICCCI 2022. CCIS, vol. 1653, pp. 317–329. Springer, Cham (2022). https://doi.org/10.1007/978-3-031-16210-7_26
8. Chen, X., Yang, R., Xue, Y., Huang, M., Ferrero, R., Wang, Z.: Deep transfer learning for bearing fault diagnosis: a systematic review since 2016. IEEE Trans. Instrum. Meas. (2023)
9. Malladi, S., et al.: Fine-tuning language models with just forward passes. Adv. Neural. Inf. Process. Syst. **36**, 53038–53075 (2023)

10. La Rosa, B., et al.: State of the art of visual analytics for explainable deep learning. In: Computer Graphics Forum, vol. 42, pp. 319–355. Wiley Online Library (2023)

11. Srinivas, C., et al.: Deep transfer learning approaches in performance analysis of brain tumor classification using MRI images. J. Healthc. Eng. **2022** (2022)

12. Kang, J., Ullah, Z., Gwak, J.: MRI-based brain tumor classification using ensemble of deep features and machine learning classifiers. Sensors **21**(6), 2222 (2021)

13. Özkaraca, O., et al.: Multiple brain tumor classification with dense CNN architecture using brain MRI images. Life **13**(2), 349 (2023)

14. Gómez-Guzmán, M.A., et al.: Classifying brain tumors on magnetic resonance imaging by using convolutional neural networks. Electronics **12**(4), 955 (2023)

15. Ghassemi, N., Shoeibi, A., Rouhani, M.: Deep neural network with generative adversarial networks pre-training for brain tumor classification based on MR images. Biomed. Signal Process. Control **57**, 101678 (2020)

16. Tummala, S.: Brain tumor classification from MRI using vision transformers ensembling (2022)

17. Zhou, X., Tang, C., Huang, P., Tian, S., Mercaldo, F., Santone, A.: ASI-DBNet: an adaptive sparse interactive ResNet-vision transformer dual-branch network for the grading of brain cancer histopathological images. Interdisc. Sci.: Comput. Life Sci. **15**(1), 15–31 (2023)

18. Asiri, A.A., et al.: Exploring the power of deep learning: fine-tuned vision transformer for accurate and efficient brain tumor detection in MRI scans. Diagnostics **13**(12), 2094 (2023)

19. Cheng, J.: brain tumor dataset (2017). https://figshare.com/articles/dataset/brain_tumor_dataset/1512427

20. Bhuvaji, S., Kadam, A., Bhumkar, P., Dedge, S., Kanchan, S.: Brain tumor classification (MRI) (2020). https://www.kaggle.com/dsv/1183165

21. Hamada, A.: BR35H: brain tumor detection (2020). https://www.kaggle.com/datasets/ahmedhamada0/brain-tumor-detection

22. Van den Broeck, G., Lykov, A., Schleich, M., Suciu, D.: On the tractability of shap explanations. J. Artif. Intell. Res. **74**, 851–886 (2022)

23. Zheng, Q., Wang, Z., Zhou, J., Lu, J.: Shap-CAM: visual explanations for convolutional neural networks based on shapley value. In: Avidan, S., Brostow, G., Cissé, M., Farinella, G.M., Hassner, T. (eds.) ECCV 2022. LNCS, vol. 13672, pp. 459–474. Springer, Cham (2022). https://doi.org/10.1007/978-3-031-19775-8_27

# MSC: A Framework with Advanced Sampling Methods for Skin Cancer Classification

Thuan Van Tran, Triet Minh Nguyen, and Quy Thanh Lu[✉]

FPT University, Can Tho, Vietnam
trietnm3@fe.edu.vn, quythanhlu@gmail.com

**Abstract.** In modern society, environmental pollution and climate change are considered the main problems affecting to increase in cancer cases. One of these, skin cancer occurs when there is an overgrowth of abnormal cells in the skin. Additionally, Skin cancer can develop in areas faced with UV (Ultraviolet) radiation. But it can also form in areas that rarely see the light. Thus, many experiments in both medicine and computer areas were realized to diagnose and treat this illness. This study introduces SMSC (Sampling in MobileNet for Skin Classification), a framework that leverages a fine-tuned MobileNet model and advanced sampling techniques to address class imbalance in the HAM10000 dataset. SMSC achieved remarkable results, with a validation accuracy of 96.93% and a test accuracy of 95.61% for classifying seven skin cancer types. Additionally, for binary classification between benign and malignant lesions, the model reached an average validation accuracy of 99.41% and a test accuracy of 98.92%. SHapley Additive exPlanations (SHAP) was employed to provide interpretability by explaining the model's decisions at the pixel level.

**Keywords:** Skin Cancer · Classification · Explanation · MobileNet · Fine-tune

## 1 Introduction

Exposure to ultraviolet (UV) radiation from the sun is the primary culprit behind the development of skin cancer [1–3]. Prolonged exposure to UV rays damages the DNA in skin cells [4], causing mutations that can lead to uncontrolled cell growth and the formation of malignant tumors. However, UV exposure is not the main reason. For instance, age, precancerous conditions, skin diseases, and even certain genetic factors contribute to the sickness [5]. Besides, skin cancer often goes unnoticed until it reaches the last stage, making early detection and prevention paramount. Regular skin examinations by dermatologists, self-checks at home, and the diligent use of sunscreen are essential steps in safeguarding against its insidious grasp.

According to Global Cancer Statistics, melanoma of the skin stood 17th on the cancer list with 331,647 new cases and sat 22nd with 58,645 dead cases

© The Author(s), under exclusive license to Springer Nature Switzerland AG 2025
Y. Zhang and L.-J. Zhang (Eds.): ICWS 2024, LNCS 15428, pp. 123–137, 2025.
https://doi.org/10.1007/978-3-031-77072-2_9

around the world in 2022 [6]. American Cancer Society estimated that skin cancer (excluding basal and squamous) would reach 104,930 new cases and 12,470 dead cases in both sexes on the United States in 2023 [7]. In 2022, the National Cancer Center of China reported an estimated 8,800 new cases of skin cancer and 5,400 cancer-related deaths [8]. Consequently, computer vision emerged as a tool to early detect and classify illness in medical images including skin cancer [9]. For example, Convolutional Neural Network (CNN) is a powerful tool in computer vision for image classification tasks due to its ability to extract features from label data [10,11].

The contributions of this paper are as follows:

- The custom MobileNet model achieved a remarkable validation accuracy of 96.93% and a test accuracy of 95.61% for a seven-class skin cancer classification task. For binary classification scenarios, the model demonstrated even higher performance with an average test accuracy of 99.41% and a validation accuracy of 98.92% which demonstrates its robustness and adaptability across different classification tasks.
- Extensive experiments demonstrated the effectiveness of the SMSC framework across various datasets. Moreover, the SMSC framework's high accuracy across diverse datasets underscores its potential as a reliable tool for skin cancer classification tasks.
- To address the class imbalance in the HAM10000 dataset, a data augmentation strategy using sampling and mix up techniques was implemented. Sampling methods balanced the number of images in each class, while mixup created new training samples by combining pairs of images and their labels
- SHAP was applied to enhance the interpretability of the deep learning model used for skin cancer classification. This interpretability facilitated better collaboration between human experts and the AI model
- The use of K-means clustering for skin cancer image segmentation significantly enhances the analysis and diagnosis process. This unsupervised learning algorithm aids in isolating the lesion from the surrounding healthy skin, thereby enabling dermatologists to focus on regions of interest and potentially improving the accuracy of identifying malignant areas.

This paper includes six main sections. Firstly, the introduction offers an overview of the research. In the related works part, the section illustrates a review of related papers. Next, the methodology provides explanations of the structure of the proposed model and employed technique. Fourth, the study indicates insight into experiments running for the demonstrated effectiveness of the model. Next, the fifth section presents the results of the most important experiment and compares them with existing methods. Finally, the sixth section summarizes the findings and offers an analysis.

## 2   Related Works

The use of CNN in classifying skin cancer images has been an area of active research, producing significant advancements in dermatological diagnostics.

Karar Ali et al. utilized the EfficientNet family to classify images in HAM10000. Their results reached a high accuracy in the EfficientNet B4 model with an f1 score of 87% and a top accuracy of 87.91 % in seven classes [12]. Besides, Md Shahin Ali et al. also classified images of two classes (i.e., benign and malignant) in the HAM10000 dataset and used the proposed DCNN model to reach the training and test accuracy of 93.16% and 91.93%, respectively [13]. In addition, Saket S. Chaturvedi et al. used a CNN model called ResNeXt101 to reach the highest accuracy of 93.20% for seven classes of classification [14].

Recent studies have explored ensemble methods and hybrid models to enhance the robustness and reliability of skin cancer classification systems. By combining the strengths of CNN architectures and other techniques, these models have achieved superior performance metrics compared to individual networks. For example, Soumyya Kanti Datta et al. combined soft attention and the CNN model to propose IRv2+SA Approach and reached a great accuracy of 93.40% in seven classes of the HAM10000 dataset [15]. Besides, Solene Bechelli et al. proposed an ensemble phase in includes a custom CNN and pre-train model to classify 2-class (i.e., benign and malignant). Thus, the proposed method showed great accuracy of 86% and other metrics recall, precision, and f1 reached 62%, 79%, and 70%, respectively [16]. Additionally, Duggani Keerthana et al. suggested a hybrid model (i.e., including DenseNet-201 and MobileNet) with SVM (Support vector machine) classifier and achieved the best accuracy of 88.02% [17].

The application of Vision Transformer (ViT) in classifying skin cancer images represents a cutting-edge shift from traditional CNN to transformer-based models in medical image analysis. Chao Xin et al. proposed a Vit-based network to classify skin cancer and reached 94.3% accuracy in seven classes on the HAM10000 dataset [18]. Muhammad Asad Arshed et al. used the vision transformer and CNN-based transfer learning models to classify seven different forms of skin malignancies in their work. They discovered throughout several investigations that using pre-trained vision transformers produced an astounding accuracy of 92.14% [19]. Besides, Guang Yang et al. presented a novel ViT model for skin cancer classification called ViTfSCD and achieved a classification accuracy of 94.1% in 7-class [20].

# 3   Methodology

## 3.1   Research Implementation Process

This research proposed the SMSC (Sampling in MobileNet for Skin Classification) framework including 10 steps explained in detail in Fig. 1. The details of each step are indicated as follows:

1. Dataset: The HAM10000 (Human Against Machine with 10000 training images) dataset addresses these issues by providing a comprehensive collection of dermatoscopic images from various populations acquired through different modalities. This dataset includes seven classes of skin lesions and

consists of a total of 10,015 images making it a robust training set for academic machine-learning purposes.

2. Data Preprocessing: In the preprocessing step, the dermatoscopic images from the HAM10000 dataset are resized and normalized. Resizing ensures that all images have uniform dimensions suitable for input into neural networks, while normalization scales pixel values to a standard range improving the ability to learn effectively from the data.

3. Data Augmentation: To address the class imbalance within the dataset, data augmentation techniques such as sampling and mixup are applied. These techniques generate new training examples by combining existing images in various ways, thereby increasing the diversity and balance of the dataset, which helps the model generalize better to unseen data.

4. Divide The Dataset: The dataset is divided into training, validation, and test sets using an 8:1:1 ratio. This means that 80% of the images are used for training, 10% for validation, and the remaining 10% for testing. This division ensures that there are enough samples for training while maintaining separate sets for unbiased validation and testing of the model.

5. Transfer Learning: Transfer learning is employed to leverage the pre-trained knowledge from existing models. By using a model that has already been trained on a large dataset, the training process for dermatoscopic image classification can be significantly accelerated and the model can achieve better performance with limited data.

6. Fine-tuning: Fine-tuning means adjusting the parameters of the pre-trained model by unfreezing some of its layers and allowing them to learn specifically from the dermatoscopic images. This step refines the model's performance to make it more accurate for the specific task of diagnosing pigmented skin lesions.

7. Validating and collecting performance: The result is validated and evaluated by measuring key metrics such as accuracy, precision, recall, and F1 score on both the validation and test sets. These metrics provide a comprehensive understanding of the effectiveness of diagnosing skin lesions.

8. Applying SHAP: SHAP values are used to interpret the model's predictions by highlighting the contribution of each feature to the final decision. This step ensures transparency and helps in understanding how the model arrives at its diagnoses, which is crucial for clinical applications.

9. Applying K-means clustering: K-means clustering is applied to segment the dermatoscopic images, particularly focusing on identifying and isolating areas that might indicate skin cancer. This unsupervised learning technique groups similar pixels together to raise the model's ability to analyze and classify lesion areas accurately.

10. Define the best hyperparameters for other scenarios: To ensure the robustness and effectiveness of the approach, the entire cycle is rerun with the best parameters in the first experiment with other models including ResNet50, VGG16, Xception, and MobileNet. Comparing the performance of these models allows for the selection of the most accurate and efficient model for diagnosing pigmented skin.

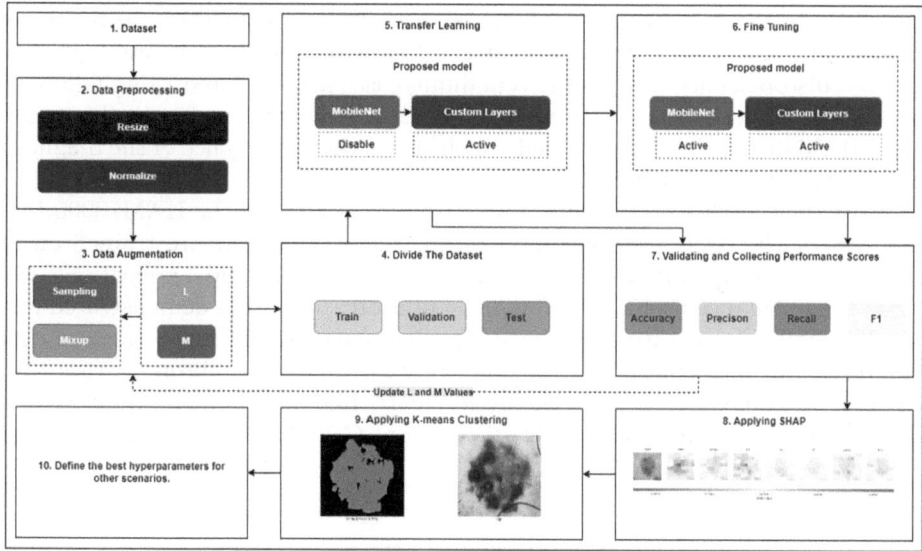

**Fig. 1.** The SMSC framework indicates a summary step-by-step of the research flow.

## 3.2  Dataset

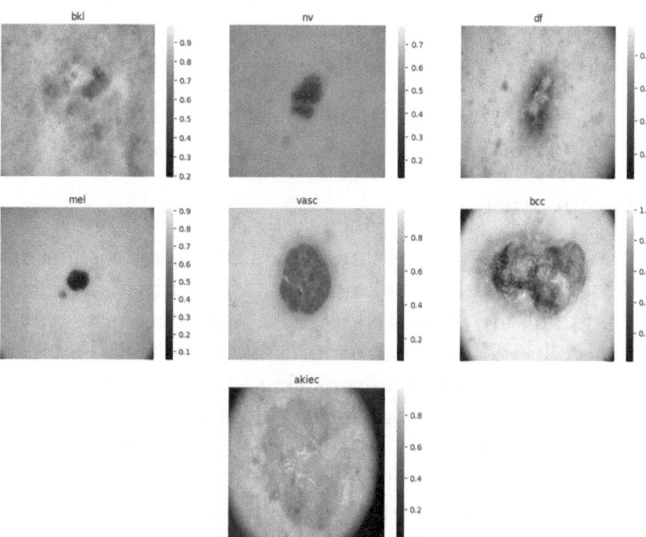

**Fig. 2.** The figure illustrates the description of seven classes including bkl, nv, df, mel, vasc, bcc, akiec in the dataset HAM10000

The HAM10000 dataset [21] includes all significant diagnostic categories for pigmented lesions. More than 50% of the lesions in the dataset are confirmed through histopathology, while the remaining cases are validated using follow-up exams, expert consensus, or in-vivo confocal microscopy (confocal). To understand HAM10000, Fig. 2 is provided which shows the importance of the diagnosis and treatment of skin conditions.

Nevertheless, there is a significant imbalance issue with the HAM10000 that may distort the results of machine learning algorithms that are trained on it. To improve the quality of the dataset in machine learning applications and lessen the imbalance problem. Data augmentation approaches demonstrated useful. Through augmentation in Fig. 3, the instances within akiec (i.e., Actinic Keratoses and Intraepithelial Carcinoma), df (i.e., Dermatofibroma), vasc (i.e., Vascular Lesions), nv (i.e., Melanocytic Nevi), bkl (i.e., Benign Keratosis-like Lesions), mel (i.e., Melanoma), bcc (i.e., Basal Cell Carcinoma) classes can be changed to 999, 997, 982, 962, 962, 962, and 962, respectively.

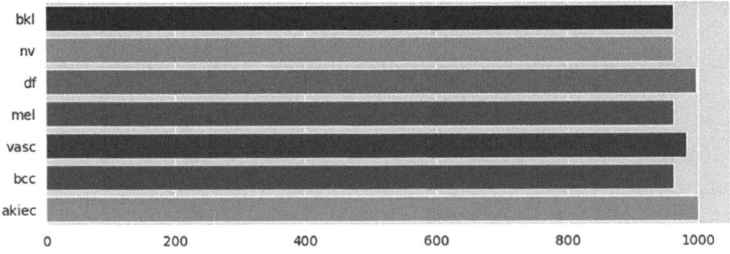

**Fig. 3.** The contribution between three classes in the dataset after augmentation

### 3.3   Data Augmentation

Sampling methods are essential techniques in machine learning used to reduce training times and deal with imbalanced datasets. In this research, undersampling and oversampling are presented for data augment strategy. Undersampling limit images can collected per class from a huge dataset. For instance, setting $L = 500$ is the largest number of images that can picked from a dataset. Based on $L$, each class does not allow for pictures higher than the default setting. On the other hand, oversampling is used when the total of pictures is lower than $L$. Calling $M = 1000$ as the maximum number of images in one class, oversampling employs a mixup method for creating new pictures in every cycle with $B = 42$ as the maximum of images generated per round.

The MixUp method described in Algorithm 1 is a data augmentation technique for image classification tasks. It works by combining images and their corresponding labels to create new synthetic samples, which can help improve the robustness and generalization of a neural network model. For each class

**Algorithm 1.** Image MixUp Augmentation

---

1: **Parameters:**
2:     image_per_class ← 1000
3:     mix_per_batch ← 42
4:     mixup ← Augmenter([MixUp()])
5:     root_label_df ← pd.DataFrame({"dx": root_labels})
6: **Initialize:**
7:     x_tensor_mix ← None
8:     y_tensor_mix ← None
9: **for** each (label, count) in count_dict.items() **do**
10:        num_mix_least ← image_per_class - count
11:        num_batch ← num_mix_least // mix_per_batch
12:        num_mix ← num_batch * mix_per_batch
13:        **for** i ← 0 to num_batch - 1 **do**
14:            indices ← random(count, mix_per_batch)
15:            real_index ← root_label_df[dx == label][indices]
16:            x_mix ← tf.gather(x_tensor, real_index)
17:            y_mix ← tf.gather(y_tensor, real_index)
18:            mix_out ← mixup({"images": x_mix, "labels": y_mix})
19:        **end for**
20: **end for**

---

label in a dictionary of label counts, the algorithm calculates how many additional mixed images are needed to reach the desired count of images per class based on batch size.

## 3.4   Transfer Learning and Fine-Tuning in MobileNet

To adapt the MobileNet model to the task of skin cancer classification, several custom layers are added after the base model in Fig. 4. First, a Global Average Pooling layer is used to reduce the spatial dimensions of the output feature maps from the base model. This helps in reducing overfitting and the computational burden. Following this, a series of fully connected layers are introduced. The first dense layer has 512 neurons with ReLU activation, followed by a Batch Normalization layer to stabilize and accelerate training. A Dropout layer is added to prevent overfitting by randomly dropping 20% of the neurons during training. This is followed by another dense layer with 256 neurons and ReLU activation, another Batch Normalization layer, and a second Dropout layer with a higher dropout rate of 35%. Finally, the output layer consists of a dense layer with a number of neurons equal to the number of classes. By integrating these custom layers, the model becomes better equipped to learn and generalize from the specific features present in skin cancer images, ultimately improving its classification accuracy.

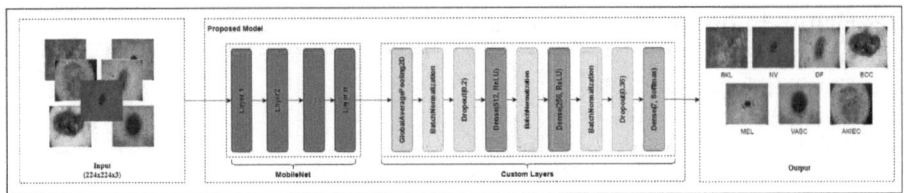

**Fig. 4.** The architecture of proposed model including MobileNet and custom layers

## 3.5 Explain the Decision with SHAP

SHAP is a method used to interpret complex machine learning models by providing consistent and locally accurate feature importance values. In Fig. 5, SHAP pays attention to a pixel or a region of the image, and the output is the model's prediction. Mathematically, SHAP values are calculated using the formula:

$$\phi_i = \sum_{S \subseteq N \setminus \{i\}} \frac{|S|!(|N| - |S| - 1)!}{|N|!} [f(S \cup \{i\}) - f(S)] \tag{1}$$

In Formula 1, $\phi_i$ represents the SHAP value for feature $i$, $N$ is the set of all features, and $S$ is a subset of $N$ that does not include $i$. The term $f(S \cup \{i\}) - f(S)$ measures the change in the model's prediction when feature $i$ is added to the subset $S$. The coefficients $\frac{|S|!(|N|-|S|-1)!}{|N|!}$ ensure a fair distribution of the contribution among all possible subsets. By understanding which features the model relies on, clinicians can better trust the automated system and potentially discover new patterns or markers indicative of skin cancer.

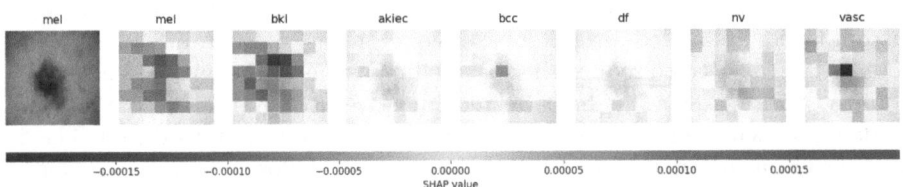

**Fig. 5.** The figure indicates a result when applying SHAP in melanoma skin cancer

## 3.6 Segmentation with K-Means Clustering

When applied to the segmentation of skin cancer images, k-means clustering can effectively group pixels with similar characteristics. This segmentation helps in isolating the lesion from the surrounding healthy skin, facilitating better analysis and diagnosis. Mathematically, the k-means algorithm (2) aims to minimize the within-cluster sum of squares (WCSS), which is the sum of the squared distances

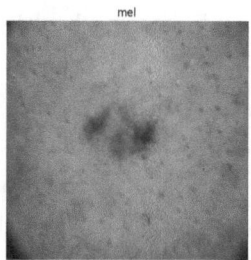
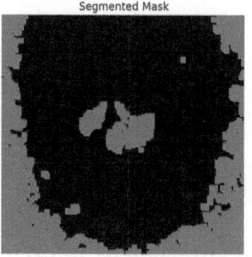

**Fig. 6.** The figure highlights a segmentation area when applying k-means in melanoma skin cancer

between each point and the centroid of its assigned cluster. The formula for WCSS is given by:

$$\text{WCSS} = \sum_{i=1}^{k} \sum_{x \in C_i} \|x - \mu_i\|^2 \tag{2}$$

Once the clusters are formed, each pixel is assigned to a cluster resulting in a segmented image where different clusters highlight different regions. In Fig. 6, one cluster corresponds to the lesion, while others represent healthy skin or background. By analyzing these clusters, medical professionals can gain insights into the shape, size, and boundaries.

## 4    Experiments and Evaluation

### 4.1    Performance and Metrics

In this study, the use of NVIDIA TESLA P100 GPUs with 16GB of memory significantly accelerates the training process by providing substantial computational power. For optimizing the model, the Adam optimizer is employed with a learning rate set to 1e−3. In more detail, this process will stop the training if no improvement is observed for 15 consecutive epochs. Besides, evaluating the performance of a skin cancer classification model requires a thorough analysis of several key metrics. Firstly, accuracy (3) is the ratio of correctly predicted instances to the total instances. Accuracy provides an overall measure of model performance, but it can be misleading in cases of class imbalance. In math formula:

$$Accuracy = \frac{TruePositives) + TrueNegatives}{TruePositives + TrueNegatives + FalsePositives + FalseNegatives} \tag{3}$$

Precision (4) is defined as the ratio of true positive predictions to the total predicted positives and it focuses on the accuracy of positive predictions. In addition, high precision indicates a low false positive rate, which is crucial in medical diagnoses to minimize the risk of misdiagnosing healthy individuals as having cancer:

$$Precision = \frac{TruePositives}{TruePositives + FalsePositives} \qquad (4)$$

Recall (5) known as sensitivity or true positive rate, which measures the model's ability to correctly identify all positive instances. Recall is particularly important to ensure that as many cases of cancer as possible are detected:

$$Recall = \frac{TruePositives}{TruePositives + FalsePositives} \qquad (5)$$

The F1 score (5) is the harmonic mean of precision and recall providing a single metric that balances both concerns. The F1 score is especially useful when dealing with imbalanced datasets, as it considers both false positives and false negatives, offering a more comprehensive assessment of model performance:

$$F1 = 2 \times \frac{Precision \times Recall}{Precision + Recall} \qquad (6)$$

## 4.2 Scenario 1: Finding the Most Suitable Hyperparameters for Sampling Methods in Classifying Seven Classes

**Table 1.** The result in different hyperparameters of sampling methods on seven classes of skin cancer classification.

| Configuration | Phase | Accuracy | | Others metrics | | |
|---|---|---|---|---|---|---|
| | | Validation | Test | Precision | Recall | F1 |
| L = 300, M = 600 | Transfer Learning | 82.97% | 85.40% | 85.58% | 85.40% | 85.18% |
| | Fine Tuning | 92.94% | 95.86% | 95.91% | 95.86% | 95.83% |
| L = 400, M = 800 | Transfer Learning | 86.81% | 84.43% | 84.74% | 84.43% | 84.28% |
| | Fine Tuning | 94.51% | 94.32% | 94.28% | 94.32% | 94.21% |
| **L = 500, M = 1000** | Transfer Learning | 83.89% | 84.19% | 84.12% | 84.19% | 84.05% |
| | **Fine Tuning** | **96.93%** | **95.61%** | **95.63%** | **95.61%** | **95.61%** |
| L = 600, M = 1000 | Transfer Learning | 83.74% | 82.15% | 82.27% | 82.15% | 81.84% |
| | Fine Tuning | 95.07% | 93.61% | 93.74% | 93.61% | 93.58% |
| L = 800, M = 1000 | Transfer Learning | 81.34% | 77.55% | 77.82% | 77.55% | 77.34% |
| | Fine Tuning | 93.59% | 93.59% | 93.59% | 93.59% | 93.55% |

Table 1 presents the results of different hyperparameter configurations for sampling methods used in a skin cancer classification task. The configurations vary the limits on the number of images in the dataset (L) and the maximum number of images required per class (M) reflecting the use of undersampling and oversampling methods to manage data distribution. Analyzing the results, it is evident that fine-tuning consistently outperforms transfer learning across all configurations. This suggests that fine-tuning is more effective at leveraging the augmented dataset to enhance model performance. Additionally, the impact of varying the L and M parameters shows that the choice of these hyperparameters influences the model's performance. For instance, the configuration with L = 800 and M = 1000 results in the lowest performance for transfer learning (i.e., test accuracy of 77.55%) suggesting that excessively large L values may not be beneficial. Conversely, configurations with L = 300 to L = 500 seem optimal for both methods, particularly for Fine Tuning, which achieves its best performance at L = 500.

## 4.3    Scenario 2: The Performance of the Proposed Model in Classifying Binary Classes

**Table 2.** The comparison on average results in classifying binary classes

| Malignant | Benign | Accuracy | | Others metrics | | |
|---|---|---|---|---|---|---|
| | | Validation | Test | Precision | Recall | F1 |
| mel | bkl | 97.40% | 97.41% | 97.41% | 97.41% | 97.41% |
| | nv | 100.00% | 99.16% | 99.17% | 99.16% | 99.16% |
| | df | 99.15% | 97.46% | 97.47% | 97.46% | 97.46% |
| | vasc | 99.46% | 99.14% | 99.15% | 99.14% | 99.14% |
| bcc | bkl | 98.44% | 98.45% | 98.45% | 98.45% | 98.45% |
| | nv | 100.00% | 99.48% | 99.49% | 99.48% | 99.48% |
| | df | 100.00% | 98.47% | 98.51% | 98.47% | 98.47% |
| | vasc | 99.48% | 98.97% | 98.99% | 98.97% | 98.97% |
| akiec | bkl | 98.98% | 98.48% | 98.52% | 98.48% | 98.48% |
| | nv | 100.00% | 100.00% | 100.00% | 100.00% | 100.00% |
| | df | 100.00% | 100.00% | 100.00% | 100.00% | 100.00% |
| | vasc | 100.00% | 100.00% | 100.00% | 100.00% | 100.00% |
| **Average** | | **99.41%** | **98.92%** | **98.93%** | **98.92%** | **98.92%** |

Table 2 compared the average results for binary classification. Analyzing the results, Table 2 observed exceptionally high performance across all metrics and class pairs, with an average test accuracy of 98.92%. The high performance across different malignant and benign pairs indicates that the model is well-generalized and capable of maintaining accuracy across diverse data subsets. The consistently high metrics across different pairs and phases highlight the efficacy of the model and the sampling methods used, which demonstrates that the model can accurately classify skin lesions with minimal errors.

## 4.4    Scenario 3: The Comparative Between the Proposed and Other Models in Classifying Seven Classes

Table 3 compares the performance of various models, including ResNet50, VGG16, Xception, MobileNet, and the proposed model in classifying seven classes of skin cancer. From the data, the custom model demonstrates the highest performance across all metrics. It achieved a validation accuracy of 96.93% and a test accuracy of 95.61% larger than the other models. The proposed model stands out as the most effective in classifying the seven skin cancer classes. Its superior accuracy and consistent metric values suggest that it has been optimized well for this specific task.

**Table 3.** The comparison of results of different models in classifying seven classes

| Model | Accuracy | | Others metrics | | |
|---|---|---|---|---|---|
| | Validation | Test | Precision | Recall | F1 |
| ResNet50 | 94.44% | 92.97% | 93.02% | 92.97% | 92.87% |
| VGG16 | 95.75% | 94.58% | 94.61% | 94.58% | 94.57% |
| Xception | 94.88% | 94.14% | 94.22% | 94.14% | 94.10% |
| MobileNet | 95.61% | 94.14% | 94.11% | 94.14% | 94.08% |
| **Proposed Model** | **96.93%** | **95.61%** | **95.63%** | **95.63%** | **95.61%** |

## 4.5    Scenario 4: The Comparative Between Different Datasets

**Table 4.** The comparison of results of different datasets in classifying skin cancers

| Dataset | Number of classes | Accuracy | | Others metrics | | |
|---|---|---|---|---|---|---|
| | | Validation | Test | Precision | Recall | F1 |
| Melanoma Cancer Image Dataset | 2 classes | 92.19% | 96.89% | 96.97% | 96.89% | 96.89% |
| ISIC 2019 Skin Lesion images for classification | 8 classes | 89.52% | 88.37% | 88.42% | 88.37% | 88.33% |
| HAM10000 Dataset (Our Experiment) | 7 classes | 96.93% | 95.61% | 95.63% | 95.61% | 95.61% |

In Table 4, the research compares the performance of different datasets. The datasets included are the Melanoma Cancer Image Dataset, ISIC 2019 Skin Lesion images for classification, and the HAM10000 Dataset used in the current experiment. The Melanoma Cancer Image Dataset achieved the highest test accuracy at 96.89%, which is notable given it only involves binary classification. The HAM10000 dataset followed closely with a test accuracy of 95.61% and demonstrated strong performance despite handling seven classes. The ISIC 2019 dataset showed the lowest performance among the three with eight classes highlighting the complexity added by more classes.

# 5    Results and Comparison

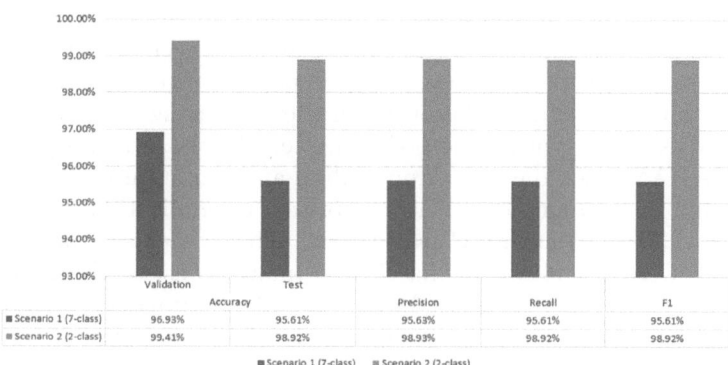

**Fig. 7.** The comparison in outcome of the proposed model

In Fig. 7, the performance comparison reveals that the model performs better in the two-class classification scenario compared to the seven-class scenario. The test accuracy improves from 95.61% in the seven-class scenario to 98.92% in the two-class scenario an increase of over 3%. This improvement is attributed to the reduced complexity of dealing with fewer classes, which simplifies the classification task and leads to higher performance metrics. In addition, Table 5 presents a comparison of various state-of-the-art methods applied to the HAM10000 dataset for skin cancer classification including CNN and ViT architecture. Overall, these comparisons are crucial for demonstrating advancements fostering continuous improvement and ensuring that new developments are both significant and relevant.

**Table 5.** Comparison with other state-of-the-art methods in CNN and ViT on the HAM10000 dataset

| Reference | Other methods | Year | Classes | Accuracy |
|---|---|---|---|---|
| Karar Ali et al. [12] | EfficientNetB4 | 2022 | 7 | 88% |
| Md Shahin Ali et al. [13] | DCNN | 2021 | 2 | 91.93% |
| Saket S. Chaturvedi et al. [14] | ResNeXt101 | 2020 | 7 | 93.20% |
| Soumyya Kanti Datta et al. [15] | IRv2+SA | 2021 | 7 | 93.40% |
| Soumyya Kanti Datta et al. [16] | Ensemble CNN | 2022 | 2 | 86.00% |
| Satin Jain et al. [12] | XceptionNet | 2021 | 7 | 90.48% |
| Chao Xin et al. [18] | Custom ViT | 2022 | 7 | 94.30% |
| Muhammad Asad Arshed et al. [19] | Custim ViT | 2023 | 7 | 92.14% |
| Guang Yang et al. [20] | ViTfSCD | 2023 | 7 | 94.10% |
| **Proposed Model** | | | **2** | **98.92%** |
| | | | **7** | **95.61%** |

# 6   Conclusion

In this study, a custom MobileNet model with additional layers significantly improved skin cancer classification. The model demonstrated robust performance, with a validation accuracy of 96.93% and test accuracy of 95.61% across seven skin cancer classes, and even higher performance for binary classification tasks, with test and validation accuracies averaging 99.41% and 98.92%, respectively. A major contribution of this research was addressing class imbalance in the HAM10000 dataset through data augmentation techniques such as sampling and mix-up methods, which improved generalization and robustness. The study validated the SMSC framework's efficacy across multiple datasets including ISIC 2019 and Melanoma Cancer Image, consistently achieving high accuracy and performance metrics. Integrating SHAP provided valuable insights into the model's decision-making process enhancing transparency and facilitating better collaboration between human experts and machine intelligence. This research demonstrates the adaptability of transfer learning combined with customized augmentation techniques for complex medical image classification tasks, emphasizing the importance of model interpretability in gaining clinical trust and improving informed decision-making in healthcare applications.

**Acknowledgement.** We are deeply grateful for Huong Hoang Luong, Hao Van Tran and Phuc Tan Huynh's collaboration and the valuable insights they have provided throughout this journey. Thank you for being an essential part of this effort.

**Availability of Data, Code, and Material.** Code and dataset for this research is published on the repository link at (https://github.com/luthanhquy/skin-cancer-2024) and (https://www.kaggle.com/datasets/farjanakabirsamanta/skin-cancer-dataset).

# References

1. Parker, E.R.: The influence of climate change on skin cancer incidence-a review of the evidence. Int. J. Women's Dermatol. **7**(1), 17–27 (2021)
2. Ahmed, B., Qadir, M.I., Ghafoor, S.: Malignant melanoma: skin cancer- diagnosis, prevention, and treatment. Crit. Rev.$^{TM}$ Eukaryotic Gene Expression **30**(4) (2020)
3. Leiter, U., Keim, U., Garbe, C.: Epidemiology of skin cancer: update 2019. Sunlight, Vitamin D and Skin Cancer, pp. 123–139 (2020)
4. Lee, J.W., Ratnakumar, K., Hung, K.F., Rokunohe, D., Kawasumi, M.: Deciphering UV-induced DNA damage responses to prevent and treat skin cancer. Photochem. Photobiol. **96**(3), 478–499 (2020)
5. Ilkhomovna, K.D.: Modern look of facial skin cancer. Barqarorlik Va Yetakchi Tadqiqotlar Onlayn Ilmiy Jurnali **1**(1), 85–89 (2021)
6. ME, J.F., Siegel, R.L., Isabelle Soerjomataram, M., Ahmedin Jemal, D.: Global cancer statistics 2022: GLOBOCAN estimates of incidence and mortality worldwide for 36 cancers in 185 countries (2024)
7. Siegel, R.L., Miller, K.D., Wagle, N.S., Jemal, A., et al.: Cancer statistics, 2023. CA Cancer J. Clin. **73**(1), 17–48 (2023)

8. Han, B., et al.: Cancer incidence and mortality in China, 2022. J. Natl. Cancer Cent. (2024)

9. Esteva, A., et al.: Deep learning-enabled medical computer vision. NPJ Digit. Med. **4**(1), 5 (2021)

10. Nguyen, H.T., Quach, Q.T., Tran, C.L.H., Luong, H.H.: Deep learning architectures extended from transfer learning for classification of rice leaf diseases. In: Fujita, H., Fournier-Viger, P., Ali, M., Wang, Y. (eds.) IEA/AIE 2022. LNCS, vol. 13343, pp. 785–796. Springer, Cham (2022). https://doi.org/10.1007/978-3-031-08530-7_66

11. Luong, H.H., Khang, N.H., Le, N.Q., Canh, D.M., Ha, P.S., et al.: A proposed approach for monkeypox classification. Int. J. Adv. Comput. Sci. Appl. **14**(8) (2023)

12. Ali, K., Shaikh, Z.A., Khan, A.A., Laghari, A.A.: Multiclass skin cancer classification using efficientnets-a first step towards preventing skin cancer. Neurosci. Inform. **2**(4), 100034 (2022)

13. Ali, M.S., Miah, M.S., Haque, J., Rahman, M.M., Islam, M.K.: An enhanced technique of skin cancer classification using deep convolutional neural network with transfer learning models. Mach. Learn. Appl. **5**, 100036 (2021)

14. Chaturvedi, S.S., Tembhurne, J.V., Diwan, T.: A multi-class skin cancer classification using deep convolutional neural networks. Multimed. Tools Appl. **79**(39), 28477–28498 (2020)

15. Datta, S.K., Shaikh, M.A., Srihari, S.N., Gao, M.: Soft attention improves skin cancer classification performance. In: Reyes, M., et al. (eds.) IMIMIC/TDA4MedicalData -2021. LNCS, vol. 12929, pp. 13–23. Springer, Cham (2021). https://doi.org/10.1007/978-3-030-87444-5_2

16. Bechelli, S., Delhommelle, J.: Machine learning and deep learning algorithms for skin cancer classification from dermoscopic images. Bioengineering **9**(3), 97 (2022)

17. Keerthana, D., Venugopal, V., Nath, M.K., Mishra, M.: Hybrid convolutional neural networks with SVM classifier for classification of skin cancer. Biomed. Eng. Adv. **5**, 100069 (2023)

18. Xin, C., Liu, Z., Zhao, K., Miao, L., Ma, Y., Zhu, X., Zhou, Q., Wang, S., Li, L., Yang, F., et al.: An improved transformer network for skin cancer classification. Comput. Biol. Med. **149**, 105939 (2022)

19. Arshed, M.A., Mumtaz, S., Ibrahim, M., Ahmed, S., Tahir, M., Shafi, M.: Multiclass skin cancer classification using vision transformer networks and convolutional neural network-based pre-trained models. Information **14**(7), 415 (2023)

20. Yang, G., Luo, S., Greer, P.: A novel vision transformer model for skin cancer classification. Neural Process. Lett. **55**(7), 9335–9351 (2023)

21. Tschandl, P.: The HAM10000 dataset, a large collection of multi-source dermatoscopic images of common pigmented skin lesions (2018). https://doi.org/10.7910/DVN/DBW86T

# Author Index

Y. Zhang and L.-J. Zhang (Eds.): ICWS 2024, LNCS 15428, p. 139, 2025.
https://doi.org/10.1007/978-3-031-77072-2